ESSAYS

IN

BIOGRAPHY AND CRITICISM.

BY

PETER BAYNE

SECOND SERIES.

Essay Index Reprint Series

 BOOKS FOR LIBRARIES PRESS
FREEPORT, NEW YORK

First Published 1858
Reprinted 1972

Library of Congress Cataloging in Publication Data

Bayne, Peter, 1830-1896.
    Essays in biography and criticism.

    (Essay index reprint series)
    Reprint of the 1858 ed.
    CONTENTS: Charles Kingsley.--Thomas Babington
Macaulay.--Sir Archibald Alison. [etc.]
    1. English literature--Addresses, essays,
lectures. I. Title.
PR99.B24 1972   824'.8   73-39681
ISBN 0-8369-2744-3

PRINTED IN THE UNITED STATES OF AMERICA
BY
NEW WORLD BOOK MANUFACTURING CO., INC.
HALLANDALE, FLORIDA 33009

ESSAYS

IN

BIOGRAPHY AND CRITICISM.
SECOND SERIES.

NOTICE OF THE AUTHOR.

EARLY in 1855, the publishers of this volume had their attention directed to a critique in the Edinburgh Witness, by Hugh Miller, upon a work entitled, "The Christian Life, Social and Individual." The book had issued from a Scottish provincial press; its somewhat commonplace title gave no promise of originality; and its author was quite unknown to fame. It was not strange, therefore, that the Editor of the Witness suffered it to lie for some time unnoticed on his table. When at length he found leisure to take it in hand, he hastened to make an apology for his neglect, and to do ample justice to its author. "The master idea," he said, "on which it has been formed is, we deem, wholly original, and we regard the execution of it as not less happy than the conception is good." "Some of the Biographies," he added, "condense in comparatively brief space the thinking of ordinary volumes." Such praise from such a source was a powerful persuasive for the re-publication of the book in this country. An edition was speedily issued, and its reception by the American public was such as is seldom accorded to the first work of an unknown author. The judgment of Hugh Miller was abundantly affirmed by men of renown among ourselves.

Soon after, the present publishers learned that the author of "The Christian Life" had been a frequent, though anonymous, contributor to the periodical literature of his native country. A correspondence with him was thereupon opened, which resulted in a contract on his part to furnish them with a selection of his published essays, together with others yet in manuscript. On their part, they made him such remuneration as was deemed by him to be amply satisfactory. The first series of the Essays thus furnished has already been given to the public. The second is presented in this volume.

The selected essays in both volumes were published, with one or two exceptions, in the author's twenty-third and twenty-fourth years. Of these essays, in their present shape, he remarks: "Some have undergone only a slight revision; others have been so modified as to be materially changed in character; while several, though, save in a single instance, retaining their original titles, may be considered altogether new." Among the contents of this volume, the papers which now for the first time appear in print, are those on Napoleon Bonaparte, Characteristics of Christian Civilization, and The Modern University. The rest have been carefully retouched, and several have received material additions. The whole constitute a body of biographical and critical composition worthy of the author of "The Christian Life."

It would be out of place to offer any criticism here on the contents of this volume; but it may gratify the reader to learn what estimate Sir Archibald Alison put upon the Essay devoted to his own writings. That distinguished Historian, after complimenting the Essay in question as " able and eloquent," proceeds to say that " it contains a more just and correct view of my [his] political opinions than has ever yet appeared in this country or elsewhere."

Some account of Mr. Bayne's personal history may be given here in answer to inquiries, by letter and otherwise, which have from time to time been made. It must be premised, however, that there is little to be told. Mr. Bayne is still a young man, — a young man devoted to literary pursuits, — and so, comparatively, without a history. His native country is Scotland. He was born in Aberdeenshire, and was graduated at Marischall College, in the city of Aberdeen. He subsequently pursued a course of theological study in Edinburgh, and also a philosophical course under

Sir William Hamilton. That great teacher and Thomas Carlyle appear to have been the two thinkers, who, more than all others, gave shape and direction to Mr. Bayne's mind. From the former he received his philosophy; from the latter, his literary culture. Of Carlyle's relation to him he makes this remark: "The influence exerted by him upon my style and modes of thought is as powerful as my mind was capable of receiving; yet," he adds, "my dissent from his opinions is thorough and total." While at Edinburgh, he wrote for Hogg's Instructor the series of articles from which several of those in this volume have been selected. The occasion of this step, he says, was "an inaptitude and distaste for private tuition, and a facility and pleasure, experienced from an early age, in literary composition." It was this "facility and pleasure," doubtless, coupled with rare success, that ultimately led him to devote himself to literature as a profession. The first fruit of this settled purpose was "The Christian Life." It furnished abundant evidence that he had not mistaken his vocation, that his genius was equal to his ambition. The work was published in his twenty-sixth year. He now projected more elaborate enterprises. In a private note he avows "a deliberate and ardent desire to execute four works of some magnitude, three of them, probably, of single volumes, and one of three volumes." The first of these works had already made good progress, when it was interrupted by a change in Mr. Bayne's circumstances, but was not, it is to be hoped, finally abandoned.

In 1855, we find him occupying the position of editor-in-chief of The Commonwealth, a newspaper published in Glasgow. From this position he retired in the summer of 1856 to recruit his failing health. In the autumn of the same year, he formed a determination to take up his residence, for a time, in Germany, for the purpose of making himself familiar with the literature of that country. He did not, however, carry his purpose into effect until the opening of the year, when he left Scotland for Berlin. On the eve of his departure, the death of Hugh Miller had made vacant the editorial chair of the Edinburgh Witness. Not long after

Mr. Bayne's arrival in Berlin, he was appointed to fill the vacancy thus created. The Witness, a politico-religious journal, was the organ of the Free Church, and under the conduct of Hugh Miller it had become a power in Scotland. That Mr. Bayne was thought worthy to succeed such a man, and to assume such responsibilities, was a compliment of the highest character. The appointment was accepted, to take effect at a future day; and meantime he continued his German studies. Before these were completed, a more tender engagement was formed by his betrothal to the daughter of Major General Gerwien, of the Prussian army.

In the summer of 1857, he returned from the continent, and on the first of August entered upon his duties as editor of the Witness. The columns of that journal have since borne constant testimony to the fertility of his resources. Among other elaborate papers, there has appeared a series in Defence of Hugh Miller's "Testimony of the Rocks," against an attack in the North British Review. These papers have excited so much attention that a pamphlet edition of them has been called for and issued. In this way, the intellectual wealth that should be concentrated into books for the pleasure and profit of all, is poured out through channels designed to reach the Scottish public alone. It cannot be, however, that journalism, worthy and noble though it be, will be allowed to divert Mr. Bayne, for a long period, from what he has demonstrated to be the true mission of his life; and the expression of an earnest desire to that effect, in behalf of his numerous admirers in America, may fitly close this notice.

BOSTON, APRIL, 1858.

CONTENTS.

VI.

VII.

VIII.

IX.

X.

XI.

ESSAYS

IN

BIOGRAPHY AND CRITICISM.

I.

CHARLES KINGSLEY.

THERE are cases in which, by reason of certain postulates which he finds himself entitled to assume, the task
of the critic is simplified and facilitated in an important
degree. These postulates enable him to strike the key-
note, to determine the ground-tone of his criticism.
Towards all that can be characterized as fault, he must be
severe; towards what is merely error, he may be mild,
however decided. If he perceives that the author or book
on which he comments is radically ignoble, radically promotive of laxity in principle or licentiousness in practice,
however marked exceptions may be, and however dexter-
ously the mask may be worn, it is his duty, with stern hand,
to tear aside the angel's veil, and show the features of the
demon. If he perceives that the heart of the book or
author is sound, that, whatever errors may mingle with the
words spoken, their general sense is unequivocally and
firmly in favor of the good, the true, the beautiful, he must

remember that the value of such a voice is too great to permit the use of any harshness, that every objection or hint must be tempered by deference and toned by love. We feel ourselves at present in the happy alternative. However widely opinions may differ regarding Mr. Kingsley, there is one point upon which all are agreed : that his voice is that of a noble, earnest, generous-hearted man; that his whole nature vibrates with strong and perpetual sympathy with his fellow-men; and that the gifts which his heart prompts him to turn to the service of his country and his race are of no common order. With such men we may differ, but such men we cannot condemn. The spirit of their whole writings is a pledge that words of honest suggestion, of manly disagreement, will be cordially accepted and soberly weighed. Nay, in criticism we may pay them what is perhaps the highest compliment which can be paid to one of high literary eminence, that he would gladly see his fame and his writings go up in one holocaust and vanish, if a grain of precious truth, hitherto unseen, remained for his fellow-men upon the altar. Mr. Kingsley, we feel assured, will put but one question to any man who dissents from his conclusions — "Are you honest, and do you love the people?" If he can believe an affirmative answer, he will at once invite him to express his dissent to one who cannot be offended. We dissent from many of Mr. Kingsley's views, much as we value his writings; but we acknowledge that the light in him points to heaven, and that our only difference is as to the mode in which its illumination can be shed around on earth.

It is but to extend the application of these remarks from Mr. Kingsley to his writings, to say, that there is much in each and all of them which merits instant recognition and applause. A spirit of brotherly kindness breathes over

them all, of generous, hopeful ardor, of integrity, nobleness, purity; and, we have no hesitation in adding, of sincere reverence towards God, as well as love towards man.
The general influence of these books is good. If the intellectual food they afford be slight or questionable, the food
for the heart is wholesome and abundant. There are books
which cultivate the intellect, while they chill the heart;
books which one might imagine produced by a logical
machine, instead of a living man; books which seem all
fuel, and no fire. Such books are invaluable if rightly used,
but, on the whole, the want of heart in a book is dangerous. In Mr. Kingsley's volumes the emotions play, we
suspect, rather too important a part; yet their prevalence,
attuned, as they always are, to nobleness and valor, spreads
a general healthfulness around. To read his works, is like
travelling in a pleasant hilly country, where the fresh hearty
breeze brings you the strength of the mountains, and the
clear atmosphere shows you every line, and curve, and
streamer, of the clouds that race the wind. You may be
compelled to remark that the corn-fields are not so heavy
as in the rich plain, that perhaps the poppy and the corn-
flower, beautiful to the eye, but light on the granary-floor,
are somewhat too abundant, and that there is an ample
allowance of gay copse, and heath, and fern. But you feel
that, at least, there is no miasma, that there is no haze, such
as floats suspiciously over the rich, moist meadow, that you
are in a land of freshness, freedom, health.

We cannot, however, disguise the fact, that we have
hitherto stated what is short of the whole truth. There is
one other remark to be made concerning all such books as
Mr. Kingsley's, which will more than justify us in applying a searching criticism to his works. Nature has not the
slightest respect for men's intentions: with her, bulk and

2*

ornament go for nothing. If you have spent half your
lifetime in attempting to bridge a chasm, and have, in any
way, misplaced the key-stone, your arch will just fall when
the scaffolding is removed. Deck your barge in the beauties of Cleopatra's, let its sides glitter with gold, and its
sails gleam like the iris, if some unseen worm has bitten
through its timbers, it will sink just as fast as so many
tarred boards rudely nailed together. To get over the
ford, how many water-lilies, fairly dispread, and basking in
the radiance of their beauty, against just so many step-
ping-stones, bare and rugged, as will enable you, though
with difficulty, to get across?

This is certainly very plain, and may appear trite or
irrelevant; we believe that, in the present day, its importance is incalculable. In a time when thousands write,
when a brilliant, ornate, emphatic style is extremely fashionable, and when youthful ardor and impetuosity are so
commonly combined with peremptory dogmatism, it is
of real moment that men constantly remember, that it is
the bare fact, the simple truth, which can be of real avail.
Language has such powers of disguising error, that it were
no very absurd philosophic paradox to assert, that every
false opinion has arisen from its misuse. And it is a nobly
human task to perform the operation, which nature ultimately performs, upon every proposition presented for consideration; to rub off every hue, to draw aside every veil,
to remove every flower, and gaze on the naked fact; to
disrobe the glowing, the charming figure, till it is as bare
as a diagram of Euclid's. It is precisely the diagram which
nature will own. We would earnestly recommend readers
to apply this test to certain of our exuberant and meta-
phoric modern writers. Let them take a paragraph which
has dazzled them by its sparkling imagery, and borne them

away in the stream of its fervor; let them test the application of each simile; let them for the time close their ears to each appeal; let them hush every murmur of passion; and then let them apply to the simple argument of the passage the dry light of careful, unagitated thought. Well is it, when the book itself honestly invites this scrutiny; well is it, when the moral earnestness of the writer awakes in the reader such a conscientious desire for truth, that he feels himself urged to apply such criticism. We honor Mr. Kingsley, in believing, as we said, that he would have us treat his books in this way.

Mr. Kingsley is one of those men whom we could with most decision fix upon as representative of his age. By this we mean no assertion of extraordinary intellectual powers; we even intend to exclude the idea of his being a leader among his fellows; our assertion is, that sympathy is his determining characteristic, that the influences of the time are largely represented in his mode of thought and composition. His is precisely that order of mind of which it can be asserted, that its whole character and actings would have been changed, if it had arrived ten years earlier or ten years later in the world. He is one of those men who seem to be intended to serve as beacons, blazing fiercely *after* they have been once kindled, and showing, by the direction of the flame, how the wind of tendency is blowing. All men are moulded and moved by sympathy; a man cannot live by himself; he is bound to his race as no other being on earth is bound. But he also reacts upon his generation, upon circumstance, by force of individual character. These two facts are decisive in determining a man's rank in the scale of greatness, when by greatness we mean power. The dull man obeys, mechanically, the ruling ideas of his time, following his neighbors and feeling little in any way; the impulsive, the sympathetic, the superiorly gifted, are moved by that new force in the agencies of the time which voices itself most powerfully; the master minds feel the influences of their age, but see through them and over them, in free, independent strength, and utter words, or perform deeds, which will direct or influence, not their own generation only, but we know not how many succeeding generations. It were an extremely profitable mental exercise to solve, concerning any great man, the problem — What would he have been if placed in a different age? Had Plato and Calvin changed centuries, to what extent would their minds have been affected, and their work modified? We can confidently say, that though each would have been materially altered, yet each would have towered over his contemporaries, listening certainly to all they said, but speaking ever a louder, a more decisive word, of instruction, of guidance, of command. Of the second class of minds, in the descending order, the receptive, the emotional, the distinctively sympathetic, it is characteristic that their grasp of truth, in itself, is not so strong as to rid them sufficiently of influence from the fact, that other men have spoken for it or against it. They love truth sincerely and earnestly, but their power does not second their will; the emotional part of their nature so far intoxicates the intellectual, that what comes fairly attired in eloquence, pleading fearlessly, and sincerely, and well, is at once received as truth. If we were asked to eliminate the radical, unconscious, determining element in such minds, we would assert it to consist in this: that the instinctive axiom on which they proceed, is rather, that the voice of man cannot be wrong, than that the voice of God alone, simple truth unsupported by one vote under the sun, is eternally right. "He," says Coleridge, "who

asserts that truth is of no importance, except in the signification of sincerity, confounds sense with madness, and
the word of God with a dream." Yet, so mighty in its influence over man is man's voice, although all would assent
to the theoretic proposition, its practical application is of
extreme difficulty. Rigorously apply the test of thought
to the system of Shelley, and its value is nearly impalpable;
yield to the influence of his marvellous powers of expression, consent like a babe in its cradle to listen to his song,
until it lulls you into soft dreams, and bears you away to
its own gorgeous cloudland, and how completely you are
mastered! Some clever fellow might give us a *jeu d' esprit*,
entitled, "The works of Shelley translated into the language
of Butler;" two or three pages of a magazine would contain it. And how strange were the metamorphosis! From
the entrancing smiles, and rich glowing tones, and perfect
curves, and deep, passionate glance of a living goddess of
love, to a slight, wind-raised fringe of atheistic foam! Mr.
Carlyle is a very different man from Shelley; his knowledge of man and his pure intellectual power render any
comparison between the two absurd; yet we believe his
mind to be of the poetic type as distinctively as Shelley's,
and we say, without hesitation, that his influence on his
time — extending, as it does, mainly, if not solely, over
those who have become acquainted with his writings during the period of their youthful ardor — had been nowise
so mighty, if his powers of thought had been unaided by
his truly poetic powers of expression.

Mr. Kingsley has been profoundly influenced by the
writings of Mr. Carlyle; so profoundly, that at times he
seems almost to lose his personal identity. The axioms of
Mr. Carlyle's system of thought meet us, perhaps twice
repeated, in each chapter, and we must allege that they are

often given in their original bareness, without being materially unfolded, or pointing the way towards further truth.
Mr. Carlyle's forms of expression and of sentence are continually recurring, while we are forced to own the absence
of that original and piercing observation, and that occasional rhythmic cadence, which redeem their singularity in
his works.

But Mr. Kingsley is a minister of the Church of England,
a believer in Christianity. This is the second explicative
fact in determining his mental constitution and analyzing
his works. Christianity must be true; but Mr. Carlyle
cannot speak falsely: a union must be devised between
the two. And so Mr. Kingsley becomes one great representative of the influence of Mr. Carlyle upon believers in
Christianity in the nineteenth century. We speak not in
any tone of censure. It is, indeed, much the reverse. We
firmly believe that such men as Mr. Carlyle are not sent
into our world for nothing — that they may speak truth
which it is the duty of Christians to hear, expose errors or
delinquencies which it is the duty of Christians to amend.
We thank Mr. Kingsley for reminding us of an important
truth, when he tells us, "That God's grace, like his love, is
free, and that His Spirit bloweth where it listeth, and vin-
dicates its own free-will against our narrow systems, by
revealing at times, even to nominal heretics and infidels,
truths which the Catholic Church must humbly receive as
the message of Him who is wider, deeper, more tolerant,
than even she can be." Surely it is not well with a Christian church, when those who refuse the Christian name
exclaim, that they have applied to her the test appointed
by her Master, that they have looked round upon her works,
and have gained such a knowledge of her by so doing, that
they must assail her. We cannot, indeed, on any hypoth-

esis defend those who confound Christianity with hierarchy, in their attacks on the church.   When they have exhausted Christian morality, when they have raised the standard of holiness and of love higher than " Christ and his disciples " raised it, then they may speak against the Gospel of Jesus but the church must look warily and ponder well, when infidels assert that their standard is higher than hers, that the ancient, all-conquering banner is draggled in the mire. Mr. Kingsley is right in accepting Mr. Carlyle's writings as a stern and momentous warning to Christian churches to awake and bestir themselves.

From the influence of Mr. Carlyle, and all that he represents of modern doubt, modern inquiry, modern philosophy, come those two applications of Christianity to distinct phenomena of our time, which Mr. Kingsley has embodied in *Alton Locke* and *Hypatia*.   In the former, he endeavors to apply Christianity to the arrangements of our social system; in the latter, his chief effort is to show that Christianity alone allays and satisfies the cravings of the earnest philosophic skeptic.   It is unnecessary to dwell upon *Yeast*, since it is an exhibition rather than a removal of difficulties, a 'problem' without its solution.   We doubt not Mr. Kingsley would permit us to say, that the answers to the questions proposed in *Yeast* are to be found in the two works we have just referred to; not, perhaps, the complete and final answers, but, at least, the general outline of those methods by which national and individual health, moral, social, intellectual, are to be attained.   To these two works, then, we propose first to direct our attention, after quoting two short passages from *Yeast*, the first declarative of Mr. Kingsley's faith in the final victory of Christianity, the second very appropriately and cheeringly conclusive on the point that, however dark may be the revelations of

2*

Alton Locke, we have reason even in our century, to thank God and take courage.

"I believe that the ancient creed, the eternal gospel, will stand, and conquer, and prove its might in this age, as it has in every other for eighteen hundred years, by claiming, subduing, and organizing those young anarchic forces, which now, unconscious of their parentage, rebel against Him to whom they owe their being."

This is a good hope, and the man may act courageously in whose bosom it dwells. Yet we must remark, that such general declarations, except when based on a very wide and accurate induction, are of little value. If the period at which Christianity is to triumph is at an indefinite distance, the announcement is little better than a truism; a noble, a glorious truism, indeed; but of application to all times as well as the present. If Mr. Kingsley intends to declare that Christianity has hitherto prevailed over every form of infidelity, in such a manner and within such a time as to dispel all fear for its victory over skepticism in our century, we must demur to his correctness. It is as stern a duty to compute the force and to weigh the triumphs of the adversary, as it is to bare the sword, and march into the conflict. Whatever the shame and agony with which we accompany the concession, we must grant that the doctrines of Voltaire have been extensively victorious on the Continent. The fact is one of unspeakable sadness; but, like every fact honestly accepted and interpreted, it reads us important lessons. It points us to the Continent, where thrones totter, where armies march, where, for sixty years, human blood has been flowing in torrents from battle-plain and barricade; in these fearful characters it holds up to us the truth, that religion is the sheet-anchor of national stability, that the nations which know not God must perish. It tells us also that it is a dangerous thing to dally with error, to lay the beautifully-tinted, slumbering snake in the bosom. How little did many a philosophic abbè dream whither all that encyclopædism was leading! The ultimate tendency of principles is hard to define. Men may plant gardens on the sides of a volcano, and rejoice as the heat beneath insensibly increases, warming the roots of their flowers, and causing them to put forth fresh buds; until suddenly all are flung into the air. The doctrines of Carlyle and Emerson may lend a fresh vigor to Christianity; but let them who use them for that purpose, at the least, beware.

Now for our second preliminary extract:—

"How dare you, young man, despair of your own nation, while its nobles can produce a Carlyle, an Ellesmere, an Ashley, a Robert Grosvenor; while its middle classes can beget a Faraday, a Stevenson, a Brooke, an Elizabeth Fry? See, I say, what a chaos of noble materials is here — all confused, it is true — polarized, jarring, and chaotic — here bigotry, there self-will, superstition, sheer atheism often, but only waiting for the one inspiring Spirit, to organize, and unite, and consecrate this chaos into the noblest polity the world ever saw realized!"

A deliberate consideration of the great and hopeful fact expressed in this passage, the fact that, at this moment, in this island, there are, perhaps, as many noble intellects at work, and as many noble hearts beating, as were ever collected in the same space since the world began, might, we think, have spread a general air of moderation, and forbearance, and deference, over Mr. Kingsley's works, for which we look in vain.

Such occasional passages as the above do little more than excite our astonishment at the dogmatism of Mr. Kings-

ley's general opinions, and the asperity of his general
appeals. "It might seem incredible," said the cool and
large-minded Mackintosh, "if it were not established by
the experience of all ages, that those who differ most from
the opinions of their fellow-men are most confident of the
truth of their own." It is a kindred observation, and
equally true, that those whose opinions are hastily adopted,
those who refuse the long drudgery of thought, and think
with the heart rather than the head, are ever the most
fiercely dogmatic in their tone. Mr. Kingsley deals round
his blows at political economists, at evangelical clergymen,
at Calvinists, and others, with such fierce decision, that
we might reasonably expect to find him prepared with
some all-healing scheme, before which every other philanthropic or political device would hide its diminished head,
or, at least, with some carefully-thought refutation of opposing theories. But, instead of this, we find the remedy he
proposes to apply to our social ills to be one concerning
which the most ardent friend of the people may entertain
serious doubts; the answer he affords to our philosophic
questionings, however true, to be neither very novel, very
precise, nor very profound; and his refutation of opposing
theories to be little else than strong appeals to our feelings,
with certain disputable axioms from Mr. Carlyle. We are
happy, however, to be able to state, that Mr. Kingsley's
ablest work, *Hypatia*, is marked by a great improvement
in this respect. If a certain patronizing, pitying, condescending tone towards an old rheumatic church, and a
slow, un-ideal generation, still lingers on the page, we
gladly admit that it is nowise so conspicuous as elsewhere,
and that the dogmatism has as good as disappeared.

Alton Locke is a didactic novel, suggested by the sorrows of the tailors and needlewomen of the metropolis.

Its objects are, to open the eyes of the public to the horrors endured by large numbers of our working-classes, and to advocate a scheme by which these horrors can be removed.

The hero, Alton Locke, is a talented youth, born in extreme poverty; who becomes a tailor, a skeptic, a Chartist, an author, and ultimately an advocate of Christian socialism. The book opens with a sketch of his early life. He was quite a remarkable child. Not only was his moral nature superhumanly faultless, but his love of nature was so intense, that he found his delight in zoölogizing among the beetles and worms, which children in general shun.

His mother was also, in her way, remarkable. She was a Calvinist, who carried Calvinism further than we ever saw it carried; to an extent, indeed, which we consider impossible. She is represented as exceeding logical. "She dared not even pray for our conversion, earnestly as she prayed on every other subject. . . . . . Had it not been decided from all eternity?" Yet "her clear logical sense" failed to perceive that just as God knew from all eternity who would be his redeemed in time, so He knew every other matter; that this was not his single act of omniscience and omnipotence. Calvinism sets its foot upon the fact of God's foreknowledge, implying, as it does, certainty; an honest opponent of Calvinism must allow that it enjoins the use of all possible means. We cannot but think Mr. Kingsley has here drawn a supposititious character, has rather looked at what he conceived to be Calvinism, and embodied what he believed to be its inevitable results, than drawn from actual life. There never was a more decided Calvinist than Jonathan Edwards; we recommend his works to Mr. Kingsley as an answer to the question whether Calvinism destroys active endeavor after conversion or all-embracing and earnest prayer. If Mrs. Locke was too logical to pray for the conversion of her children, it was by a breach of logic that she prayed for anything in the world.

His mother's Calvinism develops precocious skepticism in young Alton, so that, when he comes in contact with clever infidelity, among the journeymen tailors with whom he goes to work, he speedily loses his early belief in the Bible as the Word of God. He becomes acquainted with an old Scotchman, named Sandy Mackaye, shrewd, speculative, warm-hearted, and an intense admirer of Mr. Carlyle. The influence of Sandy, and of John Crossthwaite, an intelligent Chartist tailor, prevails so far with Alton, as to make him an ardent Chartist. He gives early indications of high literary ability, and soon commences to rhyme. In a picture-gallery he falls vehemently in love with the daughter of a dean, in his affection for whom he is thwarted by a malicious and selfish cousin. He is on the Chartist side on the famous 10th of April, but takes no part in the proceedings. At length he expires, just as he comes within sight of the American coast, whither he had set out, in conformity with the last will and testament of Sandy Mackaye. Besides Alton Locke and Sandy, there are several other characters of importance; a philanthropic, scientific dean, who is so devoid of aristocratic exclusiveness as to invite a journeyman tailor to reside for some time in his house, on a footing of perfect equality, merely because he has displayed uncommon talents; a variety of distressed tailors; and a Lady Eleanor Staunton, who marries a cultivated and benevolent nobleman, becomes a widow, expends her fortune in works of charity, is ahead of her whole age in Christian philanthropy and philosophy, converts Alton and Crossthwaite, and in every way approves herself what the heroine of a philanthropic novel ought to be.

We shall not enlarge upon the fact that probability is unceremoniously violated in *Alton Locke*. That such is the case, is undeniable, and has been elsewhere very forcibly pointed out. This, indeed, is no unusual circumstance in the novels of Mr. Kingsley. His characters very often move in an atmosphere of their own — exhibit qualities and experience emotions peculiar to themselves. That ride of Lancelot's after the fox, in the commencement of *Yeast*, is a remarkable illustration of the fact. If Mr. Kingsley himself performed that notable ride, we will take his assertion as indisputable; but we must be permitted to doubt whether any other man ever rode after a fox in the like fashion. With the prize in view, and coming down hill, Lancelot checks his horse to sentimentalize on the affecting circumstance that the hounds have leaped over the paling of a churchyard; he sees a lady emerge from the church, who quite changes the current of his ideas; he dashes on again after the fox; but, as the saddle, during a steeple-chase, is a peculiarly fitting place, from its repose and safety, for philosophic dreaming, he thinks nothing of his horse, but only of the ladye-love he has just seen; "his understanding was trying to ride, while his spirit was left behind with Argemone." He comes back to himself precisely at the moment when he ought to have stayed away, just as his horse is clearing a high paling; his first act of returning consciousness is to check the steed in mid-air, and of course bring him down on the palings. Really, the probability would have been rather enhanced than otherwise, by our being informed that the whole apparatus, horse and man, was constructed of timber, and went by steam. In violence of emotion, again, and sudden change of scene, we might back Mr. Kingsley's novels against any production of the Minerva Press. The period

and scene in which the plot of *Hypatia* is laid, were so
confused and tumultuous, that there is an apology at hand
for considerable commotion and excitement. But, even
with this concession, we must submit that the whole book
wears too much the aspect of a frenzied dream, and that no
mere mortal could possibly weep so much, swoon so much, be
enraptured so much, as that sorely-tried youth Philammon,
within a few days, and yet survive. Mr. Kingsley's figures
seem beyond the influence of those sedatives which nature
has kindly appointed for the excited brain. "Day and
night successive, and the timely dew of sleep," of which
Adam spoke to Eve, seem not to affect them. Nay, the
usual tranquillizing effects of mere eating and drinking,
the mere clogging of the ethereal principle by the body to
which it is chained, appear to be escaped by them. All
their emotions are in the superlative degree; if extremes
are always false, we tremble for Mr. Kingsley's reputation
as a depicter of character. We have our own objections
to bring against Mr. Thackeray, but here he deserves all
praise; his characters, however devoid they may be of any
important power to instruct or animate, are just the poor,
dull human beings, or the supposably clever people, one
meets in actual life. Mr. Kingsley's figures appear to move
about in an atmosphere of fire-mist.

In his hero, Alton Locke, Mr. Kingsley has, perhaps unconsciously, drawn a character which is very common in
the present day. His radical quality, little as he or Mr.
Kingsley thinks so, is intellectual weakness. He staggers
on from opinion to opinion, taking his ideas always from
the more powerful minds with which he comes in contact;
when he dies, we are by no means sure that, had he lived
seven years, he would not have returned from America
with his opinions entirely altered once more. We have

long admired and wondered at the power of Shakspeare in portraying such men as Alton Locke. He has a large class of characters, whose distinguishing quality it is, that persuasion has absolute power over them. Such are Coriolanus, Othello, Cassius the friend of Othello; our readers may recollect many others. They are noble fellows all; full of fire, of generosity, of intensity; their words are metaphorical and far-sounding; but, somehow or other, the reason is always led captive; the will stoops to receive the yoke; despite asseveration, despite determination, the point at which they will yield to entreaty can be calculated and assigned. Of this radical type is Alton Locke; with sufficient eloquence of voice and smile, Lillian could have turned him to anything; his actions are impulsive and headstrong, his feelings occupy the throne in his mind. We agree most cordially with the grand truth, whose promulgation brings this book to a conclusion; the grand truth that Christianity alone can save the working-man: but certainly, the fact that a beautiful benefactress converts Alton to this faith, as the last of a variety of opinions, would weigh very little with us in its adoption.

Sandy Mackaye is certainly a very ably-drawn and instructive character. He has been recognized as the best figure in the book, and we care not to combat the opinion; yet we think that Alton Locke is, in his way, just as true to nature. Sandy is a fierce realist, who reads old history and politics, and the works of Mr. Carlyle; who cannot away with any high-flown mysticism, or wanderings in the regions of the ideal; who loves the people with a profound and unquenchable love; whose talk may at times be crabbed, but whose heart is always warm; and who rests immovably in the fact, that moral excellence is the only hope for the poor man. It were absurd to deny that Mr. Kings-

ley has displayed extraordinary powers in depicting Sandy
Mackaye. Yet, even here, we have one word of objection,
and again its application extends beyond the present instance. Mr. Kingsley exhibits on various occasions an
intimate acquaintance with Mr. Carlyle's and Goethe's great
doctrine of unconsciousness; he must also from the great
"Harpocrates-Stentor" have heard a great deal about
silence. How is it, then, that his characters are so extremely conscious, and so extremely talkative? There is
no law of which we can more confidently affirm the universality — witness nature and Shakspeare — than the law
that those who act greatly and feel deeply do not talk
much. Great men are marked by their power to dispense
with human sympathy: "silence is the perfectest herald of
joy;" and who does not know that the proud heart, in its
moments of deepest anguish, scorns to vent its sorrow in
words? Mr. Carlyle rightly rejects the story that Burns
was seen by some tourists in a theatrical garb and attitude,
knowing that his manly mind would have shaken away
such frivolous distinction. Cromwell was no man to make
collections of bits of armor from his various fields, or of
flags from the various castles he reduced. Does Shakspeare
make mighty Julius talk much? We cannot believe that
Sandy Mackaye's room was decorated as Mr. Kingsley
avers. Political caricatures dangling from the roof; obnox-
ious books impaled; Icon Basilike "dressed up in a paper
shirt, all drawn over with figures of flames and devils, and
surmounted by a peaked paper cap, like an *auto-da-fe;*"
— all this is too trivial, too external, for the man who will
risk his life for freedom. Go into the room of the juvenile
amateur Chartist, whose valor all evaporates at the sight
of a baton, and you will probably find the whole. Mr.
Kingsley's characters are always opening up to you their

whole hearts; every emotion must reach the tongue; Eleanor alone, of all his figures that we at present recollect,
exhibits a slight trace of most refreshing taciturnity. One
is reminded, in listening to their incessant parade of emotion, of those regarding whom Guizot, quoting from Petrarch, says, that their "tongue was at once their lance and
sword, their casque and buckler." We really mean to give
Mr. Kingsley a friendly hint, when we remind him of that
masterly stroke in Sallust's portraiture of Jugurtha, "plu-
rimum facere, minimum de se loqui."

We cannot dwell upon particular scenes in *Alton Locke*,
but we must express our unqualified admiration of that
chapter in which Sandy Mackaye, after listening to Alton's
poetry about the island in the Pacific, suddenly drags him
away to visit certain scenes which he knows in London,
and which, by Sandy's irresistible recommendation, become
thenceforth the sole subjects of Alton's muse. The boy's
rhymes about his adopted island, which was to be colon-
ized and converted by missionaries, are remarkably good;
one is tempted to imagine them real productions; the lowest praise that can be given them is, that they are fac-
similes. The fragments of the description of the isle, with
its central volcano, which,

> " Shaking a sinful isle with thundering shocks,
>   Reproved the worshippers of stones and stocks,"

admit of no improvement. Sandy laughs heartily at this
rhyme, but, relapsing into a very serious mood, leads the
youth swiftly away to give him a glimpse of the poetry of
reality. He brings him first to an alley, where, on the one
hand, a gin-palace, and on the other, a pawnbroker's shop,
feed, like two hell-born monsters, on the poor. The scene
is depicted with harrowing distinctness: —

"But all this," whines Alton, "is so — so unpoetical."

"Hech!" exclaims Sandy, "is there no' heaven above
them there, and the hell beneath them? and God frown-
ing, and the devil grinning! No poetry there! Is no' the
verra idea o' the classic tragedy defined to be, man conquered by circumstance? Canna ye see it there? And
the verra idea of the modern tragedy, man conquering circumstance? And I 'll show ye that, too, in many a garret
where no eye but the gude God's enters, to see the patience,
and the fortitude, and the self-sacrifice, and the luve stronger
than death, that 's shining in thae dark places o' the earth.
Come wi' me, and see."

Sandy then guides Alton to a miserable garret, where a
wretched family drag out a wo-stricken existence in utter
want. Yet the pride of other days lingers there, and the
work-house is recoiled from. One girl lies dying on a cold
bed, yet enjoying the purest joys of religious rapture. Another is driven, to avert the absolute starvation of her
mother and the rest, to that resource which is worse than
death, which is suggestive of the most profoundly melancholy reflections to which even our dark world can give
rise. No part of *Uncle Tom's Cabin* seems to us to
reach the pathos which has been reached by Mr. Kingsley
in this passage. The mother prefers absolute starvation to
shame, and appeals to Sandy to expostulate with her daughter as to her conduct. The latter, in such tones as may be
imagined, breaks in thus: — "Repent — I have repented
— I repent of it every hour — I hate myself, and hate all
the world, because of it; but I must — I must. I cannot
see her starve, and I cannot starve myself." And then
what inexpressible pathos is here! — "Oh! if that fine lady
as we 're making that riding-habit for, would just spare
only half the money that goes in dressing her up to ride

in the park, to send us out to the colonies, would n't I be an honest girl there!—Maybe, an honest man's wife! Oh, my God! would n't I slave my fingers to the bone for him!"

Sandy, on their departure, thus sums up all to the young poet:—"Poetic element? Yon lassie, rejoicing in her disfigurement, like the nuns of Peterborough in auld time —is there no poetry there? That puir lassie, dying on the bare boards, and seeing her Saviour in her dreams, is there no poetry there, callant? That ould body owre the fire, wi' her "an officer's dochter," is there no poetry there? —tragedy

> ' With hues as when some mighty painter dips
> His pen in dyes of earthquake and eclipse.'

Ay, Shelly's gran'; always gran'; but fact is grander— God and Satan are grander. All around ye, in every gin-shop and costermonger's cellar, are God and Satan at death-gripes; every garret is a haill 'Paradise Lost' or 'Paradise Regained,' and will ye think it beneath ye to be the people's poet?"

That whole chapter is masterly.

We think also that the description of Sandy's death is a singularly felicitous effort of genius. The old man had doubted and speculated long, clear only of one thing, that it was his duty to love his neighbor as himself, and give his every faculty to resist the empire of darkness here on earth. The times were perplexing, ominous, dreary; he could not fathom or explain God's dealings with men; but he stood firm in his integrity; and closed his lips with these words, "Shall not the Judge of all the earth do right— right—right——" Higher than this "ground plan of the universe," than this simple faith in infinite Wisdom and infinite Love, no finite intellect has gone.

Mr. Kingsley has an immovable conviction that the
evils of society can be cured by bringing Christianity to
bear upon them. It was the idea of the life of Chalmers.
We need not say that our hope, too, lies here. Mr. Kingsley, in *Alton Locke*, and in all his books, invokes Christians to commence the aggressive Christianization of the
masses of our population. He cuts mercilessly into what
is now becoming generally known by Mr. Carlyle's nick-
name, "respectability." The Christianity of custom, the
comfortable religion that is anxious, for safety's sake, to
show a good example, all Christianity that does not recog-
nise the equalizing energy of the gospel of Jesus, stripping
men to the bare souls, and showing them all brethren if
they are in Christ Jesus,·he lays bare with ruthless hands,
and bids away. Disguise it as we will, the fact pointed at
in the following paragraph is as undeniable as it is portentous : —

"Is not," asks one, "the Church of England the very
purest form of apostolic Christianity?"

"It may be," is the answer, "and so may the other sects.
But, somehow, in Judea, it was the publicans and harlots
who pressed into the kingdom of heaven; it was the common people who heard Christ gladly. Christianity, then,
was a movement in the hearts of the lower order. But
now, my dear fellow, you rich, who used to be told, in St.
James's time, to weep and howl, have turned the tables
upon us poor. It is *you* who are talking all along of con-
verting *us*. Look at any place of worship you like, orthodox and heretical; who fill the pews? the pharisees and
the covetous, who used to deride Christ, fill his churches,
and say still, 'This people, these masses, who know not
the gospel, are accursed.' And the universal feeling, as
far as I can judge, seems to be, not, 'how hardly shall

they who have,' but hardly shall they who have *not*, 'riches enter into the kingdom of heaven.'"

This is put into the mouth of a working-man, or one who has but partially emerged from the ranks of those who work with their hands. We shall hope there is somewhat of exaggertion in the words, particularly in application to one part of the island. Yet, granting that the representation is in the main correct, we are forced to remark, that the fault lies as much with working-men themselves, as with any other class. Can any class expunge from the Bible those declarations which make it emphatically the book of the poor? or hide the fact, that Christ and his apostles were poor? Why, then, must Christianity ever be confounded with the short-comings of Christians, the Church in which all are kings and priests, with a priesthood? Let working-men ponder this other passage:—

"Take all the heroes, prophets, poets, philosophers, where will you find the true demagogue, the speaker to man simply as man, the friend of publicans and sinners, the stern foe of the scribe and the pharisee, with whom was no respect of persons? Socrates and Plato were noble; Zerdusht and Confutzee, for all we know, were nobler still; but what were they but the exclusive mystagogues of an enlightened few, like our own Emersons and Strausses, to compare great things with small? What gospel have they, or Strauss or Emerson, for the poor, the suffering, the oppressed? The people's friend; where will you find him but in Jesus of Nazareth?"

It is to Christianity, then, that Mr. Kingsley looks for the regeneration of society. So far he has our cordial assent. When we come to examine his scheme for its application to our social disorders, we must confess more of hesitation. He proposes a universal union among the various sections of the working-classes, for co-operation in production and division of profits. There is nothing, at least, wild or visionary in the project. There are many associations of workmen in France, and in several instances they have been found successful. It is easy to form the idea of each trade as a vast joint-stock company, in which the workmen are both owners and laborers. Mr. Kingsley proposes no arbitrary levelling of ranks; he perceives that, in countless cases, individual cupidity and individual helplessness produce, on the one hand, exorbitant wealth, on the other, destitution and slavery; he would substitute the economy of working owners for the cupidity of one, the superintendence of indispensable functionaries for the fortuitous extortion of middle-men. In this there is really nothing absurd or chimerical. The era of the equal enjoyment of comfort by each class of the community is still beyond ken in the remoteness of the future; but the period when an attempt may be made towards the approximation of classes has, we hope, arrived; and we see no danger in adopting, as the basis of this attempt, the principle of co-operation among the laboring class.

But when we lend this cautious sanction to the essential principle of Mr. Kingsley's schemes, he must bear with us while we give him two brief but emphatic counsels, attention to which is necessary to even a possibility of success. First, we must assure him that the difficulties which stand in the way of a practical realization of his plan are of the gravest description. For an exposition of these difficulties, we refer our readers to Mr. Greg's very able essays on the subject. We cannot consider the reasonings of that talented writer absolutely conclusive; but we can say, that they render the tone in which Mr. Kingsley advocates his scheme utterly indefensible. Only in calm and deliberate moods can such questions be treated; not when the blood is on fire with excitement, and the eye blind with burning tears; in the anxious recollection of what Goethe says about the danger of "active ignorance," and in the conviction that the problem to be solved in theory and practice might demand the abstraction of a Newton and the sagacity of a Napoleon, must such proposals be entertained. We must hear no more about "the fiend of competition." The sympathies of all save those who have a selfish interest in the prolongation of present distress, are with the philanthropic reformer. The boyish mistake must not be committed, of confounding with the rancor of cupidity that which may be the anticipation of nature's decision. Our second counsel to Mr. Kingsley is of kin to our first; we advise him to speak no more in a tone of contempt of political economy. It is true, that he mentions Mr. Mill with respect, but there is no disguising the sneer with which he greets the science of which Mr. Mill is a leading exponent. We may grant he is not quite consistent here; we suppose he would have Christian pastors acquainted with the principles of social science; but he cannot rid himself of the influence of Mr. Carlyle's denunciation of political economy. Now, if there is one opinion in the circle of ideas in which every reflective man may be expected to agree, it is, that Mr. Carlyle is here absolutely wrong. It can be no defence to say, that political economists advocate such and such a scheme; this is merely attributing to Mr. Carlyle a vulgar and childish error. Political economists are not men who advocate any scheme whatever, any more than astronomers are men who advocate any particular theory of light or of gravitation: astronomers are men who devote themselves to the discovery of what the laws regulating the heavenly bodies are; political

economists are those who bend their powers to the elimination of one great class of the laws which regulate the
social system.   Their only postulate is one which Mr. Carlyle reiterates, " ubi homines sunt, modi sunt; " where men
exist together for an hour, and act together in any particular way, there will spring up certain modes of thought and
action.   If there are no such modes in our economic affairs,
if this is the only province in the universe where sequence
is, *prima facie,* as untraceable as in the domain of the An-
arch old, or if it is an evil that men, before proceeding to
work, should simply and without further assumption *know*
the elements with which they have to do, then can Mr.
Carlyle be defended in his attacks on the economists.   His
tone is not that of remonstrance; it is that of unmeasured
contempt and indignation; and the thunder and flash of
his aimless artillery have deafened and dazzled Mr. Kingsley.   The fact is, that the arguments which can be adduced
against political economists, as such, are almost unanswerably absurd; they remind one of Shelley's differently-ap-
plied expression, "invulnerable nothings; " they are ghosts
too filmy for lead or bayonet, but which the first glimpse
of daylight resolves into invisibility.

In *Alton Locke,* Mr. Kingsley weighs Christianity as a
gospel of temporal salvation for the people.   In *Hypatia,* he
measures it as a substitute for ancient and modern philosophy.   We shall not say that the execution in *Hypatia*
corresponds to the grandeur of the idea or the importance
of the subject ; but we accord Mr. Kingsley the high praise
that he has in this work correctly read one great sign of
the times.   The thesis he attempts to prove in *Hypatia* may
be concisely expressed thus : — Christianity brings philosophy into life, and life into philosophy : on the one hand, it
brings down into the hearts of men the ideas of purity which

floated formerly in a few rare minds; on the other, it hallows all those social relations with which philosophy has in
all ages shown such a willingness to meddle. We might
expatiate on the power displayed in separate passages in
this book. We might congratulate Mr. Kingsley on the
fact, that his colors retain all their richness and brilliancy,
being, indeed, rather deepened and enriched than otherwise. But, on the whole, we must pronounce *Hypatia* a
failure. We have a general and grave objection to the
method adopted by its author for the promulgation of his
views. Even waiving the consideration of the fitness of
the novel for the discussion of any controverted question
— and here Mr. Greg's objections have considerable weight
— we put it calmly to Mr. Kingsley, whether the momentous
interests he desires to serve are best promoted by a series
of fictions? It is a new thing, surely, to reconstruct society
on a foundation of brilliant and fashionable novels. Really,
if this example prevails, discussion will become, in the
happy ages of our children, a different thing from what it
has been hitherto. Its liveliness will be indescribable. Only
conceive the change that will come about in the matter of
citations. No longer will one groan over such references
as these: — Thom. Aq. Summ. Theol. (lib. x., cap. xi., sec.
xii.); Duns. Scot. de Sent. Lombard. (prop. iii., sec. iv.);
Grot. de Jure Belli et Pacis (vol. i., lib. ii., cap. iii.). We
shall be charmed by such authorities as these: — "The
Christian Religion and the Rights of man " (see exhort. at
bedside of Alt. Locke, by Elean. Lyne. stand. nov., vol. xi.
Kings.) ; "The Fundamental Distinction between Religion
and Philosophy" (see speech declar. of Ed. Clifford to
Angel. Goldfinch. Bent., ser., vol. xix.). There is a good
time coming, boys and girls, sure enough! But joking
apart, we seriously think novels are not the best vehicle

for such important proposals as Mr. Kingsley's. Surely the
suffrage of the boarding-schools is not of such extreme
value. Would not a few calmly-argued treatises, which
men might read and ponder, be of more real weight than
an indefinite number of drawing-room fictions? To this
extent our objection applies to all such novels as Mr. Kingsley's. But of *Hypatia* we are compelled to say yet more.
We think it is a failure on its own ground. We cannot be
charged with bias in favor of philosophy against Christianity, yet we acknowledge our impression, after witnessing
the part each plays in the book, to be rather in favor of the
former than the latter. Surely Mr. Kingsley, in almost
morbid candor, permitted an adversary to choose his facts.
To assail philosophy by a picture of its loveliest and one
of its purest martyrs; to advocate Christianity in a book
many of whose darkest scenes are pictures of Christian
atrocity, and whose catastrophe is one of the blackest crimes
ever gloated over by a Gibbon:—we pause in astonishment
at the anomaly! But, rejoins Mr. Kingsley, it was my
object to teach a lesson to Christians also; to show them
that force and fraud can never be wedded to Christianity,
without a baneful progeny being the result. Such, it is
true, was Mr. Kingsley's aim; but he leaves himself very
much in the case of him who wrote a severe attack upon
himself and neglected the intended vindication. We see
the evil in full operation, there is a dramatic exhibition of
that; but we discover only from a few didactic hints, that
matters would have been mended by a different state of
circumstances. With all its gorgeousness of coloring, and
sustained intensity of interest, and general correctness of
conclusion, *Hypatia* must be pronounced a failure.

In the composition of *Westward Ho*, Mr. Kingsley had
a purpose less expressly didactic than that of the novels

we have mentioned. He approached his subject more entirely from the artistic point of view, desirous not so much to illustrate or enforce an argument, applicable at a particular time and to one class of circumstances, as to depict scenes fitted to evoke universal and perpetual admiration, and to delineate characters with which all generations might sympathize. To emerge thus into the wider sphere of general art must have been felt as a decided advantage by Mr. Kingsley; and an advantage corresponding to that experienced by him, might have been looked for, in a more natural and easy freedom of narrative, and in didactic inferences less strained and premeditated, by readers. This expectation would not have been altogether disappointed. *Westward Ho* is in some respects the most hearty, healthful, and true, of Mr. Kingsley's fictions. His sympathy with the old heroes whom he endeavors to portray, is genuine and profound; in the rocky coves of the coast of Devon and on the pleasant hills of its interior, his step is elastic and joyous as if he had known them in his youth; and although he never wrote without a present glow of enthusiasm in his subject, it may easily be believed that neither in the description of the Greeks of the Nile, nor in the exposure and treatment of our social maladies, was he, on the whole, so much at home, as in company of the Raleighs and Drakes, with ancient philosophy and modern economics both in the distance. But it cannot be alleged that any radical change has taken place in Mr. Kingsley's style of thought and expression. Sympathy with all that is strong, fearless, honorable, and beautiful, — richness and profusion of color, — hopefulness, buoyancy, breadth of sunny light and general cheerfulness, — these we were formerly accustomed to from Mr. Kingsley, and these are present still. But the old recklessness of assertion, the

old excitement and feverish haste, the old boisterousness
of tone, the old extravagance of conception, meet us still.

The object set before himself by Mr. Kingsley in writing
Westward Ho was, as he informs us in his opening chapter,
to do honor to the memory of England's heroes of 1588,
the time of the Armada, the Drakes, the Hawkinses, the
Gilberts, the Raleighs, the Grenviles, the Oxenhams, men
not only of England but of Devon; and, honoring them,
to proclaim to Englishmen the "same great message which
the songs of Troy, and the Persian wars, and the trophies
of Marathon and Salamis, spoke to the hearts of all true
Greeks of old."

Both the aim here indicated and the subject chosen
merit high commendation. The period of British history
to which Mr. Kingsley leads us back, affords rich and varied
materials for the epic poet, the historian, and the historical
novelist. Stirring and lofty incident, well-marked, strong,
and noble character, splendid and diversified coloring,
equally abound. It was the time when the nations were
arranging themselves after the mighty convulsion of the
Reformation. The work occupied several centuries, and
Mr. Kingsley contemplates one of the most important parts
of the imposing process. The spirit of Protestantism had
awakened. Superstition, its eye bleared and dim with the
darkness of a thousand years, had staggered and reeled,
with groping hands that seemed about to fall powerless, in
the shafts of the far-stretching moral dawn. But another
spirit had come up upon the earth, a spirit whose birth-
place, can we hesitate to say, was in the nether deep of
hell: the spirit of Jesuitism. Into the tottering frame of
Superstition this spirit entered, lending a new throb to its
fainting heart, arousing it once more to assert its sway.
Then began a great contest: its theatre the old and new

worlds, and the great oceans by which they are encompassed; its actors the nations that led the van of civilization. The nations which, at the period chosen by Mr.
Kingsley, specially supported the contest, were England
and Spain. In England, reigned Elizabeth. Her character
was not of the noblest. Vanity might be pardoned; but
the hand of time will never efface the dark stains of cruelty
and hypocrisy from that queenly brow: and Mr. Kingsley,
chivalrous as he is, might have attained a higher nobleness
than that of chivalry, the nobleness of dauntless and un-
deviating devotion to truth, by rather damping, on this
account, his enthusiasm for "Gloriana." But whatever her
failings, Elizabeth represented much of what was noblest
in her time: her intellect was calm and sagacious: and she
had the will of a sovereign born. She was surrounded by
a constellation of able and courageous men, who served
her with the loyalty of subjects to their monarch, and with
the devotion of true knights to a noble lady. Flattery, in
the court of Elizabeth, seems to deserve a less ignoble
name. We shall not say it was in small and sordid selfishness that Raleigh laid his mantle under her feet, or that
the gentle Spenser warbled silver strains of adulation in
her ear. Turning from England to Spain, the prospect,
though contrasted, is perhaps equally remarkable. Perhaps
no nation of modern times has presented an appearance so
well fitted to attract the poet or dramatist, as that presented
by Spain in the sixteenth century. The Spaniard alone
among Europeans retained the ancient devotion to Rome;
a devotion unaffected by doubt, unbroken by inquiry; a
devotion unmeasured in degree and which suggests the
infinite. Such devotion cannot exist without imparting to
the character of man or nation a certain austere grandeur, a certain epic sublimity. But this was not the only

circumstance which renders the Spaniard of the sixteenth century an object worthy of contemplation. His countrymen had led the way to the new world. His country was the leading power in Europe. Combining the pride and valor of antiquity, with the spirit of enterprise then beginning to mark itself as a characteristic of modern times; strong in faith as an old Hebrew, yet crafty, cruel, and indomitable; he exhibits the finest effects of light and shade, the subtlest blending of good and evil. His figure might have been painted by a Rembrandt: his character might have been studied by a Shakspeare.

To all this we must add a consideration of the stage on which such actors as these played their part. The grandeurs of the western world were then unfolding themselves, like a mighty panorama, to the eyes of Europe; and if we would conceive aright the effect produced by that grand panorama, we must heighten its natural colors, as now known and defined by us, with all the hues cast over it by an awakening and excited imagination. In our own time, we have seen the nations startled, allured, and set in motion, by gold. Westward and southward, to the ends of the earth, men have rushed to its witching gleam. But the poetry, the wonder, the enchantment, which hovered over the gold regions of the sixteenth century, are here no longer. We know all about the matter now. We examine the country geologically. We pound the quartz with engines. We search the dross heap with mercury. All is clear, precise, scientific, prosaic. We call the auriferous localities, diggings; a word hardly yet adapted for an epic poem! We know exactly what we have to expect when we go out. If we find one or two nuggets, we are fortunate men; but our principal occupations must be digging, with aching back, in a grave-like pit, and splashing and

rinsing among mud and puddle. The country, too, in which
we must work, is of the commonplace. Venturing into
the interior, of Australia at least, we may perish for
want of water. The natives are wretched Bushmen; the
animals opossums and kangaroos. How different was it
in the days of Cortes and Pizarro, of Drake and Raleigh!
If you went out with a few venturous companions, you
might found a kingdom, amass untold treasures, and eat
from dishes of gold. You expected to see the yellow metal
glittering on the mountain-side. The roots of the herb
you plucked up by the wayside might be intertwined with
wreaths of silver. You had heard of the golden city of
Manoa, in the midst of its sacred lake, where the eye lit
only on gold. Wise and sober men assured you of the
existence of this city, and the wandering Indians who told
the tale, themselves believed it. The known wonders of
Mexico and Peru seemed to make nothing impossible. Far
away in the west, bosomed in forests to which the woods
of Europe were shrubberies, and over which gleamed a
thousand flowers, seated in that mystic lake, Manoa was,
for at least a century, the point towards which the eyes of
the daring and adventurous in the old lands were turned.
The magnificence of the other physical conditions of the
New World corresponded with its interest as the region
of exhaustless wealth. The Andes overtopped the Alps,
the European rivers dwindled to rivulets beside Amazon
and La Plata. The condor soared among the peaks and
snows of the mountains, the jaguar prowled amid the endless forests. Birds, whose plumage vied with the brilliancy
of the flowers around them, thronged the river banks,
perching on the boughs of gigantic trees, at whose foot
crocodiles lay basking in the sun. Let it now be conceived
that all this was borne to the nations of Europe on the

4*

shadowy wings of rumor, and came with all the power of
novelty upon peoples still apt to wonder; and some idea
will be formed of the witching splendors which encircled
America in the eyes of Europe, in the sixteenth century.

With such materials as these, the fervid imagination of
Mr. Kingsley could scarcely have failed to produce a powerful effect.   No one can arise from his pages, however hasty
his perusal of the book, without having had his conception
of all connected with the period brought out in vivid clearness.   What we have said can convey but a very faint idea
of Mr. Kingsley's luxuriant description and fine enthusiasm.
His delineations of character, too, are by no means unsuccessful.   The English sea-captains of the period, those

> " Adventurous hearts who barter'd bold
> Their English blood for Spanish gold,"

are brought before us face to face.   There is, indeed, no attempt made to depict the highest minds of the time in
their highest employments.   We are brought once or twice
to glance for a moment into the councils of the nation, and
have a pretty distinct idea of the views entertained by the
great actors in the event of the book — the defeat of the
Armada.   But Sir Amyas Leigh is really nothing better
than a rough, shrewd, resolute sea-captain; one of a class
which may have influenced the destinies of England, but
hardly such an one as would individually exercise an important influence on them.   We doubt not, however, that
precisely such men as this Sir Amyas wrested their gold
from the Spaniards in that century, burned and ravaged
along the Spanish main, and prowled like wolves of the
ocean for the silver fleet.   As we should have expected,
Mr. Kingsley has made them somewhat too talkative, but
we think that, in knowledge of the value of silence, and

conception of the energy which seeks no vent in words, there has been, since the days of *Alton Locke* and *Yeast*, a marked improvement.

Nor has Mr. Kingsley failed on the side of Spain. He succeeds in fixing in his reader's intellectual vision, with a power and boldness which give assurance that it will not pass away, that figure of the Spaniard of the sixteenth century. We mark his intense egotism, his national pride, his boundless avarice, his cunning, and, above all, his cruelty. We hate his cold, clear, inevitable eye, his iron brow, his closed and determined lip. But just as we are about to turn from him in loathing, he is brought within the limits at once of art and of nature, and we feel that we have still a sympathy in which to embrace him; for we mark his dauntless valor. The contrast and the union of his qualities Mr. Kingsley skilfully brings out; and what acquaintance we have with the history of the period, convinces us that the distinct and striking portrait is closely accordant with fact.

So far we can proceed with honest heartiness in admiration and applause of *Westward Ho!* But now we must change our tone. It is not too much to say that every element of truth and beauty in the book is all but neutralized, by the presence of other elements, neither of truth nor of beauty. In construction of plot, Mr. Kingsley never displayed remarkable skill. But his plot here — the whole machinery of his novel — is an agglomeration of extravagance and absurdity. The love affair, though in some of its touches drawn from the life, is, on the whole, preposterous. As one passes from volume to volume, he is beset by all the adjectives his vocabulary commands expressive of prodigy, abortion and folly, each seeming to claim a part in characterizing the successive absurdities. Once we lose sight of the love stories and their dependent circumstances, all becomes comparatively right and true. Mr. Kingsley, if his gaze is at times unsteady, if his hand is somewhat apt to shake, may yet be said to be at home with reality. His descriptions of South American river-scenery are masterly. A comparison of his pictured pages with those of Humboldt demonstrates minute accuracy. His sketches of the landscapes of Devon are still better; distinct, bold, beautiful. Of his treatment of strictly historical characters, we have spoken. But of his management of plots and love stories, we should rather *not* speak. Readers shall judge for themselves. We must be excused for glancing somewhat particularly at the incidents of *Westward Ho!* Their eloquence will prove far more expressive than ours.

In the first chapter of the book, we are introduced to the hero, a boy of fourteen, by no means clever, but extremely good-natured, and in physical proportions, a young Hercules. Of course he is good-looking, has yellow locks, etc., etc. His name is Amyas Leigh. He is the son of Leigh of Burrough, near Bideford, then a considerable town on the coast of Devon. Strolling through the streets of Bideford, he is attracted by a group around a certain Mr. Oxenham, a mariner, who has sailed to the Spanish Main, and proposes to sail again. The right-hand man of this Oxenham is a wild, rude, stalwart seaman, named Salvation Yeo, who, in the course of the tale, becomes a Puritan of the Ironside order, and approves himself, if sharp and biting as vinegar, yet true as steel. Young Master Amyas has scarcely come up with the group, before we learn that his heart is already set upon sea-life, and that his dreams by night and by day are of the Spanish Main. But he knows he is yet young, and being a sensible fellow, is contented to wait. Mr. Oxenham sails on his voyage,

Salvation Yeo along with him; for a time both go off the
boards. Meanwhile the father of Amyas dies, leaving two
sons — the hero of the book, and Frank, older than he, a
scholar, courtier, perfect gentleman, and bold as a lion,
yet of tiny frame and delicate intellectual texture. After
a time, Amyas, tired of being flogged by a school-master
whom he has outgrown, one day playfully breaks his slate
over the pedagogue's head; whereupon his godfather, Sir
Richard Grenvile, and the disrespectfully-treated instructor,
conclude that his studies of the humanities may be considered complete. At this point we hear of Rose Salterne,
yclept the Rose of Torridge, who, albeit she has no engaging quality, beyond beauty and a fondness for romantic
narrative, has struck to the heart and vanquished every eligi-
ble youth in the neighborhood, and among the rest both
Frank and Amyas. We consider it a libel upon Devonshire to relate this universal falling in love. It is true
that Rose turns out better than was to have been expected;
but in her girlhood she is nothing but a gay, sprightly,
frivolous, village belle, of kind heart enough no doubt, and
clear harmless nature, but without a trait of such power as
might lead captive a strong man. And were there no
other pretty girls in Devon? The fact is, Mr. Kingsley's
ladies, especially in the commencement of the book, are
insipid; we have not been able to care a straw about any
one of them. Be the case as it might, it is distinctly
asserted of the young men of Devon that they all, with
one accord, fell in love with the Rose of Torridge; and as
the proceeding was at first extremely foolish, its folly was
persevered in with admirable consistency. Rose probably
appreciated the silliness of their conduct, for, as the reader
will be gratified to hear, she cared for none of them.

In due time, Amyas sails on his first voyage, going round

the world with Drake, whom, ever after, he regards as a
chief and hero among men. Of the voyage we have no
particulars, but, after much festivity on his return, he goes
to Ireland, to fight the Spaniards who have landed at Smer-
wick, and meets Raleigh and Spenser. Here he has the
misfortune to take a prisoner, named Don Guzman Maria
Magdalena Sotomayar de Soto, who at first is all that could
be wished, and gives prospect of a rich ransom, but is the
cause ultimately of wo without end. Amyas finds something to engage him in Ireland, and sends his captive over
to Devon, to wait his arrival. Here the Don has, of course,
little to do, and being a handsome fellow, with a knack of
telling tales of his escapes and valorous deeds, with an
interesting sadness hanging about him — having, in short,
touches of Othello, of the Childe, and of Rochester, in his
composition — he is far more likely to be successful with
the young ladies than the mealy-mouthed lovers of Rose
Salterne. Many of the matches in the power of this young
lady would have been excellent. Amyas was sure of promotion, and was a hearty, noble fellow. Frank was perfect
in courtesy, and sunned in the favor of Queen Elizabeth.
There were bonny estates enough in Devon which she
might have called her own. In fact, whether they had
declared or not — Amyas had not — there were multitudes
of suitors to choose among, any one of whom would have
made her happy. But this Don Guzman was decidedly
objectionable. He was a Spaniard, a Papist, a captive, one
who came with no introductions, and of whose prospects
you could have no distinct idea. He falls in love, however, with Rose, though not in the fiery way in which
the Devonshire youth chose to do so, and she now, finding
a suitor for once independent and able to do without her,
responds passionately to his affection. Rose elopes with

her lover, and goes across to America, his wedded wife;
a spirited proceeding, though, we allow, not unexampled.
But now the mischief begins to thicken. Frank had, ere-
while, persuaded the Devonshire suitors to form themselves
into a brotherhood, united by common devotion to the
lady, and bound both to confer their friendship on the man
she finally preferred, and to stand like good knights between her and any evil. Finding themselves outwitted
by the Don, the young gentlemen are, of course, consider-
ably irritated, and since it is now an impossible case that
any good can result from an attempt at interference, they
forthwith resolve to interfere. They find a ship, call it
Rose, elect Amyas captain, and set sail after the bridal party
for the Spanish Main. One of the ship's company is Salvation Yeo. He, it may be remembered, sailed with Mr.
Oxenham. That individual, a person of very imperfect
character, came to no good. The last words Yeo heard
from his lips were an entreaty to take care of his little
girl, a child of seven; and the fixed idea of Yeo's life is
now to find this "little maid." She unfortunately has got
into the hands of the Spaniards, and her chances of turning up, unless she happen to be needed by the novelist,
are few indeed. It is not mentioned that, on the occasion
of the departure of the good ship Rose, the shore was
lined with spectators, who expressed their interest in the
enterprise by shouts of laughter. But certainly no expedition so ridiculous ever set sail before or after, in fact or
fiction, and we can only pronounce the whole affair a joke
too far overdone to be amusing. Meanwhile, the married
pair had been as happy as possible. Rose declared afterwards, that at this period she was in Paradise. At least
we may conclude that there were no serious quarrels. But,
lo! there appears a cormorant, to bring dismay into this

South American Eden. It is a young Roman Catholic,
formerly a lover of the bride, and a cousin of Frank and
Amyas, wholly under the influence of the Jesuits, and disposed, in this household, to do as much mischief as he can.
He is perhaps the most watery edition of Iago that has appeared, as is Rose of Desdemona; for in the *skeleton* of
Mr. Kingsley's tale there is here a singular resemblance to
that not very recondite history of Othello. The modern
Iago strives to awaken jealousy in the breast of Don Guzman. In this his attempt would probably have been vain,
had not those moonstruck lovers come peering across the
Atlantic, at a time when every sensible friend knows he is
not wanted. Of course, if a whole cargo of lovers come
after your wife, you may have some qualms about the exclusiveness of her affection; and if the most insane of these
come into your garden at night, when you are from home,
and your wife, though with the purest intentions, finds
herself in the garden at the same time, is it in human penetration to pierce the falsehood and malice of a Jesuitic
backbiter, who is on the watch for suspicious circumstances,
and probably believes in an assignation himself? The end
is, that the Inquisition gets hold of both Frank Leigh and
the Rose of Torridge, and they die at the stake. The ship
Rose now engages in a bloody conflict with certain Spanish
vessels, and, being unable to stand a homeward voyage,
and proper refitting being impossible, is run ashore, and
burned. Its crew, with Amyas at their head, set out on
the search for Manoa, and wander for years amid the South
American forests.

After the death of his brother, and his former beloved,
it becomes the one aim of the existence of Amyas to wreak
his vengeance on the Spaniards, and particularly to come to
mortal combat with Don Guzman. Yeo still keeps looking

out for his "little maid," and, as every reader of discern-
ment will have guessed, he is ultimately blessed with the
attainment of his wish. How this comes to pass; how a
fair being, holding partly of Helen of Loch Katrine, partly
of Dido queen of Carthage, partly of Diana, huntress of
the Aonian wilds, and partly of an Indian squaw, suddenly
appeared on an island in the Meta; how, by slow degrees,
she came to honor the white men and love one of them;
how she was the queen and something like the goddess of
an Indian tribe; how she followed the party when they
departed, and could not be got rid of even when they
arrived in England; how her savagery was eradicated, and
she became all that Wordsworth demanded in a perfect
woman nobly planned; and how, as is so often the case,
the course of true love comes, in the long run, straight and
smooth; all this is deliberately detailed to us by Mr. Kingsley! It would be difficult to say whether the incidents
connected with the love story of which the Rose of Torridge is the heroine, or those of the touching tale in which
this interesting beauty of the woods is made to figure, are
the more childish and extravagant. It gives such narratives a peculiar and exquisite zest, to remember that they
are from the pen of a clergyman of the Church of England,
of decided philosophical leanings, and who believes himself not to belong to the Minerva Press or Rosewater
schools. It is strange that a writer, with not a little historical knowledge, and some command over reality, should
take his place as a constructor of plot, somewhere between
a nursery-maid and an Arabian romancer.

We are strongly moved to hazard the assertion, that Mr.
Kingsley has never yet found the most suitable channel for
his genius. His personal likings are too intense for a dramatist; he possesses not the calm thought or invention ne-

cessary in the construction of an effective plot or the conduct
of a protracted narrative; his province is not that of pure
argument.   But he lacks not lyric fire, and every tone that
he would draw from the lyre would be a tone of nobleness.
Were he to cast off every trammel of plot or action, and
break forth into glorious choral songs, tingling with sympathy for the poor and oppressed, glittering in those hues
which are too dazzling in prose, he might, perhaps, give
the age a few lyrics as certain of immortality as *The Psalm
of Life*.

On the whole, Mr. Kingsley must be pronounced a man
of rich and versatile genius, his powers of great range and
excellent quality, his nature kindly, aspiring, and free from
guile.   His deficiencies are no less obvious, and we cannot
hesitate to affirm that he lacks in many matters of capital
importance.   So devoid is he of calmness, method, and the
power of seeing things in their relative proportions and
bearings, that he scarcely deserves the name of thinker.
His mind is of that kind, in dealing with which it is even
more than ordinarily absurd, to confound the actual beliefs
with the logical, to consider assertion of fact or promulgation of theory, as necessarily implying acceptation of
the collateral circumstances of the one, or intelligent belief
in the philosophical grounds of the other.   Mr. Kingsley's
system of thought is an eclecticism without a central point.
Platonism, Fichtean Ego-worship, Carlylian hero-worship,
Christianity, mingle their elements in his mind, chaotic in
their confusion, though gorgeous in their tints.   He seems
as one sailing on a wild sea, the view obscured with flying
foam, but the sun, from above, lighting the prospect, here
and there, with glorious bursts of illumination.   He cannot
plant his foot firmly on the deck, and look fixedly, until he
once for all knows that the shore lies *there*.   His eye glan-

ces from point to point of the horizon, wherever a sun-gleam breaks out, wherever a new iris passes wavering along the foam. Every flash of beauty he hails; into every opening, under the fringe of foam and cloud, he peers. But he forgets that the essential point is to learn the precise bearings of the shore; for the night cometh, and the shore of truth is one. It is not an altogether seemly spectacle, this of a man tossed about at the mercy of his instincts, restless and agitated, not impressed with manly consistency and calmness by a reason that believes and a faith that knows! The great problem of the place occupied by Christianity in human history, its relation to human interests, its connection with human ethics, he cannot be said to have solved. In his novels, with all their elevating morality, there is no solution expressly given; what is still more important, there is none tacitly implied. We do not see that the virtues of his characters bud upon the Christian Vine. We cannot perceive in what sense he understands that Christianity makes all things new. And, as a Christian minister, this is what all men have a right to demand of him. You cannot claim of a man that his intellect be profound or his taste exquisite, but you may demand of every man that he hold what light he has clearly before you, that he have strength and honesty to say he is this and not that, that he have a faith and know it.

II.

THOMAS BABINGTON MACAULAY.

THOMAS BABINGTON MACAULAY was born in 1800, the eldest son of the well-known Zachary Macaulay, a wealthy West Indian merchant. By birth he is English; by extraction he is Scotch. The early part of his education was conducted at home; in 1818, he commenced his university studies at Trinity College, Cambridge. Of his university career we know nothing more than that it was precisely what might be inferred from his course and character in after years. He was very highly distinguished as a classical scholar, was known as a leading speaker in college societies, and, for his wide and varied acquirements, which he displayed in brilliant conversation as well as in debate, was called by his fellows " the omniscient Macaulay." He was still a youth when he produced two pieces in verse — the one a fragment, the other a finished and remarkably fine production — entitled, respectively, the *Armada* and *Ivry*. Then, we think, one who could read the literary auguries, and who had his eye on the young student, might have discerned some distinct glimmerings of that light that was to shine with so clear and fascinating a radiance. The classical distinction might be witnessed every day, the brilliancy of conversation and spirit in debate might excite neither surprise nor expectation, thousands of young men have versified, and with considerable vigor; but when very high classic attainments were united with singular knowledge of modern history and literature, and a fine, strong, clear gleam was thrown over all by poetic fire, the union might be pronounced rare and hopeful. We would form no common ideas of the youth who could offer us for inspection such a picture as this:—

"With his white head unbonneted the stout old sheriff comes;
   Behind him march the halberdiers, before him sound the drums;
   His yeomen round the market-cross make clear an ample space,
   For there behooves him to set up the standard of her Grace.
   And haughtily the trumpets peal, and gayly dance the bells,
   And slow upon the laboring wind the royal blazon swells.
   Look how the lion of the sea lifts up his ancient crown,
   And underneath his deadly paw treads the gay lilies down.
   So stalk'd he when he turn'd to flight, on that famed Picard field,
   Bohemia's plume, and Genoa's bow, and Cæsar's eagle shield.
   So glared he when at Agincourt in wrath he turn'd to bay,
   And crush'd and torn beneath his claws the princely hunters lay.
   Ho! strike the flagstaff deep, sir knight; ho! scatter flowers, fair
        maids;
   Ho! gunners, fire a loud salute; ho! gallants, draw your blades
   Thou, sun, shine on her joyously; ye breezes, waft her wide;
   Our glorious SEMPER EADEM, the banner of our pride."

Here are displayed an eye for the picturesque, a power of grouping, and a command of color, which the first painter in England, either with pen or paint brush, might have emulated. In the same piece, the faculty which has been used with such signal success in the *Lays of Rome*—the faculty of perceiving the musical cadence of particular names, and introducing them to deepen and strengthen the melody of his verses—was displayed as finely and effec-

tively as it has ever since been. In *Ivry*, a warm, youthful
enthusiasm burns through every line, and an attentive
observer might have discerned that there was much in its
glowing fervor to distinguish it from early productions in
general. The picturesqueness found its origin in a happy
selection and grouping of telling facts and events, with
neither the dimness nor the glare of verbiage; the spirit
and ardor were an echo of the feelings of the time and
scene which formed the subject of the poem, and owed
nothing to sounding commonplace or redundant adjective.
The flowers were the lilies of France; the snow-white plume
was the very one which Henry wore; the flag of Lorraine
was historically painted; and they all took their places in
the artistic picture without any aid from Minerva, or Vulcan, or the steeds of Mars. Already it might be said that
this man rode a Cappadocian courser of rare breed, and no
common hack; he was already far beyond the general band;
he had bidden adieu to commonplace. He was not yet
known to his countrymen in general; but the time was at
hand when he was to emerge from the calm regions of
privacy and silence, and become a name forever.

He was about twenty-five years of age when he left college; he was "fresh from college" when he wrote his essay
on Milton. The step was now taken irreversibly; the author of "Milton" became at once a marked and applauded
man. He might well be so; there were few such essays in
our literature at the time. It was written in that speaking
style, where the eye of the author, writing in all the fervor
of generous enthusiasm, seems to flash from every line; it
rolled on like a molten stream, glowing and impetuous;
and, when you looked, it seemed as if gold and pearls had
been lavishly thrown in, and all rushed down in princely
magnificence. Amazement at the range of learning was

heightened by its rare accuracy and minuteness; astonishment at the profusion of imagery was enhanced by its
splendor, freshness, and exquisite point; and the sound
heart rejoiced above all, that the genius, which was ministered to by such taste and such treasures, was kindled and
presided over by noble sentiment and devotion to truth.
The hand that drew the portrait of Dante, it was felt, possessed a strength and a precision of touch, which might
add many a deathless portrait to our national gallery of
fame; the magazine of literary adornment, in which were
ranged — all, it appeared, equally ready to the hand — the
terrors of Æschylus and the flowers of Ariosto, the facts
of history and the colors of fiction, seemed inexhaustible;
and the eye which, with sympathetic fire, gazed across the
intervening years to the men of England's noblest time,
with a glance of proud recognition, was at once believed
to possess a power of vision capable of penetrating far and
deep into the recesses of our history. The sensation created by the appearance of this essay was, from all we have
been able to learn, profound. Mr. Gilfillan mentions that
Robert Hall, when sixty years old, commenced the study
of Italian, in order to verify Macaulay's references to Dante.
We think any amount of applause was justifiable; Mr. Macaulay wove a brilliant crown of amaranth and gold for one
of the noblest men that England ever produced, and it was
right that its gleam should be reflected on himself.

We have now arrived at a turning-point in Mr. Macaulay's history. In the essay on Milton, he wrote with a
fervor which seemed scarcely restrainable by the forms of
composition; he scattered his riches around him like an
ancient Peruvian monarch, with inexhaustible wealth, but
knowing not its value; his decisions were firm and clear,
but brightened by a rapture as of poetry. That this would

to some extent alter, was plain; but there were various
ways in which it might change. The thought might deepen,
the decoration might be laid on more sparingly, but the
fervid, poetic sympathy with what was noble and true,
might endure or even strengthen; then might the panegyr-
ist of Milton, though certainly with no such regal tread as
his mighty countryman, emulate Milton himself. Or, all
exuberance might be restrained, and the most rigid censor-
ship be established over every portion of the style; while
the enthusiasm and fervor of youth might be chained submissively to the car of a carefully-going logic. We speak
in the language neither of censure nor of applause; we
mention merely a fact, when we say, that the latter of
these two supposable cases was, approximately at least, the
actual one. Mr. Macaulay's style became measured, careful, and comparatively cold; in his mode of thought, he
exchanged the fervid brilliancy of poetry, for the clear,
frosty light of bare logic.

We must here be permitted to express the extreme difficulty we have experienced in endeavoring to analyze Mr.
Macaulay's history, as a writer and thinker, and exhibit it
as a consistent and complete development. We feel that
we require some more information than his works afford to
account for the phenomena. To trace the formation of
his style to a certain point, is easy; to discern the consistency of his system of opinion, and the strict correspondence of his style with this system, when each is completely
developed, is also a practicable task; but to assign and
trace the causes which transmuted the impetuous, aspiring,
impassioned writer of the essay upon Milton, into the calm,
unimpassioned, practical Macaulay, who wrote the essay
upon Bacon and the essay upon Ranke, is a problem of
which we can offer nothing better than a conjectural solu-

tion. We have sometimes fancied that the glowing fires of youthful enthusiasm had been damped by some youthful sorrow; that, from the pinions of those golden dreams, on which in boyhood and early youth we float, he had been dashed suddenly upon the hard, actual ground of life, and had risen a calm scrutinizer, a logical examiner, and a scorner of the ideal: and we have very often imagined that it was all brought about by a too impetuous recoil from anything approaching to bombast, from any appearance of commonplace; that he heard the general vociferation and rant about ideals and infinites, about tyrants and slaves, about liberty and despotism, and, feeling his English common sense outraged by the din, took refuge in a strictly practical set of opinions, and a measured, unimpassioned style. Whatever the cause, the Macaulay of youth was different from the Macaulay of manhood; and we proceed to set forth, to the best of our ability, what the Macaulay of manhood is.

To indicate what we deem the highest order of mind, we shall instance that of Plato; the example is trite, but we have not space for one which cannot be speedily despatched. And we need scarcely say that it is but in one aspect that we glance at the mind of Plato. That aspect we in a word define, its attitude towards the infinite. It was a mighty force, and, being a mighty force, could not spend itself in shattering small fences; it directed itself mainly to penetrate the clouds of mystery above and below, to answer the dread questions which, like swords of flaming fire, tokens of imprisonment, encompass man on earth. Such a mind sees the practical, but holds it of small comparative value; in every direction it penetrates as far as a human mind can penetrate, and then, with a tear such as angels weep, gazes up the height which it cannot scale;

if we have here our all, it exclaims with Fichte, then a doctrine of universal suicide is the only gospel for man.

In strong contrast to this order of minds, is that at the head of which, by universal consent, stands that of Bacon. Why forever attempt, it says, to scale the infinite? why still invest a city whose walls reach unto heaven, and round which the human race has sat in vain since its infancy? Let us sow fields and plant vineyards here in the plain below, and then may we hope for a happiness that is realizable.

To this last order of minds, of which the grades are innumerable, Mr. Macaulay belongs, and has belonged ever since his mind settled into manhood. He speaks not of ideals; he generalizes calmly and cautiously; he rests content, where he deems a difficulty insoluble, in the conviction that it is so. He will have only the good things he can see, and will fly to no others that he knows not of. His mind is of that sort which rests satisfied in the fabric of human knowledge as it is, and is urged by no insatiable longings to discover how its foundations are connected with the infinite; which declares the barriers that obstruct man simply insuperable, and which contentedly devotes its energies to improve and beautify the space distinctly within those barriers; which concerns itself with the actual, not the ideal; which keeps by the natural as distinguished from the supernatural. This character is seen in all his opinions. It is ministered to by faculties of a high order: a memory of amazing range and minuteness; a judgment, in the questions which alone it discusses, clear, discriminative, sound; a taste delicately fastidious; and an imagination, not creative, or, to use a more correct word, combinative, but extremely clear-seeing. We shall endeavor to exhibit his fundamental opinions, in a brief survey of his

views on *religion*, on *philosophy*, and on *government;* and
shall then notice his manner of communicating these as a
writer and speaker.

In his religion, Mr. Macaulay is certainly not ideal. A
certain set of virtues are to be practised, a certain set of
vices are to be shunned; and the whole is transacted, as it
were, by rule and measure. We do not like to speak of
the infinite element in humanity, and far less of the organ
by which, according to some, we become acquainted with
the infinite. Yet we assert that there is undoubtedly in
the human mind a feeling of wants which earth cannot
supply, and a set of questionings which time cannot answer.
It is this looking, earnestly gazing aspect which distinguishes man as man; and we can recognize little in the
religion which does not, directly and constantly, concern
itself with the agency of God and the scenes of eternity.
In Mr. Macaulay's religious system, we can discern little or
none of this connection with what is infinite; we have
seen no traces of fiery conflict with doubt, we have seen
nothing which would lead us to believe that he did not
consider those doubts which shake strong, nay, the strongest minds, mere delusions, and esteem the victory, which,
in an agony of eloquent joy, they proclaim that they have
won, a mere dream. We shall prove and illustrate our
remarks by an instance or two.

In his far-famed essay on Ranke's *History of the Popes*,
Mr. Macaulay remarks of the Church of Rome: — " She
saw the commencement of all the governments, and of all
the ecclesiastical establishments that now exist in the world;
and we feel no assurance that she is not destined to see
the end of them all. She was great and respected before
the Saxon had set foot in Britain, before the Frank had
passed the Rhine, when Grecian eloquence still flourished

in Antioch, when idols were still worshipped in the temple
of Mecca.   And she may still exist, in undiminished vigor,
when some traveller from New Zealand shall, in the midst
of a vast solitude, take his stand on a broken arch of London Bridge to sketch the ruins of St. Paul's. . . . . When
we reflect on the tremendous assaults which she has sur-
vived, we find it difficult to conceive in what way she is to
perish."

We shall not pass in review the temporal and earthly
causes which Mr. Macaulay examines as bearing on the
question of the endurance of the Papacy; we shall merely
suggest a view of the subject which he does not take, and
a possible method of destruction which has escaped his
notice.   Suppose there are elements in the settlement of
the question which are out of the sphere of earth altogether; suppose it is true that a God, whose will is expressed in millions of solar systems, really manages the
matter; and suppose that he has breathed into one system
the breath of life, and made it a living, an immortal soul,
while he has destined the other to abide for a time, and
then to pass away forever!   This belief Mr. Macaulay cannot consider very crude or antiquated; we should not much
value the Protestantism of him who did not put his trust
in this for the endless existence of his system; and yet it
is ignored.   We can scarce conceive anything more ghastly
or barren than the view which Mr. Macaulay gives us;
looking down the vista of the ages, he sees nothing but
the old war of systems and names, a haggard, cheerless
region, inhabited by fogs and sleety showers, and cold,
biting tempests, without any ray of beneficent light from
above, to irradiate the gloom and restrain the confusion.
We acknowledge a brighter hope: we look for a dawn
whose beams of heaven-born light will smite the woman

of the Seven Hills with blindness, and bid her pass, in her
garments draggled with the best blood of earth, into ever-
lasting night. We still believe there is light thrown on
the matter by that old and singular passage, which, on any
hypothesis save ours, is surely a difficult enigma, and which
speaks of a certain "wicked" which was to be revealed,
and which, it is said, "the Lord shall consume with the
spirit of his mouth, and shall destroy with the brightness
of his coming." We must concede to Mr. Macaulay that,
counting on the operation only of earthly causes, his arguing has great force; but his practical religion is utterly
insufficient to give a satisfactory decision on the point.
And, even on the lowest hypothesis, Mr. Macaulay's conclusion excites our utter astonishment. Reason and Scripture,
he tells us, were on the side of the Protestants; and does
he really feel satisfied, under the shade of a creed which
grants to what is contrary to reason — that is, what is untrue — an equal duration, an equal possibility of duration,
with that which is true? It is a doctrine to drive mankind
mad. We believe that truth bears with it the seal-royal of
Jehovah, nay, that truth, in all its forms, is the voice of
Jehovah, which originally created and ever supports the
universe; and, if this belief is taken away — though we
can certainly have no more grief, since every sorrow is
swallowed up in one unutterable wo — it is mockery to
talk of joy. With a man of earnest religious mind, the
first question in settling the matter would surely be —
"Which system is true?" Here is a complex and marvel-
lously perfect mechanism; as perfect in all its adornments,
and as during, to all appearance, as that famed palace,
which once arose like an exhalation, and which owed its
origin, as we poor fanatics believe, to a somewhat similar
agency; it is said to be false in the core. Here, on the

other side, is an unassuming system, divided, shattered, talking in many dialects, deficient in machinery; but in it there is believed to lie somewhere the very truth of God. Which will endure, and which will pass away? If there is a God who is true, the question is simply—which is true? if there is no God, the matter is more complicated. Here, then, very strikingly, does Mr. Macaulay hold by the natural as distinguished from the supernatural.

We may here, as fitly as elsewhere, glance at Mr. Macaulay's strongly expressed opinion respecting the source of the gross immorality of the Restoration. He traces it simply to the Puritans: their rule, he says, produced public hypocrisy, which, when it could, flung off the mask, and showed the face of public infamy. Now, we do not deny that the Puritans, earnest, godly, truly noble men as they were, directed themselves too much to externals, and proscribed, in some instances, what they should not have meddled with. But Mr. Macaulay's analysis is, we must think, superficial: the source of the phenomenon he explains lies deeper—in the corrupt nature of man. We believe the principle was radically the same which we see acting, so often and so banefully, in the history of the Hebrew commonwealth. After each period of marked national godliness, there was a period of marked national decay; it was so after the era of Joshua, so after the era of Samuel, so after the era of David, so always. And was it the godliness of those periods that occasioned the iniquity of the succeeding time? Surely not: it was the recoil from godliness of the evil heart of man. The sun shone clear and bright, and beneficently warm; but a mist arose from the earth which darkened his face; and shall we say it was the shining which caused the darkness? No; we shall rather say that England at the Restoration "closed her Bible;"

that the radiance of that time was too bright for her dazzled eyes; that men love darkness rather than the light. Mr. Macaulay's account of the phenomenon embodies truth, but neither the whole truth, nor the most important truth in the matter.

When we turn to consider Mr. Macaulay's decisions concerning the religion of individuals as distinguished from that of systems, we find the same ignoring of the supernatural which meets us elsewhere. We hear of the "hysterical tears of such a soldier as Cromwell:" "Scarcely any madhouse," we are told, "could produce an instance of delusion so strong, or of misery so acute," as those of Bunyan in his early doubts, and struggles, and victory. Now, we can hardly think it possible that a man who ever passed through such mental conflicts as those of Bunyan or Cromwell could talk so; and Mr. Macaulay seems to ignore, as simply out of the question, the Christian doctrine — with which strict Christianity stands or falls — that there is really such a thing as spiritual influence from on high upon the human mind. *If* there is no God — *if* heaven and hell are illusions — *if* time is a reality, and eternity a dream — then Bunyan's woes and Cromwell's "hysterical tears" deserved a smile of mingled pity and contempt; but *if* there is a God — *if* heaven and hell are realities — *if* eternity is an infinite reality, and time a fleeting vision — or even if Bunyan and Cromwell *believed* so — then surely, when they considered their infinite concerns in danger, it was conceivable enough, or even logical, that they should be moved regarding them. "The hysterical tears of such a soldier as Cromwell!" Singular as it may look, such tears have not in general unnerved the arm of action. King David could wield his sword, could rule his kingdom, could hew the nations in pieces with right valor and energy; but he wept more even than Cromwell. Paul felt his sins to be a fearful burden; yet he was no vague arguer, and no loitering worker. In fact, if we examine, the mystery seems to vanish. The belief that there is an Eye that "slumbers not nor sleeps"—an Eye which guards the universe—continually fixed upon each motion, and penetrating every thought—seems to have a tendency, which can be traced, to make one do his work with his might, uncaring what earth can do to him or give to him, but caring, with unmeasured concern, to perform the task appointed him.

This fatal defect in Mr. Macaulay's religious views vitiates his opinions on two subjects, to which we can but refer: on the great religious revolution of the sixteenth century, and the *Pilgrim's Progress* of Bunyan. It renders his account of the Reformation, actually and literally, an account of the growth of a forest, without once mentioning the principle of life which gave it animation. To explain this principle of life is not requisite, but to acknowledge its presence is utterly indispensable. Mr. Macaulay gives us those few causes of the great movement of the sixteenth century, which may be found in the state of the respective reformed nations at the time of the Reformation; but he never asks whether the doctrine of Protestantism was an emanation from the throne of God, and we never hear that intense personal earnestness to flee from the wrath to come really kindled the flame which set Europe in a blaze.

There is incorrectness—at least, deficiency—in Mr. Macaulay's views respecting the *Pilgrim's Progress*. These have been much spoken of, and much admired, but we cannot join fully in the applause. Here, again, the *vital* element is ignored—the fact that Bunyan believed he was clothing in a garb, which is formed almost entirely of Scriptural imagery, the truths of Christian experience. It is not because it is a literary masterpiece, or for any literary reason, that Bunyan's work has been so popular with all classes; but because it reads off, in a dialect which every peasant-Christian can understand, the feelings which every peasant-Christian has known. That the literary excellence of Bunyan's famous work is very high, we admit; that Mr. Macaulay has spoken beautifully of that excellence, is also true; and we deny not that the work has been admired by many who could not read it in the spirit thereof; yet we must assert that Mr. Macaulay, in criticising it, has omitted an all-important element.

The order and the depth of Mr. Macaulay's religious sentiments may be illustrated by a momentary glance at the man whom, of all others, he appears to have selected for admiration. In speaking of Addison, the cold, accurate measurement of his developed style seems to warm into something akin to the fervid enthusiasm which guided his pen when he wrote of Milton. Addison is the model virtuous man; immaculate, unoffending, turning a smiling face on all; but by no means a penetrating, fiery soul. Him Mr. Macaulay delights to honor, and by his creed, as it appears to us, Mr. Macaulay has shaped his own. Milton was a very different man from Addison; a much more questionable and daring spirit; one who believed his creed to be written in heaven, or to be none; a man in whose life may be found certain points which make even an ardent admirer question and doubt. But every spot is a spot in a garment of brightness; we can liken him to one of his own martial angels, passing over the earth, upon whose celestial armor certain stains, imparted by the foul atmosphere, abide for a time. Addison walked according to the

6*

rules of virtue, and his path was smooth; Milton trod along
his rugged way, urged by the fire within, and found his
path through this world a very stern and toilsome journey.
Mr. Macaulay in his youth wrote of Milton in a strain
which would have kindled the eye of the princely bard
with sympathy; Mr. Macaulay, in the fulness of his years,
wrote of Addison in a strain of such softened beauty, with
such a thorough appreciation of his virtue and talents, that
the mild author of the *Spectator* would have approved and
rejoiced.

In every instance, then, Mr. Macaulay's religion is seen
to be of the easy-going, unoffending order; it concerns not
itself with any of the mysteries which torture the individual mind; it ignores conversion in the sense in which Bunyan and Cromwell used the word; it recognizes Christianity
as a system of virtues and rules, and seems to proceed in
the ignorance that it can be anything essentially different
from a mere ethical system; it is not pervaded with the
spirit of that Book which the most earnest of the sons of
men have believed to be a message from Heaven. His religion is the normal product of his mind; it suffices for all
ordinary matters of life, and concerns not itself with the
ideal or the infinite. And here we must differ essentially
with Mr. Macaulay; whatever else may be bounded, religion must be ideal, must hold of the infinite, or is nothing;
its aim must be the glories of heaven, its morality the holiness of God.

Of Mr. Macaulay's philosophy, it is unnecessary to speak
at length; it corresponds strictly with the general structure
of his mind. It is practical, wholly practical, immediately
practical. In his essay on Bacon, his views are unfolded
with unmistakable clearness. He contrasts the two grand
orders of human intellect in the person of Bacon and of

Plato, and he speaks thus: "To sum up the whole, we should say that the aim of the Platonic philosophy was to exalt man into a God; the aim of the Baconian philosophy was to provide man with what he requires while he continues to be man. The aim of the Platonic philosophy was to raise us above vulgar wants; the aim of the Baconian philosophy was to supply our vulgar wants. The former aim was noble; but the latter was attainable. Plato drew a good bow; but, like Acestes in *Virgil*, he aimed at the stars; and therefore, though there was no want of strength or skill, the shot was thrown away. His arrow was indeed followed by a track of dazzling radiance. but it struck nothing: —

> "Volans liquidis in nubibus arsit arundo,
> Signavitque viam flammis, tenuesque recessit
> Consumta in ventos."

Bacon fixed his eye on a mark which was placed on the earth, and within bowshot, and hit it in the white. The philosophy of Plato began in words, and ended in words; noble words, indeed, words such as were to be expected from the finest of human intellects exercising boundless dominion over the finest of human languages. The philosophy of Bacon began in observations, and ended in arts."

It is not in our province at present to inquire, whether Mr. Macaulay has, here and in the other paragraphs of his essay, given a precisely correct estimate of the Platonic and Baconian systems of philosophy; what we have quoted is sufficient to indicate the philosophical tendencies of the writer, and it is with him we here concern ourselves. Of his criticism of Plato, in this view, and his own philosophy as thence inferred, we say simply, that it again restricts itself to the finite, the temporal, the immediately practical. If there is no infinite towards which the mind of man must gaze, then is the philosophy of Plato, in great part, a mere abortion, born of vacancy; if the thoughts which wander through eternity indicate nothing, then is it a mere vagary. But, if this insatiable longing, which has moved the mightiest human minds; this profound feeling that the earth can never satisfy the immortal soul; this earnest calling, in all generations, to the earth below and the heaven above to tell us why and whence we are, and whither we go, are all intimations of some state whence we have fallen, and monitions towards some nobler dwelling-place than we now occupy; then the philosophy which concerns itself with these is a noble attendant upon humanity. I come not, it may say, to tell you how to till your ground, or to spin your flax; I cannot with demonstrable certainty tell you anything; but I can at least, in the voices of the noblest of earth's sons, warn you that there is something to be known, beyond what is seen; that the little world does not bound the wants or capabilities of man. The human mind has in all ages exclaimed, "I care not though you carpet my world with flowers, and roof my house with gold, and cover my table with dainties; I shall forever gaze up that wall, over which some clusters of heavenly fruit I can still discern hanging, though I cannot now touch them; and I will rather gaze wistfully at what reminds me of my ancient glory, and awakens a hope for eternity, than spend all my energies on what is really and utterly unable to make me happy." But, even on Mr. Macaulay's own grounds, we cannot grant that he has fairly represented the work done by the Platonic philosophy and ancient philosophy in general. He asks triumphantly what it did, and we venture to answer, It did much. Were we to shelter ourselves behind the grand fact, that "nothing

is which errs from law," we should hold ourselves justified
in saying, that such an amount of human intellect was
never absolutely wasted. But we must also express our
conviction, that ancient philosophy did perform a most important part in the history of our world, and that its work
is traceable. That work we can express in a single sentence: it prepared the nations for that better light which
was to dawn, it slackened the fetters which bound the
human mind, it turned the eyes of earnest men from the
sensuous to the spiritual, and, sapping the foundations of a
religion which was the product of human nature and of
earth, made room for that spiritual, supersensual religion,
which came down from God. What more it did, we need
not inquire; we consider this a most important work.

But truth is one; there is no schism in the family of
nature, there is no useless force in the armory of God. If
the truth embodied in the philosophy of Bacon is carried to
its limits, it must recognize the philosophy of Plato; if the
philosophy of Plato is carried out, it in no way counteracts,
but should beneficently shelter, the philosophy of Bacon.
The philosophy of Bacon is based on the constancy and
wisdom of nature; it bows down to facts. And is not the
Platonic philosophy, and what represents it in all ages, at
lowest, a great fact? Is it, then, the one fact in nature
which is meaningless and futile? Is every talent of every
handicraftsman made use of by the great thrifty Mother,
and have her noblest and mightiest sons been mere harps,
of the rarest mechanism, and of ravishing melody, which
she has recklessly hung out to be played on by the vacant
winds? No true Baconian can say so. Can the Platonist,
again, deny that man, though, from his whirling sand-grain
of a world, he gazes with wistful eye on the immensity
around, and though that gaze be the most important fact

in his history, is yet a denizen of earth, and for the present has, as his first duty, to live? Surely not. The truth is, partiality of view always implies error. Bacon and Plato each represented a great class of minds, and each is valuable in the great world. In the temple of Time, which stretches over the long centuries, we seem to see Plato as one pillar, with his lit eye gazing on the empyrean; and, in the distance, Bacon, another pillar, looking earnestly upon the earth, where he discovers that fine gold, unobserved hitherto, is gleaming. Which order of mind is essentially the grander and greater of the two, it is not necessary to examine; we think, as we have said, it is that which Plato heads. At all events, Mr. Macaulay, in his philosophy, as in everything else, belongs with marked distinctness to the other.

Once more, Mr. Macaulay's theory of government is in perfect consistence with his philosophy and his religion. "We consider," these are his words, "the primary end of government as a purely temporal end, the protection of the persons and property of men." He permits governments to concern themselves with other matters, such as those of religion and education; but they are strictly subordinate. He does not endeavor to penetrate into the origin of government, he aims at no ideal perfection. To realize what I propose, he says, is practicable; to realize ideal theories, is impossible, and I have neither time nor inclination to weave cobwebs. It is interesting to contrast the views of Mr. Macaulay on this point with those of Mr. Carlyle. The latter traces it all to hero-worship. It is the right of the foolish to be governed by the wise, he exclaims, and it is the duty, often a stern one, of the wise to guide the foolish; government arose from the necessity of guidance and the power to guide. This government, if it is

that of a true-born king, must concern itself with much
more than the protection of life and property; that alone
is simply "anarchy *plus* a street constable." To find your
wisest is a work of difficulty, indeed; but it is one which
must be done, or all is fatally out of course. Mr. Macaulay, on the other hand, utters his opinion on this point with
clear, unfaltering decision, in these words: — "To say that
society ought to be governed by the opinion of the wisest
and best, though true, is useless. Whose opinion is to
decide who are the wisest and best?" The day will come,
Mr. Carlyle rejoins, if you fail utterly in finding the wisest
and best, when nature will step in to your aid, and, by
some world-shattering earthquake like the French Revolution, attempt an adjustment.

We shall not pronounce an unqualified opinion upon Mr.
Macaulay's views of the functions of government; but we
must state, that two considerations have presented themselves to our mind which seem to cast a shadow of doubt-
fulness over the whole. In the first place, we can hardly
imagine a government, whose aims were of no more exalted
a character than those which Mr. Macaulay declares distinctively its own, gathering round it the sympathy, the
loyalty, the love of mankind. Men will die for a king or
a commonwealth; the name of liberty will make them fight
valiantly, when the darts shut out the mid-day sun: but
for a policeman men will hardly die. Surely something
loftier than mere security must, either rightly or wrongly,
have lent fire to the eye of patriotism, and drawn men in
serried phalanx round their king; surely it were an imperfect theory of government which would deprive men of
that loftier feeling and motive. In the second place, we
cannot but think that government must be ·progressive in
a nobler sense than this theory admits. It is manifest that

a skilful machinery, a system of invisible rails pervading society, is all which Mr. Macaulay's theory primarily embraces; and this might operate as well under a Montezuma as under a Cromwell — under a Jove, a Vishnu, or a Mumbo Jumbo, indifferently. But we trust that, with every advancement of humanity, government also advances; that, with every fresh burst of light which streams over the nations, it becomes more bright. We hold by the personality of governments; we think they should have a will and a voice; and then will every improvement in the general knowledge and condition of mankind be centred in them. Mr. Macaulay's theory is, we think, inadequate to the phenomena of the past, and the requirements of the future; but, as we have said, we do not mean to examine it at length, and submit that it is quite sufficient for us to exhibit that theory, and indicate its correspondence with his general mental state.

We have now finished our brief survey of those fundamental views which lie at the basis of Mr. Macaulay's system; we have found them agree in those grand features which mark them as products of one mind; we proceed to consider the mode in which he has given the system, of which they are the foundation, to the world.

Mr. Macaulay's style is by far the most popular of those which are at present devoted to the conveyance of sound instruction. He

> " Has set all hearts
> To what tune pleased his ear."

He is admired with an eager, unbounded admiration, such as used to be reserved for novelists and popular poets; and the causes of his popularity are patent. He writes in a calm, sensible manner; he startles not by any of those apostrophic bursts which astonish and thrill us in perusing the prose of Milton and Carlyle; he calls not on the mind for sustained enthusiasm or penetrating thought: but he can lay his hand upon such rare means of adornment as he can alone command; he has culled only those flowers which grow far out of the common path, in the byways of history and poetry, and these he scatters over his pages with what we might call an elaborate carelessness and profusion. His imagination, too, is clear and, of its kind, powerful; so that in his pages everything is reflected with the vivid force of reality. The result of his knowledge, taste, and care, is a style which, for elegance, grace, and quiet force, is a rare model.

His mode of composition bears marks of the revolution wrought in his general mode of thought. When he wrote *Milton*, he was impetuous and brilliant, but he altered soon and forever. He recoiled with fierce impatience from any semblance of commonplace; his words and imagery would all be chosen with the most searching scrutiny. Concerning that vast store of imagery, the Greek mythology, we gather his decision from the following clauses uttered long after in speaking of the poetry of Frederick of Prussia:—
"Here and there a manly sentiment, which deserves to be in prose, makes its appearance in company with Prometheus and Orpheus, Elysium and Acheron, the plaintive Philomel, the poppies of Morpheus, and all the other frippery which, like a robe tossed by a proud beauty to her waiting-woman, has long been contemptuously abandoned by genius to mediocrity." In Mr. Macaulay's writings, allusions to the Greek mythology have scarce an existence, and, though the remark is here incidental, we must say we regret the fact. If the old religion of Greece was a personification of natural powers; if, above all, it was the most perfect

embodiment, in ideal forms, of ideal beauty, that ever was produced by the mind of man, its beauty is perennial and inexhaustible. And such it surely was. We count the Greek mythology as true and strict a product of nature as the silky leaves of the birch, or the rosy clouds of the morning; and, after a million of poetasters have done their worst, the petals of the roses will be undimmed in beauty, and untainted in fragrance, when they once more bind the brow of the Spring whose footsteps we are just beginning to hear. In the works of Carlyle, the Greek mythology is used with a power and splendor which dazzle and delight as effectively as if the whole had been discovered, in some ancient tomb, last year. Need we remind Mr. Macaulay that the song of the lark was, according to Mr. Rogers, old in the time of Homer? Would it not be hard to have forbidden all subsequent poets from listening in rapture to its morning carol, or endeavoring to catch a few of its notes? It is the prerogative of genius to shed a new light over every form of beauty, as the sun every morning sheds a light, old and yet ever new, over the lakes, and flowers, and mountains, arraying them in a beauty that is ever fresh.

But Mr. Macaulay, we say, would have imagery which no other could show; he would set out — to use his own words, which strikingly illustrate our remarks — only "an entertainment worthy of a Roman epicure; an entertainment consisting of nothing but delicacies — the brains of singing-birds, the roe of mullets, the sunny halves of peaches." His sentences are irresistibly fascinating from the succession they present of new and interesting facts, instructing while they illustrate, and amusing while they instruct. He is totally destitute of pretension; he "rolls no raptures;" he treads calmly along in the confidence that he has a strength of which word-mongers know nothing. His pictures float past the reader, like the cumulous clouds on a summer's day, clear, swiftly flying, and touched with the loveliest hues; or like the meadows, gardens, and lakes, which glide past, when you sit in an open carriage, going at an easy pace, through a beautiful land, in a crystal atmosphere. The following pair of sketches are done with the minuteness of Teniers, but with a warm glow of color which Teniers could not command : — " The correctness which the last century prized so much resembles the correctness of those pictures of the Garden of Eden which we see in old Bibles. We have an exact square, enclosed by the rivers Pison, Gihon, Hiddekel, and Euphrates, each with a convenient bridge in the centre, rectangular beds of flowers, a long canal, neatly bricked and railed in, the tree of knowledge, clipped like one of the limes behind the Tuilleries, standing in the centre of the grand alley, the snake twined round it, the man on the right hand, the woman on the left, and the beasts drawn up in an exact circle round them. In one sense the picture is correct enough. That is to say, the squares are correct, the circles are correct, the man and the woman are in a most correct line with the tree, and the snake forms a most correct spiral.

"But if there were a painter so gifted that he could place on the canvas that glorious paradise, seen by the interior eye of him whose outward sight had failed with long watching and laboring for liberty and truth, if there were a painter who could set before us the mazes of the sapphire brook, the lake with its fringe of myrtles, the flowery meadows, the grottoes overhung by vines, the forests shining with Hesperian fruit, and with the plumage of gorgeous birds, the massy shade of that nuptial bower which showered down roses on the sleeping lovers, what should we think of a connoisseur who should tell us that this painting, though finer than the absurd picture in the old Bible, was not so correct?"

Consider this other picture, too; it is that of young Maria Theresa, when the troubles of war were beginning to darken round her imperial brow:—"Yet was the spirit of the haughty daughter of the Cæsars unbroken. Hungary was still hers by an unquestionable title; and although her ancestors had found Hungary the most muntinous ot all their kingdoms, she resolved to trust herself to the fidelity of a people, rude, indeed, turbulent, and impatient of oppression, but brave, generous, and simple-hearted. In the midst of distress and peril, she had given birth to a son, afterwards the Emperor Joseph II. Scarcely had she risen from her couch, when she hastened to Presburg. There, in the sight of an innumerable multitude, she was crowned with the crown, and robed with the robe of St. Stephen. No spectator could restrain his tears when the beautiful young mother, still weak from child-bearing, rode, after the fashion of her fathers, up the Mount of Defiance, unsheathed the ancient sword of state, shook it towards north and south, east and west, and, with a glow on her pale face, challenged the four corners of the world to dispute her rights and those of her boy. At the first sitting of the Diet, she appeared clad in deep mourning for her father, and, in pathetic and dignified words, implored her people to support her just cause. Magnates and deputies sprang up, half drew their sabres, and with eager voices vowed to stand by her with their lives and fortunes. Till then her firmness had never once forsaken her before the public eye: but at that shout she sank down upon her throne, and wept aloud. Still more touching was the sight when, a few days later, she came again before the Estates of her realm, and

held up the little archduke in her arms. Then it was that
the enthusiasm of Hungary broke forth into that war-cry
which soon resounded through Europe, 'Let us die for our
king, Maria Theresa!'" There is a silent, unostentatious
power here which is irresistible; the grand fact stands
grandly forth, in its simple majesty, like a Greek statue,
where not one superfluous fold of drapery encumbers the
silent loveliness; there is not a word that could be spared,
and yet there is not a word too few. It is upon such pictures that the distinctive English reader loves to gaze; there
are no sentimental raptures to dim its transparent clearness,
there is no trifling prettiness unworthy of its greatness,
there is no affectation; all is manly, simple, beautiful.

At times, too, Mr. Macaulay can indulge in a quiet but
hearty laugh; and exactly such a laugh as every Englishman can join with him in enjoying. Of the translations
of Homer by Pope and Tickell he thus speaks:—"Addison, and Addison's devoted followers, pronounced both the
versions good, but maintained that Tickell's had more of
the original. The town gave a decided preference to
Pope's. We do not think it worth while to settle such a
question of precedence. Neither of the rivals can be said
to have translated the Iliad, unless, indeed, the word translation be used in the sense which it bears in the Midsum-
mer Night's Dream. When Bottom makes his appearance
with an ass's head instead of his own, Peter Quince exclaims, 'Bless thee! Bottom, bless thee! thou art translated.' In this sense, undoubtedly, the readers of either
Pope or Tickell may very properly exclaim, 'Bless thee!
Homer; thou art translated indeed.'"

Of Mr. Macaulay's style we cannot say, as he says of the
eloquence of Fox, that it is penetrated and made red-hot
with passion; it is not a turbid, heavy-rolling stream, which

7*

at intervals dashes itself into spray, and thunders foaming over lofty precipices, where the gazer trembles at the stupendous height, while his·eye is dazzled by the gorgeous rainbows that wreathe it, a description which would apply to the style of Richter or Carlyle; its flow is even and smooth, or ruffled only by the mildest summer breeze. It is an honest style; and this is a matter of importance. There is no lashing of his sides to raise himself into fury; there is no outflow of tears; all is clear as an English fountain, beautiful as an English woodland, abounding in such picturesque, unpretentious attractions as an Englishman loves. We may differ from Mr. Macaulay in his general modes of thinking; we may hold that he seldom or never rises into the highest regions of descriptive or didactic composition; but, for point, purity, clearness, and elegance, we repeat, his style is a rare model, and will ever continue to be esteemed such.

We have been very much astonished, indeed, to meet with a severe attack upon Mr. Macaulay as an orator; we think in no character is he more true to himself. He is not a passionate, fiery soul; it were affectation to assume the oratorical language or gestures of such. His eloquence is calm, clear, unimpassioned, the placid deliverance of a placid mind. Rich in historic adornment, fascinating from the flowing continuity of the sentences, and never exchanging the plain garb of common sense for the tawdry drapery of nonsense, it trims between dulness and passionate fire, between transcendental nonsense and transcendental truth. We had the pleasure of hearing him address his constituents·in Edinburgh a few months since; and a more perfect correspondence between his oratory, his works, and his whole character, than that which was discernible on that occasion, we cannot conceive.

It were unpardonable to omit mention of Mr. Macaulay's poetic efforts; but, as these have been ere now noticed at some length in our pages, and as our space is well-nigh exhausted, we shall be extremely brief. Mr. Macaulay, of course, never thought of claiming the title of poet; his mind is of a class essentially different from the poetic. But all the beauties of his prose find their consummation in his stanzas; the skill in grouping, the vivid painting, the picturesque arrangement of facts, the mellifluous harmony of names. His *Lays of Rome* remind us of the fervor of his *Milton;* and with extreme admiration there is blended a shade of regret. They have been praised in all quarters, and never a word too much: in their way, we can scarcely conceive anything finer. They are full of that sort of enthusiasm which inspires delight; we are never moved to agony, we are never raised to rapture, and we never imagine that the writer was deeply stirred in their composition; but we are in the midst of the scene, we see the army of the Tuscans as distinctly as Horatius saw it, and we share the emotions of the bystanders in their pride and valor without their terror. In his verses Mr. Macaulay gives himself the rein; he curbs not his enthusiasm, he restrains not his fire: in his prose, he seems to write under the eye of some cold censor, the personification of English common sense, who rigidly damps every ardor, and dims every gleam of passion. His Lays indicate what his prose might have been, had he retained the style of *Milton:* they are, as we have said, the concentration, with an additional flash of fire, of his beauties in prose.

Mr. Macaulay's external history, as gleaned from one or two contemporary authorities, is soon told. He became a member of the House of Commons in 1831; he allied himself to the advocates of the Reform Bill, and has continued a consistent liberal.   About the year 1833, he became connected with Indian affairs, and was for several years member of the Supreme Council of Calcutta.   In 1839, he became secretary of war under Lord Melbourne, and went into opposition when Sir Robert Peel became prime minister.   In 1846, he was rejected by the electors of Edinburgh; he retired into a dignified privacy, ennobled by studies of national importance; he became the most popular of English historians; and, in 1852, he was again victoriously returned for Edinburgh.

There are three men who may be said to bear rule at present in the kingdom of British literature : their doctrines are repeated, their style is echoed, in all magazines; their conjoined or antagonistic influence will be powerful in moulding the thoughts of several generations to come: they are Alison, Macaulay, and Carlyle.   The man who would form an approximately correct idea of his time must know all the three.   Alison must be had recourse to for a general view of the time and its events.   He is of wide rather than keen vision, of fervid rather than piercing utterance; he turns the gaze of men upon the institutions which have been the growth of ages, and, in a revolutionary age, he calls upon men to preserve what is true, and beware how they unfix those pillars that have so long sustained the political system.   His works are immense magazines of facts, and of facts which every thinking man will, in the present day, earnestly ponder.   Macaulay, fervid and earnest in youth, seemed to be unsheathing a sword of.flame; but he suddenly grew calm, and the blade which, after careful polishing, he ultimately displayed, was cold as the brand Excalibur, with the moonbeams playing over it in the frosty night, but invisibly sharp.   In him is no intensity; he never awakens the profoundest tears or the deepest laughter; the fearful questions concerning God, Freedom, Immortality, at which the most thoughtful and the most noble of the sons of men have stood aghast, he simply bids away; his writings are a stream in which you may see gold grains gleam, but of which you can always see to the bottom. He is a literary impersonation of the middle class of Englishmen. Carlyle stands in a category by himself; where the others are admired, he is, so to speak, worshipped. The other two concern themselves with institutions and laws, the embodied wisdom of many. Carlyle looks to men. Had you formulas sufficient to thatch the world, he exclaims, they would not stead you; you must have the lit eye that can see, the stout arm that can do, or all is lost. He penetrates into "the abysmal deeps of personality;" he cares not so much to register facts, as to pierce into their producing principles and causes. In every direction he seeks to penetrate as far as the human intellect can go, and then, like Plato, gazes earnestly towards the infinite. His style is varied, broken and startling: in his best day it was clear as an Italian morning, and extremely beautiful; in after times, though occasionally degenerating into comparative inferiority, it at intervals rose into passages of surpassing grandeur. He has cast his eye over history with a glance whose sympathy was kindled by what had been unseen or unheeded by other men; wherever tremendous force was allied with nobleness and truth, he has recognized with rapture the union, and sympathetically traced its workings. He has broken up old modes of thought and old modes of composition; he has been studied with an earnestness, and loved with a devotion, which no other writer of the day can claim; he has been imitated by a class of writers, whose unapproachable parody could never have been produced, save unconsciously; he has spoken more sense, and given rise to more nonsense, than any literary man of the day. It may be granted to "the little kingdom" to feel a kind of pride that two of these distinguished men are her own, and the third hers by extraction.

There is an argument having some appearance of subtlety and force, often urged against Macaulay, to which it may be proper briefly to refer. It is alleged that his mind is of that order, which dwells most congenially in the region of the abstract; that he can scientifically estimate, rather than act; that he loves events, rather than men. He is, thus runs the approved phraseology, essentially a mechanical man, not a dynamical. In one form or other, this theory often appears. One man, red hot from Carlyle's French Revolution, remarks sniffingly that Macaulay is an English Girondin. Another recites the story of Gibbon, who sat looking upon Pitt and Fox in passionate conflict, in precisely the same mood, with precisely the same kind and degree of interest, as warmed his philosophic bosom when he contemplated, through the long, passionless perspective of ages, the Trajans and Tamerlanes of his Decline and Fall. Gibbon and Macaulay are then involved in a common condemnation. The general argument has been expounded with great elaboration, and a certain felicitous piquancy difficult to resist, in one of the ablest of our Reviews.* But both the reviewer in this case, and, as it appears to us, those in general who indulge in the habit of depreciating, on such grounds, our great essayist and historian, omit the consideration of one preliminary question, of vital importance in the discussion. Is not the composition of great literary works itself action, nay, action of as august and important a nature as any strictly practical operation; and if it is, and if, in its highest perfection, it admits not of combination with more ordinary exertion, is it not in all

* The National. The essay has since been republished along with others by the same author, Mr. Bagshot.

52457

senses right and noble in a man, so far to sequester himself from practical life, as to give his powers full scope and fair play for the higher achievement? Was the presence of mind of a Pitt or Fox, was their practical tact or parliamentary skill, was all that they did for us, or left to us, so much greater than that calm breadth of historical vision, which gazed over wide spaces of time, harmonizing the diverse, uniting the remote, seeing all with new clearness, and at last giving to the world a literary masterpiece, which, with all its faults, is imperishable as civilization? It has been remarked that Napoleon possessed powers which would, so directed, have secured him immortal fame as an author. No hypothetic fact seems to us more certain. But as an author, he will never be thought of; both in theory and practice, both in taste and style, he was a bad writer. Pure intellectual action, and mixed intellectual action, were incompatible. But would it have been less great and manly in Napoleon to have devoted himself to pure thought, to such work as that of the Aristotles, Newtons, Goethes, if it had been so ordered by Providence that no diadem should cast its maddening gleam into his eyes, luring him to empire and despair? It matters little to our argument in what way this question is answered: but it is plain that an answer must be given it, before a man can be adjudged of an inferior order, moral and intellectual, for having preserved himself so far from the distracting influences of life, as to permit his mind to work in an intellectual region, serene because it is lofty. For our own part, we scruple not to avow our belief that it may be a man's highest duty and noblest course thus to seclude himself. Consider the matter fairly even for one moment, and it will be found, that all the great writers of mankind, poets, philosophers, historians, men of science, have in one way or other pursued that abstract method of contemplating truths and events, which is objected to Gibbon and Macaulay. They all afford illustration of the fact that there is an antithesis between thought and action, between literary exertion and life. The one is broad, calm, and proportionately slow; its slowness renders it so far unfit for the momentary emergencies of practical endeavor: the other is fragmentary, collected into instantaneous flashes, swift as the lightning and proportionately agitated; and this agitation is totally incompatible with the highest intellectual achievement. It was certainly sublime in Milton to postpone the composition of Paradise Lost at the voice of his country; but the postponement, with the reason assigned, remains an incontestible proof of the necessity of calm to high intellectual exertion; and we can safely pledge ourselves to admit ignoble weakness in any case, where it can be shown that practical assistance was withheld, in a crisis so momentous as that which led Milton from the still slopes of the Aonian hill to join the battling squadrons in the plain. But the truth is, Mr. Macaulay can hardly be said in any sense to need defence. He has shrunk from no public duty. He has entered with ardor into the political discussions of his time. It seems universally admitted that his administration in India was sagacious and admirable. He preserved only such intellectual calm as was absolutely necessary in obedience to the highest hests of his genius. And when he has given us consummate works, we gracefully and gratefully blame him for not having given them in an impossible manner !

What has Macaulay done to deserve the thanks of his country? He has done much. He has thrown over large portions of her history the light of a most powerful fascination: he has maintained the purity of the English language in a time when it is in danger; he has never stooped for a moment to the ignoble or the low, either in sentiment or style. Of the structure which he has reared, and which is to be his monument to the generations to come, we have been unable to present a finished or complete delineation; we have been unable even to glance at its several portions in detail; but we pronounce it a consistent and stately structure, and shall deem ourselves happy if we have, with any fair measure of success, laid bare its foundations, and exhibited, so to speak, the statical laws on which it has been built. While Britain lasts, English history will be better known than heretofore; for, while Britain lasts, Macaulay's *Essays* and Macaulay's *History of England* will be read. Lastly, he has furnished to cultivated minds a source of pure and exquisite pleasure; and, in dropping our pen after this summary, we experience a feeling akin to dread, that we have said anything unworthy of one to whom we are indebted for so much knowledge, so much instruction, and so many hours of refined and manly enjoyment.

III.

SIR ARCHIBALD ALISON.

THE present is very prominently a criticizing age. From the quarterly review, whose writer aims at immortal renown, to the daily newspaper, whose writer aims at saying what will please readers, and gain him the reputation of being a smart and spirited young man, every sort of periodical is more or less critical. And yet it may be questioned, whether the facility of forming a correct, adequate estimate of any marked writer, is, in a material degree, furthered by this vast amount of reviewing. The very facility of having an opinion increases the difficulty of having a correct one. Each reviewer professes impartiality; many honestly endeavor to be fair. But it cannot be doubted that many, whatever their professions, are really and consciously influenced by motives of party or interest; that many more, striving honestly to divest themselves of all such considerations, are yet, unconsciously but fatally, moved thereby; while the utter inability to take the correct measure of a distinguished man, by no means necessarily precludes self-satisfied dogmatism in pronouncing an opinion concerning him. Thus arise innumerable errors; and, in each instance of error, the great speaking-trumpet called public opinion (which, almost as much as any other trumpet, utters sounds that are produced by another), is made to give forth uncertain or discordant sounds. Hence it is, that certain literary maxims or cries, analogous to certain watchwords in the political world, become bruited about in society respecting known authors; originating with political opponents, or struck off, more for the sake of their smartness than their truth, by some clever litterateur; and always, in part at least, erroneous. The influence such cries exert is incalculable. They seem so smart, they are so easily retailed, and they so pleasantly save all trouble. Equipped in this manner, every spruce scion of the nobility, whose intellectual furniture consists mainly of certain long-deceased conservative maxims, can pronounce decisively that the great whig essayist and historian, Macaulay, is "a book in breeches;" while every new-fledged politician, who steps along in the march of intellect, panoplied in ignorance and conceit, feels himself of quite sufficient ability and importance, to sneer at the king of literary conservatives, Sir Archibald Alison, and sublimely remark that his writings are the "reverse of genius."

In endeavoring to attain a correct opinion respecting any celebrated contemporary, almost all such prepossession must be resolutely and conscientiously laid aside. We say almost, because every cry will be found to contain one small grain of truth, and, while fatal if taken as keynote, to be valuable as a subordinate contribution. With as thorough impartiality as is attainable by any effort of the will, in full sight of encompassing dangers, the author must be studied, must be communed with, as it were, face to face, through the works he has given to his fellow-men; and as great a sympathy as is possible must be attained with him in his views and objects. The grand principle also must never be lost sight of, that God makes nothing in vain; that the moral world is as varied, as vast, and as complex as the physical; and that it is only when, coming out of the little dwelling of our own ideas and maxims, we gaze over the thousandfold developments of mind, that we perceive the harmonious grandeur of the whole. In all cases, narrow intensity marks imperfection. The worker of limited power excels in some one particular: the private soldier knows when to put his right foot foremost, and when to draw his trigger; the commissariat officer knows how to arrange the provisioning of a division; the Murat or Lambert can command a body of cavalry, and bring it down with overpowering vigor upon an enemy; but it is only the Napoleon or the Cromwell that can do all in his single person, and so prove himself born to command. The same holds good of writers. The narrow, limited author has one particular idea, by which he thinks he has taken the measure of the universe; he sympathizes with one sort of excellence, he has one formula in politics, he has one dogma in religion; while the king in literature — the Richter, the Goethe, the Shakspeare — displays a countless variety of excellences, sympathizes with every sound human faculty, and at last almost attains the serene and all-embracing tolerance of "contradicting no one." These men can take a comprehensive view of nature in all her forms and all her workings; they know well that, when the magnificent island exalts its head in the ocean, not the smallest insect that formed it has died in vain.

It is with the earnest desire to attain as close an approximation as possible, to the impartiality and width of view and sympathy we have indicated, that we approach the literary measurement of Sir Archibald Alison. Our position, purely literary, precludes political bias; and, though not subscribing to every article of his political creed, we hope to do him some measure of justice.

The fundamental stratum on which Sir Archibald Alison's character, with all its feelings and faculties, is based, is that which is in all cases indispensable, but which in many instances has been wanting. That basis is thorough, fervent, well-applied honesty. He is a man who believes with the whole power of his soul. He is not cold and formal as Robertson; he is not tainted in his whole nature, as was Gibbon, by mistaking a sinewless phantom, called "philosophy" — evoked, like some Frankenstein, from vacancy, by the literary necromancy of French savans — for an embodiment of celestial truth: friends and foes alike respect the genuine fervor, linked with earth and with heaven, which pervades and animates the writings of Sir Archibald Alison. This it is which must, we think, make his works essentially pleasing to every honest man. In one place, we may question an inference; in another, we may detect an imperfect analogy; here we may smile at the identification of the advocates of organic reform (revolution) with the powers of hell; and there we may think the laws of chaste and correct imagery infringed; but we always feel that the company of this man is safe — that his breast holds no malice or guile — that he believes really, and believes in a reality. Such is the base of Sir Archibald's character — a basis of adamant.

With this comports well the general tone of his mind. He is always animated; he is always energetic. But here a distinction must be made. Sir Archibald is not one of those men whom a class of modern writers would specially characterize as "earnest." We cannot discover that he has undergone any of those fierce internal struggles which figure so largely in modern literature, and which give such a wild and thrilling interest to certain writings of Byron, Goethe, and Carlyle. He seems never to have wrestled in

8*

life-and death struggle with doubt; he seems to have early
discerned, with perfect assurance, the great pillars of human
belief, and calmly placed his back against them; his mind
is essentially opposed to the skeptical order of intellect.
Hence it is that his beliefs, though honest and unwavering,
are not intense; that he throws all his energy out upon
objective realities; that we have no syllable as to the
author's subjective state. We believe that the two latter
writers, whom we have referred to as entering largely upon
subjective delineation, would declare this to be the more
healthy mental state of the two; it is that, indeed, towards
which all their efforts tend. We see as little of Sir Archibald Alison when he discusses any question, as we do of
Homer when he narrates. But this order of mind may be
characterized by various degrees of intellectual power;
and, as a general fact, its beliefs will not be held with such
intensity as in the other case. When one grasps a precious
casket from his burning dwelling, he grasps it more tena-
ciously, and proclaims his triumph with more intense exultation, than if he had never doubted for a moment his safe
possession of it.

Sir Archibald's beliefs, then, are not intense; we must
add, that his energy is not concentrated. The stronger
the spirit distilled from any substance, the smaller the
quantity; a small cannon will do as much as a huge bat-
tering-ram. We are often reminded of the fact in perusing the works of Sir Archibald Alison. In one point of
view, his energy may be wondered at, and in some measure commended; in another point of view, it must be pronounced defective, and almost to be regretted. That readers may obtain an idea of his powers of working — of the
amount which he can perform—we extract the following
from a very able article upon Sir Archibald, which ap-

peared, some years since, in the *Dublin University Magazine : —*

"Like all men who have durably left a name in the annals
of serious literature, Mr. Alison has immense powers of
application. The mere reading he has gone through, exclusive of study and note-taking, appears to an ordinary
person incredible. Two thousand volumes, and two-thirds
of these in a foreign language, were the basis upon which
he reared his great history; and the information on other
subjects which he exhibits in his miscellaneous writings is
not less extraordinary. Politics and history, novels and
poetry, the drama and the arts, alike engage his attention.
Every masterpiece of antiquity has been scanned by him;
every remarkable Continental work undergoes his scrutiny.
The literature of the day, the newspaper press of France
and England, of America and the colonies, are ready to
illustrate or corroborate his statements; and, in his hands,
trade circulars, blue-books, and parliamentary returns, become eloquent from the truths they unfold." To this more
may be added. Sir Archibald has all along performed the
duties of "a judicial office of greater labor and responsibility
than any other in Scotland." His collected essays form
three large volumes; his great historical work fills twenty
considerable volumes; and he has just published the first
volume of a new history, containing about six hundred
octavo pages. Besides all this, he has published four other
works, two of them of great size. That this displays an
amazing power of working, no one can deny; but we think
the further position must be allowed, that, however we
may praise the honest application which it involves, it is
to be regretted that it was not condensed, and dealt out
more circumspectly. We speak not of the history; we
direct our attention to the essays. It must be taken as, in

one point of view, quite a satisfactory account of every
defect in these able and fascinating performances, that they
were written in such haste that revision was impossible;
under the circumstances, they could not reasonably have
been expected to be better. But our very admiration of
the essays, and our profound conviction of the value of
the thought they contain, sharpen our regret that haste
should have deprived them of any polish or vigor — that
in any instance it should be suspected by the reader that
the plough is going over the top of the ground, and not
into it. It may be said, that these essays were written at
particular junctures, when it was important, for national
reasons, that they should instantly appear. We acknowledge the force of this; it is perfectly sufficient to excuse
every defect which marred the essays as they were issued
in the pages of the magazine; but did not their collection
in a form adapted to separate publication afford an opportunity for revision and condensation? Is any one more
fully aware than Sir Archibald of the value of thought?
that one grain of its imperishable gold outweighs whole
reams of printed paper? And can any one forget the fact,
that men often judge by a slip, or a deficiency, or an imperfection, and obstinately refuse to believe in excellence
which is not uniform? We again profess an extreme admiration for many of the essays of which we speak; and we
must avow that no feeling more powerfully affected our
mind, as we perused them, than a desire that their author
had, with the utmost deliberation and earnestness, applied
himself to exhibit, in clear separate form, certain of those
views and principles to which he rightly attaches so much
importance, and which he has so thoroughly mastered. As
we read such essays as those on the *Indian Question* — on
which, in all its aspects, Sir Archibald is admirable — as

we discerned great, and true, and important principles
slightly obscured, and rendered uncertain of effect, by being
connected with certain political crises, and made the basis
of certain predictions which could be but partly true, we
felt the deepest regret. It seemed anomalous too, that
discussions of high ability should occur in a volume containing such imperfect and temporary productions as the
essays on Napoleon and Mirabeau. One Damascus sabre,
whose edge is invisible from sharpness, is worth many
ill-tempered blades, clumsy in use, and obscured here and
there by rust; we wish Sir Archibald had devoted more
attention to tempering and sharpening, and comparatively
little to indefinite multiplication.

His indefatigable industry has enabled Sir Archibald Alison to accumulate very extensive stores of knowledge; by
continual practice in composition, he has them ever at hand;
and he infuses life into all by the sustained animation and
fervor of his mind. His judgment, although it cannot be
defined as penetrative, or adapted to distinguish very
minute shades of thought, is yet of extreme value in those
cases where great national characteristics are to be discerned;
it is unbiassed either by sentimentality or coldness of heart;
and, although it sometimes is led astray by too prevailing
a dread of anything like democracy, its decisions, as embodying one important aspect of human affairs, are always
deserving of serious attention and deference. In his early
days, Sir Archibald was "an enthusiastic mathematician,
obtained the highest prizes in these studies in the University of Edinburgh, and has often lain awake solving problems in conic sections and fluxions in the dark, with the
diagram painted in his mind." This early proficiency in
mathematics has characterized very many distinguished
men: Milton, Napoleon, Chalmers, Carlyle — men surely

of dissimilar, but all of great genius. We doubt not that this mathematical study has availed Sir Archibald much, in enabling him to glance over multiplex national and social phenomena, and discern the one truth which connected them all, and which lent them their signification.

Sir Archibald's sympathies are wide, and give rise at once to versatility of talent, and fairness to opponents. He is certainly Conservative; he is an uncompromising, unquestioning Tory. But we think it must be allowed that he treats his opponents generously; that here the only conservatism which attaches to him is that of honor and of chivalry. He would as much scorn to search out, with malignant scrutiny, the pardonable weakness or foible of an opponent, as the true knight of the olden time would have scorned to point his lance just at the spot where he thought the armor of his foe was cracked. He concerns himself with principles; if he overcomes his antagonist, it is by utterly smashing the arms of his trust by the force of historic truth; he disdains to take his foe at a disadvantage, but he neither asks nor gives quarter.

It is somewhat astonishing to find the same enthusiastic, rolling utterance in his critical as in his political essays; we presume in one case it is thé enthusiasm of belief — he feels he is talking to his countrymen and to posterity on matters of vital importance, and he speaks fervently and loud: in the other, we take it to be the enthusiasm of delight; "we have done," he seems to say, "for a time, with the doctrines of currency; we shall let the Manchester school alone, there being room enough in the world for it and us; let us away to hear the ringing of the squadrons around Troy, to weep or sadly smile with Dante, to see celestial softness in the creations of Raphael, or to tremble at the wild passion of Michael Angelo." And in criticism,

the same mental characteristics are manifested as elsewhere.
He does not, by natural bent, turn all his powers to penetrate into radical laws of beauty or taste. In examining a
work of art, he sees great characteristics; he does not
remark the particular waving of a curl, he does not measure
every angle, he does not refine about rhythm or euphony,
but he sees the eye of Homer glancing into the heart of
man, and he follows the hand of Angelo as it strikes out
the big bones and muscles. In all cases, he is wide and
fervid, not piercing, lynx-eyed and intense.

In opinion, Sir Archibald Alison, we have remarked, is
Conservative; this is the foundation of all his system of
thought. And we must profess our profound conviction,
however much on particular topics we might venture to
join issue with Sir Archibald, both that his conservatism
is a most honest and venerable conservatism, and that it is
of incalculable importance and value to true progress. His
conservatism is one whose object is liberty, and whose
watchword is progress. We, of course, cannot condescend
upon particular views entertained by him on particular
subjects; but, leaving the vexed questions of currency, we
think his system may all be shown to branch out from two
great stems: —

1st, Universality of representation.

2nd, National honor.

By the first of these, which is an expression of our own,
we by no means intend to represent Sir Archibald as an
advocate of universal suffrage; we design it to mean the
accordance to every interest in the state of its due representation and influence. Let the aristocracy, he says, be
represented, for then you have continually gathered round
the national standard those who are bound to defend it by
every obligation of honor, descent, and interest: who have

inherited education, by birth, who have unlimited leisure
by the possession of wealth, and who are raised by position
above the excessive influence of popular clamors. Let the
middle classes be represented, that the interests of commerce be not overlooked, and that the interests of the
farmer be not merged in those of the landlord. Let every
one who has proved himself of sufficient industry, honesty
and intelligence to rise from the working-classes, and who
has a stake in the national welfare, have a vote. But by
no means extend the right of voting to all numerically, for
then you have destroyed all radical uniformity; you have
committed a suicidal act; you have put the sceptre into
the hand of that which is so vastly the most numerous
body in the state — the populace. Their representation
in the other case will be indirect but real. Sir Archibald
strongly advocates the extension or continuance of representative rights to the colonies of a mother state.

From the second great branch of Sir Archibald's system,
the upholding, at all hazards, of national honor, proceeds
his unqualified protest against utilitarianism as the basis
of a system of policy; his untiring and eloquent advocacy
of colonial interest; his utter disdain of the political creed
whose formula is £. s. d. National honor, national justice,
national religion, national unity—these are his watchwords.
And here, again, his views are wide and practical, rather
than penetrating or ideal. He takes his stand upon those
virtues which characterize a nation as distinguished from
an individual — moderation, calmness, general purity of
manners. He trusts for the attainment of these to a national church, and has, therefore, an unmasked distrust and
dislike of dissent. The renovation of the nation from an
individual starting-point, he regards as chimerical; he looks
to national religious institutions, and not to men: for the

attainment of national virtue, he must have a national church. And here it is that the outline of his system is most liable to objection. "The contest," he says, "between revolution and conservatism is no other than the contest between the powers of hell and those of heaven. Human pride, adopting the suggestions of the great adversary of mankind, will always seek a remedy for social evils in the spread of earthly knowledge, the change of institutions, the extension of science, and the unaided efforts of worldly wisdom. Religion, following a heavenly guide, will never cease to foretell the entire futility of all such means to eradicate the seeds of evil from humanity, and will loudly proclaim that the only reform that is really likely to be efficacious, either in this world or the next, is the reform of the human heart. . . . . Conservative government, as distinguished from despotism, has never yet been reestablished in France; and religion has never regained its sway over the influential classes of society. . . . . But religion, be it ever recollected, does not consist merely in abstract theological tenets. Active exertion, strenuous charity, unceasing efforts to spread its blessings among the poor, constitute its essential and most important part. It is by following out these precepts, and making a universal *national provision* for the great objects of *religious instruction, general education, and the relief of suffering,* that religion is to take its place as the great director and guide of nations, as it has ever been the only means of salvation to individuals." However true this may be, it surely is not the whole truth; it ignores the fact that dissent may spring from religious earnestness, as well as from scientific skepticism. Such *religion* as any effort of conservatism could enable to "regain its sway over the influential classes of society," would be pronounced by most earnestly religious men a misnomer. It might be called "respectability," and so shown to be invaluable to a government; if named religion, rigorous limitations would be made. We shall not enter upon this complicated and difficult question; but we take the truth in the matter to be this:—Sound dissent is invariably based upon individual earnestness; so it was with the Waldenses, so with the Puritans, so with the Wesleyans; and it were the perfection of government, when this individual religious earnestness was permitted to diffuse itself harmoniously through the commonwealth, neither arrayed in hostility nor monopolizing regard. Sir Archibald Alison, looking entirely from a national point of view, has, we must think, failed to perceive the value, the power, nay, even the safety, of individual earnest religion in a nation: he sees not that, in the fervor of dissent, there can ever glow the true light from heaven; the iron, the brass, and the clay of false systems cannot, he thinks, be broken, unless the stone is most carefully cut and shaped by the hands of government. The sectary of limited vision, on the other hand, looking entirely from an individual point of view, ignores the vitally important distinction between the individual and national life. In both cases there is error, for in both cases there is narrowness of view: the aim of every government should be to ally to itself by the ties of loyalty every interest in the state, to steady itself by a thousand different anchors.

We deem Sir Archibald Alison's conservatism a truly noble conservatism; based on honesty, patriotism, and extensive knowledge; embracing one great department of truth, which has in all ages to be re-proclaimed. And, in the present age, we think it peculiarly useful. When Socialism, Communism, Chartism, and the rest, are perambulating the world, like so many resuscitations of Guy Fawkes,

each with a lighted brand, purporting to have been kindled
by reason and truth, and to be able to shed a paradisiacal
light over nations, and yet too evidently threatening to fire
the world with a very different kind of illumination, such
a conservatism takes the link from the red hand, and compels the ruffian to pause, to consider, and gradually to regain
his right mind. The best human system is not all truth —
the worst is not all error; but the friend of advancement
has little faith in his cause, if he goes out of his way to
denounce conservatism.

In addressing ourselves to make a few remarks more
particularly on Sir Archibald Alison, as historian and essayist, it is scarce necessary for us to premise that we must be
concise and fragmentary. The work by which he is best
known, and which has attained a world-wide reputation, is
his *History of Europe during the French Revolution.* The
origin of that great work, and the preparation for it undergone by its author, are eloquently discoursed of by the
writer whom we have already quoted; his words are so
beautiful, and his authority so reliable, that we are glad to
enrich our columns by their insertion. " Many illustrious
men have neglected their genius in youth — many more do
not become aware of possessing it till that fleeting seed-
time of future glory is past forever." "Amid my vast and
lofty aspirations," says Lamartine, "the penalty of a wasted
youth overtook me. Adieu, then, to the dreams of genius,
to the aspirations of intellectual enjoyment!" Many a
gifted heart has sighed the same sad sigh; many a noble
nature has walked to his grave in sackcloth, for one brief
dallying in the bowers of Circe, for one short sleep in the
Castle of Indolence. But no such echo of regret can check
the aspirations of our author. Brought up at the feet of
Gamaliel in all that relates to lofty religious feeling and

the admiration of art, and in not a little concerning the
grand questions of national politics, his youth was well
tended; and almost ere he emerged from that golden,
dreamy period, he had embarked on the undertaking which
was to be the mission of his life, and his passport to immortal fame.   Among the dazzling and dazzled crowds
whom, from all parts of Europe, the fall of Napoleon in
1814 attracted to the French metropolis, was a young Englishman, who, hurrying from his paternal roof, arrived in
time to witness the magnificent pageants which rendered
memorable the residence of the allied sovereigns and armies
in Paris.   Napoleon had fallen, the last act of the revolutionary drama seemed to have closed; and in the Place
Louis XV., assembled Europe and repentant France joined
in the obsequies of its earliest victims and holiest martyrs.
It was in the midst of those heart-stirring scenes that the
first inspiration of writing a history of the momentous
period, then seemingly closed, entered the throbbing heart
of that English youth — and that youth was Alison.   Ten
years of travel, meditation, and research followed, during
which the eye and the ear alike gathered materials for his
great undertaking, and the mind was expanding its gifted
powers preparatory to moulding these materials in a form
worthy of the great events to be narrated, and of the high
conceptions which the youth longed to realize.   Other fifteen years of composition were required ere the history
was brought to a close, and the noble genius of its author
awakened the admiration of Europe."

The standard of historic excellence by which Sir Archibald has been regulated, we are able to determine from his
own works; we cannot do better than quote the following:
—" Passion and reason in equal proportions, it has been
observed, form energy.   With equal truth, and for a similar

reason, it may be said, that intellect and imagination, in equal proportions, form history. It is the want of the last quality which is in general fatal to the persons who adventure upon that great but difficult branch of composition. It in every age sends ninety-nine hundredths of historical works down the gulf of time. Industry and accuracy are so evidently and indisputably requisite in the outset of historical composition, that men forget that genius and taste are required for its completion. They see that the edifice must be reared of blocks cut out of the quarry; and they fix their attention on the quarriers who loosen them from the rock, without considering that the soul of Phidias or Michael Angelo is required to arrange them in the due proportion in the immortal structure. What makes great and durable works of history so rare is, that they alone, perhaps, of any other production, require for their formation a combination of the most opposite qualities of the human mind — qualities which are found united only in a very few individuals in any age. Industry and genius, passion and perseverance, enthusiasm and caution, vehemence and prudence, ardor and self-control, the fire of poetry, the coldness of prose, the eye of painting, the patience of calculation, dramatic power, philosophic thought — are all called for in the annalist of human events. Mr. Fox had a clear perception of what history should be, when he placed it *next to poetry in the fine arts, and before oratory.* Eloquence is but a fragment of what is enfolded in its mighty arms. Military genius ministers only to its more brilliant scenes. Mere ardor or poetic imagination will prove wholly insufficient; they will be deterred at the very threshold of the undertaking by the toil with which it is attended, and turn aside into the more inviting paths of poetry and romance. The labor of writing the *Life of*

9*

Napoleon shortened the days of Sir Walter Scott. Industry and intellectual power, if unaided by more attractive qualities, will equally fail of success; they will produce a respectable work, valuable as a book of reference, which will slumber in forgotten obscurity in our libraries. The combination of the two is requisite to lasting fame, to general and durable success."

The general voice of his countrymen, and we might almost say of the world, has set the great history we have named in the list of standard national works; it is, as the Germans would say, a world-historical book. Its ground-tone is of course conservative; its style is vivid, animated, and pictorial; its study is almost a necessary part of a complete modern education. We think its study might be most profitably combined with that of Carlyle's powerful and original work on the same subject: in the one, the madness of revolutions is denounced and dreaded; in the other, there is the stern sympathy of an old Norseman, who gazes on a weltering battle from afar, and the earnest hailing of truth, though it comes "girt in hell-fire."

As an essayist, Sir Archibald Alison deserves very great commendation. He does not always excel: in the biographic essay, for instance, he appears immeasurably inferior to certain writers of the day; but, in many instances, and on various subjects, he attains very high excellence. In laying down great principles in political economy, he is manifestly in a congenial element; in historical subjects he is, as might be expected, sagacious and happy; and, in criticism, his vision is wide and his judgment powerful.

In the historical essays, we sometimes come upon paragraphs containing truths of the highest value and the widest application. We were delighted to find the following great fact so clearly stated; its historical worth we deem incalculable; were it once fairly accepted and imbibed by the human race, the gates of Limbo would be choked for three days, so much nonsense would get its mittimus : — "Sub- jugation by a foreign power is itself a greater calamity than any benefits with which it is accompanied can ever compensate, because, in the very act of receiving them *by force*, there is implied an entire dereliction of all that is valuable in political blessings — a security that they will remain permanent. There is no example, perhaps, to be found in the history of mankind, of political freedom being either effectually conferred by a sovereign in gift, or com- municated by the force of foreign arms; but as liberty is the greatest blessing which men can enjoy, so it seems to be the law of nature that it should be the reward of intrep- idity and energy alone; and that it is by the labor of his hands and the sweat of his brow that he is to earn his free- dom as well as his subsistence."

The same remark holds good of Sir Archibald's critical essays; the principle, for instance, embodied in the follow- ing sentences, lies at the foundation of all criticism:—"The human heart is, at bottom, everywhere the same. There is infinite diversity in the dress he wears, but the naked human figure of one country scarcely differs from another. The writers who have succeeded in reaching this deep sub- stratum, this far-hidden but common source of human action, are understood and admired over all the world. It is the same on the banks of the Simöis as on those of the Avon — on the Sierra Morena as on the Scottish hills. They are understood alike in Europe as in Asia — in ancient as in modern times; one unanimous burst of admiration salutes them from the North Cape to Cape Horn — from the age of Pisistratus to that of Napoleon." Were we to change somewhat the expression of this thought, and substitute "the perennial in man" for certain of its phrases, it would be astonishing how closely it would resemble a leading doctrine of Mr. Carlyle's.

The extent of information possessed by Sir Archibald; the swift glance which he can cast over it all; his animated rolling diction; his varied sympathy; his truly British absence of affectation; in a word, every excellence of his style, can be found in the following magnificent apostrophic exordium to one of his critical essays:—"There is something inexpressibly striking, it may almost be said awful, in the fame of Homer. Three thousand years have elapsed since the bard of Chios began to pour forth his strains; and their reputation, so far from declining, is on the increase. Successive nations are employed in celebrating his works; generation after generation of men are fascinated by his imagination. Discrepancies of race, of character, of institutions, of religion, of age of the world, are forgotten in the common worship of his genius. In this universal tribute of gratitude, modern Europe vies with remote antiquity, the light Frenchman with the volatile Greek, the impassioned Italian with the enthusiastic German, the sturdy Englishman with the unconquerable Roman, the aspiring Russian with the proud American. Seven cities, in ancient times, competed for the honor of having given him birth, but seventy nations have since been moulded by his productions. He gave a mythology to the ancients; he has given the fine arts to the modern world. Jupiter, Saturn, Mars, Minerva, are still household words in every tongue; Vulcan is yet the god of fire, Neptune of the ocean, Venus of Love. Juno is still our companion on moorland solitudes; Hector the faithful guardian of our flocks and homes. The highest praise yet bestowed on valor is drawn from a comparison to the god of war; the most grateful compliment to beauty that she is encircled by the cestus of Venus. When Canova sought to embody his conceptions of heroism or loveliness, he portrayed the heroes of the *Iliad*. Flaxman's genius was elevated to the highest point in embodying its events. Epic poets, in subsequent times, have done little more than imitate his machinery, copy his characters, adopt his similes, and, in a few instances, improve upon his descriptions. Painting and statuary, for two thousand years, have been employed in striving to portray, by the pencil or the chisel, his yet breathing conceptions; language and thought themselves have been moulded by the influence of his poetry. Images of wrath are still taken from Achilles, of pride from Agamemnon, of astuteness from Ulysses, of patriotism from Hector, of tenderness from Andromache, of age from Nestor. The galleys of Rome were — the line-of-battle ships of France and England still are — called after his heroes. The Agamemnon long bore the flag of Nelson; the Bellerophon combated the gigantic l' Orient at the battle of the Nile; the Polyphemus was the third in the British line which entered the cannonade of Copenhagen; the Ajax perished by the flames within sight of the tomb of the Telamonian hero on the shores of the Hellespont; the Achilles was blown up at the battle of Trafalgar. Alexander the Great ran round the tomb of Achilles before undertaking the conquest of Asia. It was the boast of Napoleon that his mother reclined on tapestry representing the heroes of the *Iliad*, when he was brought into the world. The greatest poets, of ancient and modern times, have spent their lives in the study of his genius or the imitation of his works. The Drama of Greece was but an amplification of the disasters of the heroes of the *Iliad* on their return from Troy. The genius of Racine, Voltaire,

and Corneille, has been mainly exerted in arraying them
in the garb of modern times. Parnassus is still the emblem
of poetry; Olympus, of the council-seat of supreme power;
Ida and the Cyprian Isle, of the goddess of love. The
utmost exertion of all the arts combined on the opera stage
is devoted to represent the rival goddesses as they appeared
to the son of Priam on the summit of Gargarus. With-
draw from subsequent poetry the images, mythology, and
characters of the *Iliad*, and what will remain? Petrarch
spent his best years in restoring his verses. Tasso portrayed the siege of Jerusalem and the shock of Europe and
Asia almost exactly as Homer has done the contest of the
same forces, on the same shores, 3000 years before. Milton's old age, when blind and poor, was solaced by hearing
the verses recited of the poet to whose conceptions his own
mighty spirit had been so much indebted; and Pope
deemed himself fortunate in devoting his life to the translation of the *Iliad;* and the unanimous voice of ages has
confirmed his celebrated lines: —

> ' Be Homer's works your study and delight,
> Read them by day, and meditate by night;
> Thence form your judgment, thence your maxims bring,
> And trace the muses upward to their spring.' "

We must draw our remarks abruptly to a close; our space
is already exhausted. We need not say the subject is far
from being so. We intended to say a good deal concerning
Sir Archibald's style; to show that here, as elsewhere, we
have his distinguishing characteristics displayed — wide,
not intense thought, giving rise to a flowing and diffuse,
rather than a terse mode of expression — diffused, not concentrated energy, producing a constant glow rather than a
piercing fire; and to point out a few of its defects. Upon

the repetitions, the mistakes in imagery, the sameness, frequently rendered the less pardonable by commonplaceness, of forms of phrase, we *could* descant, but must cover all up in this inuendo.

Sir Archibald Alison's writings are a continued protest against modern utilitarianism; his whole life has been an effort to break Mammon's threefold chain of gold, silver, and copper; he has exposed the dishonesty and insanity of political or party cries; occasionally he has confounded the good with the bad, occasionally his scythe has cut down the corn with the weeds. On the whole, we think he will give us his sanction in saying that change is not wrong in itself: that the frivolous restlessness of the child, which breaks one toy and cries for another, is to be despised; that the morbid fickleness of the hypochondriac, who thinks that a change of seat or the attainment of some dainty would insure health, is to be pitied; but that the calm, reasonable desire to change an old habitude or dwelling for a new, entertained by the sagacious and healthy man, is to be respected; and that it is so in the case of nations.

Sir Archibald is the son of the Rev. Archibald Alison, the celebrated writer on Taste; he became a member of the Scottish bar; and the government of the Earl of Derby conferred upon him the title which he adorns.

IV.

SAMUEL TAYLOR COLERIDGE.

AMONG the men who have led the van of British thought during the present century, who have stamped the impress of their genius upon the forehead of the age, and moulded the intellectual destinies of our time, there is one name preëminently fraught with interest to the student of our internal history. That name is Samuel Taylor Coleridge. In our schools of poetry, of philosophy, of theology — among our critics and our ecclesiastics, our moralists and our politicians — the influence of Coleridge has worked, silently and viewlessly, but with wide-spread and mighty power. As by a verbal talisman, his name opens to our mental gaze vast and varied fields of reflection, invokes grave, important, and thickly-crowding thoughts, and forms the centre round which countless subjects of discussion and investigation group themselves. For these reasons, superadded to the fact, that we know of no easily accessible account of his life and writings at once concise and comprehensive, we purpose to devote some considerable space to a biographic sketch of this celebrated poet and thinker.

Towards the latter half of the last century, there lived at Ottery St. Mary, in the southern quarter of the balmy and beautiful county of Devon, discharging there the duties

of vicar and schoolmaster, an eccentric, erudite, and remarkably loveable old man. He was the father of Samuel Taylor Coleridge. "The image of my father," says the latter,
"my reverend, kind, learned, simple-hearted father, is a
religion to me." Richter expressed pity for the man to
whom his own mother had not rendered all mothers sacred.
Both the remarks shed a beautiful and kindly light over
the characters of their authors.

The vicar of Ottery St. Mary was twice married, and
had, in all, thirteen children. Samuel Taylor was the
youngest; his day of birth was the 21st of October, 1772,
when he appeared "about eleven o'clock in the forenoon."
He speedily gave indications of superior capacity, being
able, at the completion of his third year, to read a chapter
in the Bible. We soon begin to discern the operation of
causes, bearing, with rather singular importance, upon the
formation of his character and the shaping of his destiny.
The youngest of the family, he was the object of peculiar
affection to both parents, and, in consequence, excited the
envious dislike of his brother Francis, and the malevolence
of Molly, the nurse of the latter. Hence arose annoyances
and small peevish reprisals; for the power of a boisterous
and sturdy brother, and a malignant nurse, to embitter the
cup of a bard in pinafore is considerable; so little Samuel
became "fretful and timorous, and a tell-tale." A tell-tale
is an object of united detestation on all forms of all acad-
emies; it was so at Ottery St. Mary, where Coleridge went
to school; the future metaphysician was driven from play,
tormented, and universally hated by the boys; he sought
solace at mamma's knee and in papa's books. He became
a solitary, moping child, dependent on himself for his
amusements, passionately fond of books, of irritable temper,
and subject to extreme variations of spirits. At six he

had read "Belisarius," "Robinson Crusoe," and "Philip Quarles," and found boundless enjoyment in the wonders and beauties of that Utopia and Eldorado of all school-boys, the Arabian Nights' Entertainments. The following is a portrait of him, about this time, as he sketched it in after years: — "So I became a dreamer, and acquired an indisposition to all bodily action, and I was fretful, and inordinately passionate; and, as I could not play at anything, and was slothful, I was despised and hated by the boys: and because I could read and spell, and had, I may truly say, a memory and understanding forced into almost unnatural ripeness, I was flattered and wondered at by all the old women. And so I became very vain, and despised most of the boys that were at all near my own age, and, before I was eight years old, I was a *character*. Sensibility, imagination, vanity, sloth, and feelings of deep and bitter contempt for almost all who traversed the orbit of my understanding, were even then prominent and manifest."

This has to us a deep significance, in the psychological consideration of Coleridge's character. The ideas lodged in the mind at this early period of life, and the habits formed, may, in after years, change their forms, and appear in manifold and diversified developments; but they retain their place with extreme obstinacy. This childhood of Coleridge's we cannot, on the whole, pronounce healthy. Little boys are naturally objects of dread, rather than of flattery, to old women. Little Robert Clive, for instance, utterly astonished and startled the old women by exhibiting himself on the steeple of Market Drayton; and turned out a man of clear and decisive mind and adamantine vigor. The playground and the meadow, with the jocund voices of his playmates round him, and in the constant consciousness that his independence has to be maintained and defended amid their boisterous and fearless sports, is the proper place for the development of the future man. It is our belief that, in these years, an almost instinctive knowledge of character, a thorough command of the faculties, and a power of bringing them, on all emergencies, into swift energetic action, are attained; and that no subsequent education can compensate the premature devotion of these early days to mental pursuits. May we not here find the faint and unsuspected commencement of that anomalous and mournful severance between the powers of action and the powers of thought, which the world has deplored, and may so well deplore, in Coleridge?

With all his bookishness, however, with all his indolent inaction and indifference to the sports of childhood, little Samuel had a dash of fierce stubbornness in his composition. The old women, on occasion, found cause for abating their flattery: in proof, take the following anecdote. He was about seven years old, when, one evening, on severe provocation from Frank, he rushed at him, knife in hand. Mamma interfered, and Samuel Taylor, dreading chastisement, and in fiercest fury, ran away to the banks of the river Otter. The cold evening air, it was reasonably calculated, would calm his nerves, and bring him quickly home; but the calculation was incorrect. He sat down in resolute stubbornness on the banks of the river, and experienced "a gloomy inward satisfaction," from reflecting how miserable his mother would be! It was in the end of October: the night was stormy; he lay on the damp ground, with the mournful murmuring of the Otter in his ear; but he flinched not, nor relented; with dogged determination, he resolved to sleep it out. His home, meanwhile, was in a tumult of distress and consternation. Search in all directions was instituted; the village was scared from its slum-

bers, and, ere morning, the ponds and river were dragged.
At five in the morning the little rascal awoke, found himself able to cry but faintly, and was utterly unable to move.
His crying, though feeble, attracted Sir Stafford Northcote,
who had been out all night, and he was borne home. The
joy of his parents was inexpressible; but in rushed a young
lady, crying out, "I hope you'll whip him, Mrs. Coleridge!"
Coleridge informs us, that neither philosophy nor religion
was ever able to allay his inveterate antipathy to that
woman.

Just as his youngest son was completing his ninth year,
the good old vicar of Ottery St. Mary died. Through the
influence of Judge Buller, a presentation to Christ's Hospital, London, was obtained for Samuel Taylor; and about
April, 1782, he went to London. Here he was, before
entering the hospital, domesticated with an uncle. This
uncle looked upon him as a prodigy, and was very proud
of him. He took him to taverns and coffee-houses; accustomed him to hear himself called a wonderful boy; taught
him to converse and discuss with volubility; and, in short
"spoiled and pampered him."

This fast mode of life, however, soon came to an end: a
very different regimen and environment awaited him in
Christ's Hospital. Here he found himself under the strict
discipline of Bowyer; his food was stinted; and he had
no friends to encourage him by approbation, or refresh his
heart by kind indulgence on a holiday. Though enlivened
by occasional swimming matches, and wanderings, somewhat hunger-bitten, in the fields, his existence was, on the
whole, a joyless one. "From eight to fourteen," he says,
"I was a playless day-dreamer — a *helluo librorum*." The
manner of his becoming possessed of sufficient opportunity
to indulge his keen and insatiable appetite for books, was

singular and characteristic. He was wandering one day
along the Strand: physically, he was pacing the hard pavement, jostled by the thronging crowd, stunned by the surrounding noises; mentally, he was breasting the waves of
the Hellespont, and gazing, through his vacant but glittering eyes, at a light in the distance. The hands, as in som-
nambulism, caught impulse from the mind, and were cleav-
ing the smoky air in act of swimming. Suddenly he was
awakened. By feeling beneath his feet the hard dry sand
on the banks of the moonlit Bosphorus, and the kiss of
Hero on his lips? No: but by a sudden grasp of the hand,
and an exclamation in his ears, "What! so young and so
wicked!" His wandering, unconscious fingers had come
into too close proximity with a passenger's pocket, and
pocket-picking was suspected. The simple-hearted little
dreamer told the whole truth: belief could not be withheld, for the whole, we can well see, was written on his
cheek and in his eye; and the man, interested in the boy,
obtained him access to a circulating library. Reading
was henceforth his constant occupation, his unfailing solace.
"My whole being," we quote his own words, "was, with
eyes closed to every object of present sense, to crumple
myself up in a sunny corner, and read, read, read." He
went right through the library. He was ever first in his
class, occupying that station not from any impulse of ambition or youthful emulation, but simply by his surpassing
powers. His general book knowledge was wonderful. Before fifteen, he had sounded the depths of metaphysics and
theology, was a fluent master of the learned languages, and
had comparatively lost taste for history and separate facts.
How strongly developed, even at that early age, was the
unalloyed exercise of the intellectual powers! How clearly
can we trace, gradually widening, the lamentable severance

10*

of which we have spoken! On the whole, what a wonderful boy was this Samuel Taylor Coleridge! The child, even, is father of the man; and, in the boy, his lineaments, both mental and physical, become ever more conspicuous. Already the dream of fancy, or the abstract effort of thought, had greater charms for Coleridge, than the surrounding, or even the historical, realities of life; already his mind had become its own dwelling-place, and found within its own compass a sufficiency of object to allure and delight; already he had drawn astonishment to his commanding faculties. Whether the extreme development of the receptive powers, and the constant inundation of the mind by the ideas of other men, might not, to some extent, weaken the sinews of the soul, and implant the seeds of that irresolution which clouded his latter days, were a question; we would be disposed to render it an affirmative answer. He soon displayed an inability to tread in beaten paths, to pursue common methods. He might be found, during play hours, reading Virgil "for pleasure;" but he could not give a single rule of syntax, save in a way of his own.

His reading was, as might be supposed, exceedingly varied. It reached Greek and Latin medical books on the one side, and Voltaire's "Philosophical Dictionary" on the other. This latter appeared to the boy conclusive; to Bowyer, it did not. In utter disrespect for freedom of opinion, and the finer feelings of Samuel's bosom, Bowyer did not attempt, by laborious effort of philosophical reasoning, to re-convince him; he gave him a sound flogging! It appears to have acted with potent persuasion; and Coleridge called it, in after life, the only just flogging he ever received from him.

In February, 1791, Coleridge entered at Jesus College, Cambridge. He speedily distinguished himself by winning a gold medal, for a Greek ode on the slave trade; but, in various subsequent competitions, during his university career, his endeavors were not attended with corresponding success. As heretofore, he was by no means a methodic student, but he still continued a voracious and desultory reader. He gave proofs, also, of that astonishing conversational power by which he afterwards became so distinguished. His room was the resort of the gowned politicians; and Coleridge, besides being the life and fire of debate, put them, by means of his wonderful memory and swift reading, in possession of the latest political pamphlets.

It was a time of extreme excitement. The French Revolution was exploding; the most wonderful series of events, since the Reformation, was taking place; the long imprisoned winds had burst their cavern, and their noise was going over the world: Coleridge, as all others, felt the influence. The whole atmosphere, political and literary, vibrated with excitement; the glories of the latter morning were deemed to be arising; and thousands of the fiery-hearted youth of the land hasted to enrol themselves under the banners of the good cause.

Principles are rained in blood: that has long been an ascertained fact. And what a deluge of blood did it require to rain this one principle; yea, may we not, from the general appearance of the world at present, predict that even more blood must be shed ere men are fully convinced of it — namely, that, by simply leaving mankind to the freedom of their own will, they will arrive, not at regeneration and highest felicity, but at destruction, misery, and confusion worse confounded? Surely the French Revolution might have taught us this, and instructed us to look for final regeneration to the heavens. But the lesson, if we are now to esteem it acquired, was, as we say, hard to

teach. A whole Egyptian inundation of blood was required
to water, and enable to take deep root, this one principle;
and, in pursuance of a method which nature very often
adopts, its contrary was first shown in full operation. Remove the restraints of tyranny; open wide the floodgates,
so long pent up, of human love and sympathy; and all
men, throwing up their caps to welcome the time of peace,
will, simultaneously and of necessity, rush into each other's
arms! Such was the faith of Shelley, embodied in the
"Revolt of Islam;" such was the belief, for a brief period,
of Robert Southey; such was the faith which threw some
method into, and some brilliant hues over, the wild, almost
demoniac, but yet heartfelt philanthropy of Byron; such
were the hopes which, for a time, fed the enthusiasm, and
based the dream-fabrics, of Coleridge.

Of his devotion to this creed, he found means of giving
proof when at college; it was a proof characteristic of the
man. He was, we must remark, of gentle, truly loveable
nature; honest, brave, ardent; but not by any means fierce
or truculent. He did not plan a college rebellion, for the
regeneration of society; he did not, by fiery and desperate
audacity, exasperate the university authorities; he displayed
his attachment to new era principles in the following somewhat different manner. On the green lawns before St.
John's and Trinity Colleges, a train of gunpowder was to
be laid, imprinting the grand watchwords of the new epoch,
"Liberty" and "Equality." By the ignition of the gunpowder, the words were to be burned into the grass, and
to stand forth there, seen by the sun above, and the college
windows farther down, for certain days, a monition and
benignant illumination to all the world. A "late chancel-
lor of the exchequer" executed the redoubtable plan; and

so Coleridge vindicated his claim to the title of champion of democracy.

At this period of his career, Coleridge was Unitarian in his religious principles. His grounds of belief were not those commonly held by the professors of that creed. He distinctly avowed his conviction, that the Scriptures taught the doctrine of the Trinity; and that the attempts to explain away their statements on the question, in which Unitarians indulged, were utterly unjustifiable. His reasons were almost wholly subjective. Refusing to accede to the doctrine of the atonement, and denying the divinity of our Lord, he calmly pronounced these beliefs the Platonisms or Rabbinisms of the apostles John and Paul. A fuller development of his mental powers; a wider and more searching survey of the realms of truth; and a profounder knowledge of the problems of human history, and the wants and workings of the human heart, led him afterwards to the unwavering conviction that Unitarianism was null and void.

Ere this time, Coleridge had written a considerable quantity of poetry. On the whole, it was not of a very astonishing description. A delicacy of fancy, without singular exuberance of power; a command of soft and brilliant language, at times overladen with ornament; occasional vigorous personation; these comprehend the main beauties and merits of his earliest pieces. "The Songs of the Pixies," is a piece of fine fancy-painting, indicating a true eye for nature, and a power of delicately pencilling her gentlest and fairest forms. This poem seems to lie just on the line of demarcation between the years of youth and those of early manhood.

Various circumstances contributed to embitter and darken the latter part of Coleridge's university career. Some pub-

lic competitions, as the reader will have gathered, resulted
in a way to disappoint his expectations. His Unitarian
principles, which he was far too honest to disavow, barred
the gates of preferment. And some debts, which his simplicity and want of decision had led him to contract, sub-
jected him to numerous and harassing annoyances. Besides
all this, we have found it asserted, that his mild and sus-
ceptible heart had been sorely vexed in some love affair.
The warm-hearted, dreaming youth was, in fact, peculiarly
sensible to the enchantment of female gentleness and
beauty; while, of a surety, but few girls were, or ever are,
to be found, capable of loving, and of corresponding to
the ideal of, the author of "Genevieve."

In November, 1793, he suddenly quitted Cambridge for
London. Arrived in the "great brick desert," feeling the
loneliness which a stranger may experience when surrounded by thronging myriads of his fellow-men, to him
mere automata, and finding himself speedily reduced to
pecuniary straits, occasioned partly by his Goldsmithian
readiness to give money to any distressed object, he cast
about for some means of present subsistence. Shifts there
were few; these were none of the choicest, and hunger was
menacing; he adopted the singular one of — enlisting as a
dragoon. Silas Tomken Cumberbatch (S. T. C.) was the
imposing designation by which he was known to his fellow-
soldiers; and, under such auspices as appeared, he commenced his military career.

Now it soon became manifest, that nature, whatever her
generosity or ungenerosity, had not gifted this Silas Tomken
Cumberbatch with qualities to enable him to discharge
creditably the functions of a dragoon. Far-stretching flights
into dreamland on the wings of fancy, imagined beating
of the Hellespont waves with a Hero's lamp in view, ab-

stract ponderings on theology and metaphysics, interfere objectionably with the grooming of one's horse! Besides, the man has no "ambition," and seems stupidly callous to the attractions of "glory." Accordingly, he meets with no promotion; never rises out of the awkward squad; and at drill, flounders painfully about, so as to provoke the exclamation of a facetious serjeant, "Take care of that Cumberbatch—take care of him, for he will ride over you!"

What a scene! Was there ever, since the days of the mighty hunter, such a private soldier? What have our painters been about? What more supremely appropriate theme could be imagined, for a national painting than this scene of "Cumberbatch on drill," or "Apollo as a dragoon?" "The rapt one of the godlike forehead;" the man whose impulse has probably gone deeper than that of any other into the vital springs of British thought and general mental development in this nineteenth century; the man at whose feet men of genius and fame sat, like children round a wizard, earnestly regardful of his smallest word; stumbling and staggering about, on his ill-groomed steed, the most awkward of the awkward squad! Talk of Kilmenie among the rustics, after her sojourn by the celestial streams; talk of Apollo amid the gaping herdsmen of Admetus; this of Coleridge among the dragoons beats them all hollow!

"Eheu! quam infortunii miserrimum est fuisse felicem!" This sentence, to the utter surprise of an officer who observed it, and, we doubt not, the sheer uncomprehending amazement of his brother privates, Silas had inscribed on his stable wall. With his brother soldiers he was popular; he wrote their letters, entertained and astonished them with historic narrations, and won their hearts by his gentleness; while they, in return, assisted him to groom his horse. We hear, likewise, of one of the officers—the same, we pre-

sume, who made the above discovery — condescendingly
permitting him, when their path lay in the country and
not in the town, to walk abreast with himself and enter
into conversation. How indulgent! How condescending!
He would not find such conversation in the messroom, we
daresay; such conversation was probably not to be found
in the British Islands; the day was coming when Hazlitt,
Lamb, Carlyle, and De Quincey, were to listen, in rapt
attention, to the tones of that conversation!

At length, after some four months' drill, the astonishing
dragoon was discharged. He returned for some short time
to Cambridge, but quitted it soon and forever.

In the summer of 1794, Coleridge, on a visit to Oxford,
became acquainted with a young man named Robert
Southey; a steady thoroughgoing worker, of strong literary
tastes and vast information; who also was under the influence of the Liberty and Equality mania. An acquaintance,
which soon ripened into friendship, sprung up between
them; there was a strong, perhaps radical, dissimilarity
between their characters; but the ethereal spark in either
bosom urged them together. This intimacy and this friendship gave tone to much of the subsequent history of Coleridge, and furnish us with one of the raciest and most
delicately comic of its episodes. The episode is that of
world-renowned Pantisocracy. We shall glance at it.

The scheme, as seems generally agreed, originated with
Coleridge; a beautiful dream-poem it was, which he mistook for a reality. The amelioration of the species, the
regeneration of the world, the attainment of unmitigated
felicity here below, were its objects; the excitement of the
French Revolution, with which the air was still tremulous,
gave hue to the undertaking. A coterie of choice spirits,
free from all stain of selfishness, and with every energy

devoted to the above grand ends, was to be selected: these
benign and stainless individuals were to select just as many
young ladies of similar perfection, and marry them; the
whole were then to take shipping for the banks of the
Susquehanna River, beyond the blue Atlantic.   This Susquehanna was chosen, Coleridge informed Gillman, on
account of the name being pretty and metrical!   Here the
choice spirits male were to toil, untiring and unselfish, in
the supposable manner of their father Adam *before* the
fall; the choice spirits female were to do the household
work, and perform all the delicate sweetnesses appointed
them by nature; all taint of selfishness, all deleterious ad-
mixture, of whatever sort, of human failing was to be non-
existent.   The unruffled felicity of a second Eden was to
be the unquestioned result.   Meanwhile, the world, in
amazement at its own long stupidity, and rapt admiration
at the dwellers in the new Happy Valley, was to open all
its prison gates, fling all its crowns into Limbo, and sheathe
sword from pole to pole!   Then, by slow degrees or more
rapidly, after a gently-brightening silver age or in full and
sudden glory, the long-postponed golden age was to gleam
upon the world!   All living beings were to be embraced
in the scheme of love.   Hear this:—

"Innocent Foal! thou poor despised Forlorn!
I hail thee Brother — spite of the fool's scorn!
And fain would take thee with me, in the Dell
Of Peace and mild Equality to dwell.
Where Toil shall call the charmer Health his bride,
And Laughter tickle Plenty's ribless side!
How thou wouldst toss thy heels in gamesome play,
And frisk about as lamb or kitten gay!"

From bards to donkeys the blessings of Pantisocracy were
to extend!

The pleading of this unassailable scheme, and the object of raising the terrestrial element of cash, caused much lecturing in Bristol, whence the world-renovating expedition was to sail. In this town, abode one Joseph Cottle: a man whose nature we can confidently pronounce one of the gentlest, noblest, purest, and most generous to be met with in literary annals, and to whom the world is deeply indebted for his published reminiscences of Coleridge and Southey; he was a bookseller, and warmly patronized genius. Cottle became acquainted with the schemers; enjoyed much their conversation; encouraged their efforts; and lived in hourly expectation of the sailing of the fateful ship, bound for the Elysian Susquehanna. His nerves, one fine morning, were thoroughly and conclusively calmed by the receipt of the following note:—

"MY DEAR SIR, — Can you conveniently lend me five pounds, as we want a little more than four pounds to make up our lodging bill, which is indeed much higher than we expected; seven weeks, and Burnet's lodging for twelve weeks, amounting to twelve pounds.— Yours affectionately,
S. T. COLERIDGE."

Four pounds wanting for a lodging-bill, and the regeneration of the world in hand! One begins to fear that the tough old incorrigible is not to be regenerated yet! Pantisocracy vanishes into vacuity, or is drowned in peals of "inextinguishable laughter!"

Did it all vanish then? Did the whole of the elaborate and fairly-schemed plan fleet into nonentity, and the aerial elemental stuff which dreams are made of? Oh no; very decidedly not. The golden age, as usual, hung back; the Eden on the banks of the musically-named Susquehanna could not be set agoing, without fully more than "four pounds to pay our lodging-bill;" but there was one part of the scheme, which, being of the ethereal sort, and flourishing well when fanned by the airs which blow from dreamland, took deep root. This part, as all our fair readers anticipate, was that in which the young ladies figured; Coleridge and Southey were both engaged in marriage. The union of the former with Miss Sarah Fricker took place on the 4th of October, 1795; the provision by which the youthful husband purposed to support himself and his bride being — an engagement, on the part of Cottle, to give him a guinea and a half for every hundred lines of poetry which he delivered him!

This financial scheme, it was found, would not work; in fact, to secure a competency in this way, one would outwrite Homer before his marriage coat, if very carefully preserved, was out at elbow. Cottle paid some guineas in advance; but Pegasus scorned to be yoked in the provision cart; and, on the whole, some more substantial and certain plan of subsistence was found necessary. The young couple had taken up their abode at Clevedon, a village on the banks of the Severn.

The mind of Coleridge was always scheming, and generally his plans were on a gigantic scale; Cottle tells us of a list of eighteen contemplated works, not one of which was accomplished: his schemes almost invariably, like those of Mithridates, found themselves unduly seconded, and ineffectually actualized, in execution. His schemes on the present occasion, however, were by no means of a singularly romantic or impracticable character. They were chiefly three: to found a school, to become a Unitarian preacher, and to undertake the editing of a magazine. The latter, after consideration, and with somewhat of reluctance, was adopted. The magazine was to be entitled the

Watchman;" it was to consist of high political writing,
of biographical essays, and of reviews; its date of appearance was fixed for Tuesday, 1st March, 1796, and its price
was to be fourpence.

Whether the idea of a magazine was congenial or uncongenial to the mind of Coleridge, he entered upon its
realization with ardent and manly energy. He undertook
a tour to collect subscribers; and accompanied the performance of this primary object with the occasional delivery
of pulpit discourses. His religious views were still Unitarian, and his pulpit garb would have somewhat startled an
orthodox audience; on one occasion, he appeared in blue
coat and white waistcoat. His discourses, too, were "pre-
ciously peppered with politics;" and we must shock our
readers by informing them, that subjects were afforded for
two of them by the corn-laws and the hair-powder tax!

The tour preliminary to the publication of the "Watchman," is one of the most brilliant passages in Coleridge's
history. His mind was in the warm glow of opening manhood; full of hope, ardor, courage, love; we can well imagine that the Cherub Contemplation seemed ever to lie
and dream in his dark gray eye. His conversation was at
the time perhaps at its climax; men hung in wondering
silence on the rhythmic stream which, in wild lyric grandeur, or in gentlest lute tones, rolled ever from his lips.
His eloquence attracted crowds when he appeared in the
pulpit; he was the "figurante" in all companies, and his
irresistible powers of persuasion increased his list of subscribers, beyond even his own imaginings. Of his pulpit
manner, we may form an idea from Hazlitt's description of
him a few years afterwards. Earnest solemnity, despite
his dress and politics, seems to have distinguished his mode
of delivery; poetic adornment, graphic power, and enthu-

siastic exuberance, his style. "The tones of his voice were musical and impressive," says Hazlitt; and "he launched into his subject like an eagle dallying with the wind." No wonder that he attracted crowds.

At Nottingham, he had some dealings with Dr. Darwin, who utterly scorned religion, and thought himself in position to banter Coleridge on the subject. His arguments fell of course like snowflakes on a river; they might, Coleridge said, have been of force at fifteen, but provoked only a smile at twenty. "He (Dr. Darwin) boasted that he had never read one book in favor of such stuff, but that he had read all the works of infidels." The impartial, free-thinking man! "Such," adds Coleridge, "are all the infidels whom I have known."

We said above, that his powers of persuasion during this tour were irresistible; but it is unsafe to indulge in such poetic generalizations; the dull tints and dusts of earth so obstinately mingle with all human glories. Coleridge was in Birmingham, beating up for subscribers — enchanting, astonishing, electrifying. In the strict prosecution of his design, he was destined speedily to find his perseverance and courageous scorn of difficulties put to the test. We must give his own description of the scene; it at once indicates the graphic truth of his pencil, and illustrates the fine hearty joviality which lay deep in his bosom: — "My campaign commenced at Birmingham, and my first attack was on a rigid Calvinist, a tallow-chandler by trade. He was a tall, dingy man, in whom length was so predominant over breadth, that he might almost have been borrowed for a foundry poker. Oh that face! . . . . I have it before me at this moment. The lank, black, twine-like hair, pinguinitescent, cut in a straight line, along the black stubble of his thin gunpowder eyebrows, that looked like a

11*

scorched aftermath from a last week's shaving. His coat collar behind, in perfect unison, both of color and lustre, with the coarse yet glib cordage that I suppose he called his hair, and which, with a bend inward at the nape of the neck (the only approach to flexure in his whole figure), slunk in behind his waistcoat; while the countenance, lank, dark, very *hard*, and with strong perpendicular furrows, gave me a dim notion of some one looking at me through a *used* gridiron, all soot, grease, and iron!"

This man was a friend of the species, and grand society-regenerator. Attentively he listened to "the heaven-eyed creature," as he poured forth, now like a cataract of sunny foam, now like an Æolian harp, his eloquent pleadings; the tallow fumes meanwhile wandering intrusively about the nostrils of the wondrous speaker, mournfully reminiscent of earth. Persuasion that might have melted Shylock having had due course, Coleridge paused to become aware of the effect. "And what, sir, might the cost be?" "Only four-pence (oh how I felt the anti-climax, the abysmal bathos of that FOURPENCE), only fourpence, sir, each number, to be published on every eighth day." "That comes to a deal of money at the end of a year; and how much did you say there was to be for the money?" "Thirty-two pages, sir; large octavo, closely printed." "Thirty and two pages? Bless me, why, except what I does in a family way on the Sabbath, that's more than I ever read, sir, all the year round! I am as great a one as any man in Brummagem, sir, for liberty and truth, and all them sort of things, but as to this (no offence, I hope, sir) I must beg to be excused."

From Sheffield, in the January of 1796, Coleridge wrote to a friend reporting progress. In that letter occurs the following sentence:—"Indeed, I want firmness; I perceive I do. I have that within me which makes it difficult to say No, repeatedly, to a number of persons who seem uneasy and anxious." This, so strictly true, we regard as a physiognomic glimpse of importance. With all his brilliancy, with all his marvellous powers, with all the genius which dwelt in his wonderful eye, the great disruption between the powers of thought and the powers of action had begun to be conspicuously manifest in Coleridge. He had not the power of saying No! And yet how necessary, how utterly indispensable, in this world of ours, is the ability to utter, on needful occasions, a clear, defiant No! Mentally or physically it has to be done every hour of our life; and would we not be near the mark, in dating the full development of self-sustained manhood at the thorough attainment of that power?

The "Watchman" did not succeed; the causes of its failure were manifold. Too much was expected by the public; a sufficient staff of talented men was not attached to it; and, finally, the close, accurate drudgery, necessary to the successful superintendence of a magazine, was singularly uncongenial to Coleridge's nature.

Some time after the publication of the "Watchman" ceased, we find its editor stationed at Stowey. Here, though for a brief space he enjoyed tranquillity and comfort, the frustrated hopes of his past life sunk deep into his soul. He was approaching a critical and important epoch in his spiritual development. It can be discerned, with indubitable distinctness, that his mind was in an unhealthy portentous state — feverish, excited, unsettled; now in the whirl of fiery enthusiasm and hilarity, now in the morbid disquietude of hopeless depression; now scheming stupendous epics, now cowering, anxious and trembling, to propitiate the "two Giants, Bread and Cheese." All this points to a shattered nervous state and prompts mournful forebodings.

About this time, Coleridge was of very striking appearance. In person he was somewhat full, and rather above the common size; his complexion inclined to light, but was shaded by dark hair; his eyebrows were large and protruding; his forehead, as Hazlitt describes it, was "broad and high, as if built of ivory;" his large gray eye rolled and gleamed, in the light of mild but mighty genius.

We have arrived, as we said, at a grand crisis in his character and history. We have seen him in his youth; we have marked the swift expansion of his faculties, the first meteoric blaze of his fame. His path hitherto must be pronounced brilliant. Not unshaded by sorrow, not untinctured with error, it is yet encompassed with a grand auroral radiance. The light of genius flashing from his eye, the light of hope and ardor firing his bosom, he has trod along, kindling expectant admiration in all breasts. His very errors have been those of a noble and mighty nature. The banner of human advancement had been thrown abroad upon the winds, inscribed with liberty and with love; and ardent young souls hastened to range themselves beneath it; unweeting that those golden words had been, or were to be, soaked and blotted with blood. With what in the mighty onrushing of the French Revolution was truly noble, with the perennial truths of freedom and advancement, Coleridge had deeply sympathized; in its wild volcanic fury he never shared, and, when murder and despotism sat in its high places, he utterly abjured its cause. For a time, the ardent, all-fusing love in his own bosom, had bathed the world in kindness and beauty; the tones of his own heart were those of tenderness and gentlest sympathy, and he had dreamed that he had heard respon-

sive notes from the bosoms of all his fellow men. Hence
had arisen the Susquehanna scheme, the beautiful morning
dream of the Happy Valley. Already, in various ways,
he had evinced gigantic powers. In a constellation of
rarely gifted youths, he had been the central light, the most
dazzling star; his eloquence and his conversation had shed
enchantment around him: his "Religious Musings," to
specify no other of his juvenile performances, had been the
indubitable pledge of power to scale the loftiest heights of
thought and of fame, and to sit there crowned among the
mightiest.

But his path, dazzling and wonderful as it was, had been
strictly that of youth. An element of excitement had
encompassed him; the atmosphere of his mind had been
tempestuous and fiery; and the grand question which presents itself, at the momentous period of his history at
which we have now arrived, is this:—Is his radiance to
be merely meteoric, intermittent, and youthful; or is he
henceforth, in calmer air and with steadier glory, to shine
in the placid majesty of manhood?

Southey, the friend of his youth, and the sharer for a
time in his dreams, with powers whose might was never
considered so rare or so wonderful as his own, calmly and
courageously marched from the dreamland of youth, and
in gathered energy commenced life victoriously as a man;
Wordsworth, gentle but stalwart-hearted, had virtually done
the same; and how was it with him, whose eye gleamed
with a more unearthly radiance than that of either, who
was among them the acknowledged monarch — Samuel
Taylor Coleridge?

What, in our view, marks the full development of manhood, and dissevers it totally from the states of boyhood
and youth, is a sustained *self-mastery*. When the energies

are not the slaves of excitement; when the fiery impatience of occasional effort has become the perseverent energy of continued work; when the powers are ranged in ordered submission under the will; when the motives are not the faint wavering fatui or meteors of the hour, but the guiding principle of the life is clearly ascertained and resolutely adhered to; — then the boy has passed into the man.

According to this view of the matter, it is manifest that sound healthful manhood does not necessarily presuppose any vastness of mental power, any extraordinary or astonishing genius. A William Burns, for instance, toiling calmly and with stern endurance to find sustenance for himself and his children, may be a sounder, and in stricter terms, a more fully developed man than his world-shaking son the poet, with his wildly-tossing passions and his sadly blasted hopes. The miner, who works resolutely and without flinching in the bowels of the earth, may be more a man than the feverish creature of excitement, who now soars above the clouds, and now lies prostrate and hopeless in the mire. Who ever said Byron was a fully developed man?

Still more, it is precisely where the powers are mightiest, and the passions strongest, that the difficulty of attaining calm manhood is sternest. A comparatively easy task it is for the man of common, everyday powers, to attain their proper command, to restrain them within their due mechanic circle. But when the passions are fierce and mighty as whirlwinds, when the breast heaves with volcanic fire, and the eye rolls in frenzy, when the sensibility is as intensely acute to disappointment as the hopes are bright and certain of failure; then it is, at the momentous crisis when the dreams of youth, whose light has hitherto suffused the world, vanish finally from the soul, that the struggle is tremendous. The bearing of these remarks upon the character of Coleridge will become manifest as we proceed.

After the failure of the "Watchman," we find Coleridge residing at Stowey. The urgency of a regular mode of subsistence had become more imperative, from the fact of his having become a father. Pecuniary affairs, however, wore by no means a hopeless aspect; Charles Lloyd, a young man who had conceived the profoundest admiration for Coleridge's genius, had taken up his abode with him; occasional sums were obtained from Cottle for poetry; and at length, in 1798, Mr. Josiah Wedgewood and his brother, who patriotically desired that Coleridge's marvellous powers should be untrammelled by a profession, bestowed upon him an annuity of £150. One half of this sum ceased to be paid at a subsequent period.

Ere proceeding in our history of Coleridge's character, we must indulge our readers and ourselves with a glance at his Stowey life; a sunny prospect, which we shall sood find enveloped in cloud and darkness. We avail ourselves of the words of kind and honest Cottle, who waxes hilarious and quasi-poetical on the occasion; the time was June 29, 1797. "Mr. C. took peculiar delight in assuring me (at least at that time) how happy he was; exhibiting successively his house, his garden, his orchard, laden with fruit; and also the contrivances he had made to unite his two neighbors' domains with his own. . . . After the grand circuit had been accomplished, by hospitable contrivance, we approached the "Jasmine Harbor," where, to our gratifying surprise, we found the tripod table laden with delicious bread and cheese, surmounted by a brown mug of true Taunton ale. We instinctively took our seats; and there must have been some downright witchery in the provisions, which surpassed all of its kind; nothing like it

on the wide terrene, and one glass of the Taunton settled
it to an axiom. While the dappled sunbeams played on
our table, through the umbrageous canopy, the very birds
seemed to participate in our felicities, and poured forth
their selectest anthems. As we sat in our sylvan hall of
splendor, a company of the happiest mortals (T. Poole, C.
Lloyd, S. T. Coleridge, and J. C.), the bright blue heavens,
the sporting insects, the balmy zephyrs, the feathered chor-
isters, the sympathy of friends, all augmented the pleasur-
able to the highest point this side the celestial! . . . .
While thus elevated, in the universal current of our feelings, Mrs. Coleridge appeared, with her fine Hartley; we
all smiled, but the father's joy was transcendental!"

All this was too bright to last. As yet, indeed, there
seemed no great cause for abatement of the hopes of those
who, in ever-increasing numbers and in ever-deepening
veneration, encircled Coleridge. We might say, in fact,
that it was much the reverse. The dreamy disappoint-
ments of youth might become matter for a pleasant smile;
the poetic fire, in which he had clothed nature and man,
might yet warm his own bosom and nerve his own arm.

His political opinions had attained a fuller development;
while retaining all the enthusiasm and love of early days,
they had settled into assured stability, on a foundation of
soundest wisdom. His theological views also — a fact of
momentous importance, and fraught with richest hope —
had undergone revision. More profoundly and with truer
reverence, he had acknowledged, in his inmost soul, that
the Bible is, in very truth, the articulate voice of God to
man; he had perceived that the whole history of the human
race, for the silent but mighty facts of which no youthful
imaginings could be substituted, hath, for its centre, its
keystone, and its crown, the Lord Jesus Christ; he had

begun to discern that religion, if in any sense strictly revealed, must superadd something to the dicta of nature, and be a "religation" or binding again; he had heard the deep and awful words of mystery which rise from the whole frame of nature and the whole inner world of the soul; and, in meekest but manliest adoration, he had bowed down to the triune God. Oh, how Hope now, dashing aside the veil of the shadowing years, seems still, despite our knowledge of the end, with brightest smile to point to Coleridge, as he was at the close of the last century!

In the years of boyhood and youth, Coleridge's constitution, although not peculiarly robust, was unquestionably sound and healthful; not free from weakness, not unvisited by pain, he was yet indubitably the possessor of a buoyant spirit and vigorous frame. But on one occasion, about the close of the century, he had been visited by severe and singular bodily ailment, accompanied by excruciating pain. For relief, he had recourse to — opium! Finding the relief he sought, and unaware that he was dallying with a power, whose deadly necromancy withers the arm and palsies the soul, he went on, heedless and unweeting, until resistance was vain.

Here, then, was the blasting of all hope; here was the attainment of calm manhood rendered forever impossible; henceforward the chaining of his energies in ordered submission to the car of will, was hopeless.

Beyond all doubt, this was the proximate and decisive agent in bringing about the tragic anomaly of Coleridge's after life. Yet there were other influences at work, which acted mainly as hindrances and counteracting forces to his at once awakening from his trance, and tearing from his bosom the vampire that drank his life-blood. The shattering of his youthful schemes, and the failure of his youthful hopes, had wakened tones of deepest sorrow in his soul. We hear of a "calm hopelessness," of long days of despairing anticipation and unbrightened foreboding. Besides this, we have reason for thinking it a fact, and we need do no more than mention it, that his marriage had in some respects been an unhappy one.

But for the mighty magic of opium, which, at such a crisis, came in to throw a shade of most mournful gloom over the character and life of Coleridge, these secondary disturbing influences might well have been overborne; but for the depressing effects of these influences, opium might never have succeeded in throwing its withering influence, finally, and irremediably, over his soul: in their mutual operation, they produced what we have called the grand severance in Coleridge's character.

After visiting Germany, in 1798, and making a stay there of fourteen months, Coleridge settled in the Lake country, and engaged largely in newspaper writing. In 1804, he visited Malta. Returning, after a residence of considerable length, to England, we find him, in the year 1809, commencing, once more, the publication of a periodical, this time named, "The Friend." During the period when this paper appeared, the circulating libraries were doubtless in as full operation as ever; the British public of this enlightened age were hanging over their novels, or preparing, perhaps, their ball dresses; commerce was rushing heedless onwards; Mammon was stalking abroad, with all eyes turned towards him in supplication or praise; "The Friend," being sadly over-freighted with wisdom, and having no direct bearing on cash, but only on the eternal destiny of man, and his true and lasting temporal amelioration, could not be carried on for lack of support! This is a fact; and admits of being thus broadly stated. As we peruse those volumes, now promising fair for literary immortality, in which the published numbers of "The Friend" are preserved to us, it appears strange and even humiliating, that such periodical writing should, in our century, under whatever disadvantages, have failed of adequate support. But what, after all, must we say? That, in this defective world, small worms destroy imposing gourds, that, as Richter remarks, though wings are admirable for the azure, we want boots for the paving stones, that the consummate linguistic skill and high metaphysics of Coleridge were rendered unavailing, not solely through the indifference or stupidity of his countrymen, but through such small and undignified shortcomings, as want of punctuality, want of clearness, and want of business tact.

Towards the end of his sojourn at the Lakes, Coleridge's mode of existence, as we learn from Mr. De Quincey, was cheerless and anomalous. Towards the afternoon, he descended from his bedroom; and through the still watches of the night, until the morning struck the stars, his lonely taper burned mournfully in his window. The same writer assures us, that the intense glow of sympathy and joyous admiration, with which Coleridge had once gazed upon Nature, had now well-nigh died away : the magic had passed from stream and lake, from wood and mountain, from the ocean and the stars : they woke no tones of music in his breast, they lit no fire of rapture in his eye. Ah, what a mournful change was here!

In 1810, Coleridge quitted the Lake country forever. In the early part of 1814, we find him lecturing at Bristol. Opium was now in the full exercise of its tyrannic and deadly power. Sternly, and with sincerest effort, he resisted it, but its magic became ever the more irresistible; its necromancy had smitten his energy with fatal paralysis.

The effort to free himself from the spell was vain; the thrill of temporary gladness, as of returning youth and rapture, formed so witching a contrast to the remorse and almost despair of his disenchanted hours, that he ever threw himself again into the arms of his destroyer. He seems to us to be sorrowfully, but truly, imaged by his own "miserable knight," haunted by the spectre of a bright and beautiful lady, from the ghastly gleam of whose eye he could not escape, and whom he *knew* to be a fiend.

The wild fire in his eye, and other indications, revealed to Cottle the melancholy state of affairs. In deepest distress, and actuated by his sincere and tender love for Coleridge, he resolved to address to him an expostulating letter. With Cottle, we can find no fault; the voice of duty to his friend and to his God prompted the effort; but, with deep conviction we must say, he was not the man to perform the task. The delicate and reverential kindness which every sentence should have breathed; the admiring and bewailing pity, distinguishing minutely and unremittingly between crime and disease; the manliness of friendly and most earnest advice, with no tone of censorious exhortation or blame; — these were beyond the mental capacity of Cottle. How sad are these words in reply: — "You have poured oil in the raw and festering wounds of an old friend's conscience, Cottle! but it is *oil of vitriol!*" And what an unfathomable sorrow is here: — "I have prayed, with drops of agony on my brow; trembling, not only before the justice of my Maker, but even before the mercy of my Redeemer. 'I gave thee so many talents, what hast thou done with them?'"

Ah! little did Cottle, or even Southey, with his far greater soul, know of the fearful battle which this mighty and valiant spirit had to fight; we must even say that they did not fully attend to what they might plainly have discerned. Does not the whole course of Coleridge's life indicate sternest effort? His newspaper writing, his editing "The Friend," his long researches into metaphysics and theology; do they not show an earnest and noble effort to attain "the perennial fireproof joys of constant employment?" do they not show a soul struggling, with Titanic effort and deadly perseverance, against a viewless but resistless power? Could aught which Southey or Cottle might say, instil a deeper abhorrence of opium into Coleridge's mind than was there already? Could any human hand portray its effects and influence, in darker hues, than those in which, in his own agonized and blasted soul, they were imaged already to the eye of Coleridge? It was not advice or exhortation which was needed; it was kindliest, tenderest co-operation with the efforts of the sufferer; it was admiring sympathy and respectful assistance. Good conscientious Cottle somewhat mistook his function in addressing Coleridge, and his attempt was, of course, unattended with any important result.

In 1816, Coleridge took up his abode at Highgate, in the immediate vicinity of London, under the roof of Mr. Gillman, a physician. Here he thenceforward remained; and here he terminated his career, in 1834. During this long period, he constantly displayed his astonishing intellectual powers; and exhibited, along with them, the marvellous and melancholy prostration of the powers of action. On the whole, from these years there seems to breathe a wailing cadence of unutterable sorrow. Splendors there were, beautiful, meteoric; but they appear but as the gleaming of nightly meteors over the pale Arctic snow, far different from the calm and brightening beams of morn. His mental powers were still mighty and rampant, as an army of lions; but his will, that should have guided and subdued them, was feeble and wavering as a deer.

Yet how wonderful is the power of genius! Mournfully as the lines of decision had faded from that cheek, sadly as the fire was dimmed in that eye, broken as were the tones of that once soft and melodious voice, ardent and gifted souls were drawn instinctively towards him. Week after week and year after year, did they listen attentively, did they journey patiently; drawn by the weird gleam of the halo of genius round his brow. A sort of undefined glory encompassed him; an influence proceeded from him as of some wizard power, allied to inspiration, and linked in some mysterious manner with infinitude. Round his shrine was ever a brilliant troop of powerful young minds; among the others, we can see William Hazlitt, John Sterling, and Thomas Carlyle.

The last mentioned writer, in his lately published life of John Sterling, has devoted a chapter to Coleridge; and we present to our readers the following sketch of him during his Highgate life, from Carlyle's unequalled pencil: —

"Coleridge sat on the brow of Highgate Hill in those years, looking down on London and its smoke-tumult, like a sage escaped from the inanity of life's battle; attracting towards him the thoughts of innumerable brave souls still engaged there. . . . The good man, he was now getting old, towards sixty perhaps; and gave you the idea of a life that had been full of sufferings; a life heavy-laden, half-vanquished, still swimming painfully in seas of manifold physical, and other bewilderment. Brow and head were round, and of massive weight, but the face was flabby and irresolute. The deep eyes, of a light hazel, were as full of sorrow as of inspiration; confused pain looked mildly from them, as in a kind of mild astonishment. The whole figure and air, good and amiable otherwise, might be called flabby and irresolute; expressive of weakness under possibility of strength. He hung loosely on his limbs, with knees bent, and stooping attitude; in walking he rather shuffled than decisively stept; and a lady once remarked, he never could fix which side of the garden walk would suit him best, but continually shifted in corkscrew fashion and kept trying both. A heavy-laden, high-aspiring, and surely much suffering man. His voice, naturally soft and good, had contracted itself into a painful snuffle and sing-song: he spoke as if preaching, — you would have said, preaching earnestly and also hopelessly the weightiest things. I still recollect his "object" and "subject," terms of continual recurrence in the Kantean province; and how he sung and snuffled them into "om-m-mject" and "sum-m-mject," with a kind of solemn shake or quaver, as he rolled along." He died, as we have said, in 1834.

There are four aspects under which Samuel Taylor Coleridge presents himself to our gaze:—those of poet, philosopher, critic, and conversationalist. Our glance at him in these capacities must be very hurried. The perusal of Coleridge's poetry is singularly suggestive of the idea of stupendous powers, never exerted to their full extent, and never applied to objects fully worthy of their might. To paint with delicate exactness, until the mimicry produces a titillating delight; to evoke visions from dreamland, and present them, dressed in the gaudy tinsel of fancy, to the eye of ennui-stricken maiden, demanding no effort of thought, inspiring no new and nobler life; such may have been the attempts of some, whom it would be deemed hard to exclude from the confines of Parnassus; but such we must esteem a desecration of poetry, and such could never have been the poetry of Coleridge. To flash new light upon the destiny of man, and to kindle his eye with light from heaven, must ever constitute the true mission of the poet; and to this alone could Coleridge, fully and finally, have devoted his powers.

But to these objects, it cannot be said that he ever, in full measure, devoted them. He has done much; but we are profoundly sensible that he might have done more. Strains of softest, gentlest melody he has left us, strains which will sound in the ears of the latest generations; the gift he bestowed upon his country was precious and marvellous. Yet might not the Titanic powers to which they bear witness have drawn new notes of grandeur from the great unwritten epic of human history, have thrown new and brighter light on the ways of God to man, have spread out a new auroral banner to illumine man's destiny, and lead him nearer to the celestial country? In his youth he schemed an epic, which might have set him on the same starry pinnacle with Milton; but it was his fate to scheme, while Milton, heroic in every fibre, accomplished.

We shall notice, and that but most cursorily, only four of Coleridge's poems: "Religious Musings," "The Ancient Mariner," "Christabel," and "Love."

In the Pickering edition of 1844, the date affixed to the "Religious Musings" is Christmas Eve, 1794. If this is correct, the piece was composed when its author was a dragoon; but Cottle asserts it to have been written at a later period. We are inclined, however, to suspect, that the latter has confounded subsequent revision and addition, with original production. At all events, it was a juvenile effort, and truly it was a mighty one. All through it, there glows the white heat of a noblest and holiest enthusiasm; its tempestuous rapture reminds you of Homer. Some passages gleam with a Miltonic grandeur and sublimity;

and the marvellous power with which the poet spreads his vivifying enthusiasm all over nature, is unsurpassed.

The magnificent personifications with which this poem abounds, are perhaps its distinguishing characteristic. The power of personification, we regard as one of the truest and severest tests of poetic genius; and among modern poets Coleridge and Shelley are probably its greatest masters. As a specimen of the ability of the former in this way, and also as a characteristic extract from the poem of which we speak, we quote the following lines; our readers will recollect Coleridge's early political views, and the excitement of the French Revolution:—

> " Yet is the day of retribution nigh;
> The Lamb of God hath open'd the fifth seal
> And upward rush on swiftest wing of fire
> The innumerable multitude of Wrongs
> By man on man inflicted! Rest awhile,
> Children of wretchedness! The hour is nigh:
> And lo! the great, the rich, the mighty Men,
> The Kings and the chief Captains of the World,
> With all that fix'd on high like stars of Heaven
> Shot baleful influence, shall be cast to earth,
> Vile and down-trodden, as the untimely fruit
> Shook from the fig-tree by a sudden storm.
> Even now the storm begins; each gentle name,
> Faith and meek Piety, with fearful joy
> Tremble far off—for lo! the giant Frenzy,
> Uprooting empires with his whirlwind arm,
> Mocketh high Heaven; burst hideous from the cell
> Where the old Hag, unconquerable, huge,
> Creation's eyeless drudge, black Ruin, sits,.
> Nursing the impatient earthquake."

That "giant Frenzy," we are inclined to pronounce the finest personification in the whole compass of modern poetry; and we are not sure that two such figures as this, and "creation's eyeless drudge, black Ruin," are to be found, in an equally short space, in any poem that ever was written. And this was composed ere Coleridge was twenty-five.

The "Ancient Mariner" is one of the most wonderful products of modern times. So much has been said of it, that little need now be added. It is a vivid and awful phantasmagoria, of weird mystery and terrific sublimity. A vision of wildest grandeur, which passed before the poet's ecstatic eye, it was cast into poetic unity by the vivifying power of imagination, and limned forth by the poetic hand in magical and meteoric tints, to the rivetted eyes of all men. Its graphic power is absolutely wonderful; and we need only remind our readers what an important element of poetic effect this is. What other men *hear* of the poet *sees;* in the intense glow of poetic rapture, annihilating time and space, he gazes one moment into the flames of Tophet, and the next·upon the crowns of the Seraphim; what other men speak of, he paints. It is perhaps the mingling of awe, and mystery, and wildest imagining, with terrific distinctness of picturing, that makes the spell, which this poem throws over the reader, so irresistible. What a picture is this:—

> "The upper air burst into life!
>   And a hundred fire-flags sheen;
>   To and fro they were hurried about!
>   And to and fro, and in and out,
>   The wan stars danced between.
>
> And the coming wind did roar more loud,
>   And the sails did sigh like sedge;
> And the rain poured down from one black cloud;
>   The moon was at its edge.

> The thick black cloud was cleft, and still
>> The moon was at its side;
> Like waters shot from some high crag,
> The lightning fell with never a jag,
>> A river steep and wide."

Those wan stars, that black cloud with the moon at its edge, and that river of lightning, make up surely one of the most terrific landscapes ever conceived or portrayed. What a still and awful sublimity, too, is there in these lines:—

> " Still as a slave before his lord,
>> The ocean hath no blast;
> *His great bright eye most silently*
> *Up to the moon is cast.*"

If, again, we consider the imagery of the poem, we find it also perfect:—

> " Day after day, day after day,
>> We stuck, nor breath nor motion;
> As idle as a painted ship
>> Upon a painted ocean."

The inexpressible beauty and appropriateness of this image were never surpassed.

And does not the heart thrill with the aerial melody, and serene loveliness, of these so simple lines?

> " It ceased; yet still the sails made on
>> A pleasant noise till noon,
> A noise like of a hidden brook
>> In the leafy month of June,
> That to the sleeping woods all night
>> Singeth a gentle tune."

But we can particularize the beauties of this poem no

farther.   We regard it as one of the most wondrous phan-
tasmagorias, one of the most marvellous pieces of imaginative painting, to be met with in ancient or modern poetry.

"Christabel" is a production by itself.   Coleridge wrote
no other piece like it, and no man but Coleridge ever could
have written it.   The idea of satanic enmity and malice,
under the garb of angelic innocence and beauty, seems to
have been much present to the mind of Coleridge.   Geral-
dine, and the fiend lady beautiful and bright, are personifications of the same thought; and it is one of chilliest hor-
ror.   We give no excerpts from "Christabel;" its most
striking passages have been quoted numberless times.   The
blending of undefined mystery and awe, with the most
vivid bodying forth of each portrait in the picture, and the
most delicate minuteness in laying on the tints, perhaps
distinguish it as a poem.

We lack words to speak our admiration of Coleridge's
poem called "Love."   Its melody rolls trancingly over the
soul, raising unutterable emotions; its gentle but mighty
enthusiasm, calm as a cloudless summer noon, wraps the
whole being in an atmosphere of rapture; its ideally beautiful painting laughs at our power of admiration.   There
are a few pieces in our language which stand apart from all
others, in unapproached, inexhaustible loveliness: among
these we place Milton's "Allegro" and "Il Penseroso,"
Shelley's "Cloud," and Coleridge's "Love."   Our readers,
of course, all know it; but we must once more recall to
their minds its serenely beautiful commencement:—

> " All thoughts, all passions, all delights,
>   Whatever stirs this mortal frame,
> All are but ministers of Love,
>   And feed his sacred flame.

Oft in my waking hours do I
Live o'er again that happy hour,
When midway on the mount I lay,
Beside the ruin'd tower.

The moonshine, stealing o'er the scene,
Had blended with the lights of eve;
And she was there, my hope, my joy—
My own dear Genevieve!"

The pieces we have mentioned are the most wonderful efforts of Coleridge. We have been able to do little more than refer to them as proofs of his gigantic powers, without, in any adequate measure, analyzing or displaying their beauties.

Of Coleridge, as philosopher and critic, we cannot speak, save in the briefest terms. The "Friend," the "Aids to Reflection," the "Biographia Literaria," and the "Method," are his leading contributions to criticism and philosophy. We shall not characterize them separately. They abound in profound wisdom and practical insight; a collection of aphorisms might be made from them, we venture to say, embodying all, or almost all, the great truths, religious, moral, and political, whose proclamation constitutes the spiritual advancement and attainment of the nineteenth century; their style is on all hands considered one of the most perfect of models. Of his distinction between the reason and the understanding, which was the keystone of his philosophy, and which has so widely influenced philosophic thought in our century; and of his distinction between the imagination and the fancy, to which critics have been so much beholden, we shall say nothing. Their importance may be very great; they may have led to new and rich fields of thought; but we are very far from thinking that it is by estimating their precise value, that a correct or adequate

SECOND SERIES.   13

idea of the influence which Coleridge has exerted, and the work he has done, is to be obtained. It is in the spiritual impulse which he communicated to British thought; in the new earnestness and elevated enthusiasm with which he inspired the noblest spirits of our age; in the new life which he kindled in thousands of hearts, that the extent and magnitude of his influence are to be seen. From his works, in their whole range, comes a mild but powerful influence, purging the soul of earthliness, turning the eye heavenward, and nerving the arm to noblest endeavor; while mammonism, selfishness, and baseness, like spectres and night-birds at the morning strains of Memnon, are startled and flee away. To perform this work in our gold-worshipping age, Coleridge seems pre-eminently to have been missioned by the Most High. And when the reader conceives to himself the effect of this, in its thousandfold ramifications, through our families, our churches, and our literary schools, to trace which is at present impossible for us, he will agree with us in thinking the work of Coleridge a far extending and mighty work.

To Coleridge's conversational powers, allusion has already been made. On all hands they have been recognized as wonderful; but there has been an important difference of opinion regarding them. Mr. Carlyle, in the work from which we have already quoted, says: — " I have heard Coleridge talk, with eager musical energy, two stricken hours, his face radiant and moist, and communicate no meaning whatever to any individual of his hearers — certain of whom, I for one, still kept eagerly listening in hope," etc. The importance of this is very great, and its weight cannot, by any means, be entirely nullified. It is difficult for any reader of Carlyle to believe, or even conceive, that, in any such case, his earnest and fiery eye would not see into

the heart of what matter there was. But we must listen
to another authority on the subject, which will also be recognized as of weighty import, that of Mr. De Quincey; —
" Coleridge, to many people, and often I have heard the
complaint, seemed to wander; and he seemed then to
wander the most, when, in fact, his resistance to the wandering instinct was greatest, viz., when the compass and
huge circuit by which his illustrations moved, travelled
farthest into remote regions, before they began to revolve.
Long before this coming round commenced, most people
had lost him, and naturally enough supposed that he had
lost himself. They continued to admire the separate beauty
of the thoughts, but did not see their relations to the dominant theme. . . . . I can assert, upon my long and intimate knowledge of Coleridge's mind, that logic, the most
severe, was as inalienable from his modes of thinking as
grammar from his language."

Under the shield of De Quincey, we venture to suggest,
that the practical energy of Carlyle, and the fact that long
and subtle trains of abstract speculation are not congenial
to his mind, may afford a solution of the circumstance, that
he failed to discover order or continuity of argument, where,
to the more practised metaphysical intellect of De Quincey,
all was beautifully and emphatically perspicuous.

We have finished our cursory survey of the life and
works of Samuel Taylor Coleridge. Around his career
are glories as of empyrean light; and sorrows that might
draw tears from the Seraphim. Of kind and gentle nature,
and by constitution and early education ill adapted for the
sore buffetings of the life-battle, his intellectual vision was
wide as that of the eagle, and piercing as that of the
lynx; his love of nature was deep and delicate as a Naiad's
that has dwelt forever by a fountain in the silent wood;

his youth was bright, and radiant with the beams of promise; his intellectual prowess, in its full expansion, was gazed on with dumb astonishment; while, in beautiful union with this, was a fantastic, almost childish playfulness and geniality of heart. His religion, despite the sad anomaly in his character, and the baleful influence of the power under whose magic he lay, we must, from the whole spirit of his writings, from the deep devotion of his private letters, and from the agonized struggle of his life, declare to have been profound and all-pervasive. In a fatal hour, he quaffed the enchanting draught of opium, and there was not enough of rugged vigor in his soul to break the spell; henceforward it was as if the spirit of an eagle was closed in the heart of a dove. We image him to ourselves as a desert-born steed, with hoofs to outrun the wind, and eyes to outgleam the lightning, but smitten, at the bright morning hour, by the withering Samiel, and thenceforward staggering, with eye dimmed and limbs tottering, along the burning sand.

V.

WELLINGTON.

AMONG the many wonderful phenomena of human history, war holds a prominent, if not the most prominent, place; in the web of human destiny, it has marked itself by a deep and continuous stain of red; it has directed every national development, it has called forth every human emotion, it has entered into the composition of every language. It is, withal, a phenomenon whose meaning is extremely difficult to read, and of which, we must make bold to say, the readings have been extremely unsatisfactory.

To discern that war is essentially an evil, demands no singular amount, and no extraordinary exercise, of penetration. The fair Earth that smiles daily to the sun, decked in flowery garlands by the hand of Summer, might surely serve a nobler end than to be the dwelling-place of self-exterminating beings; the lordly rivers, wandering through stately champaigns, and, like beneficent queens, scattering rich bounties around them, were surely not designed to be reddened and thickened by the gore of brother men; the mountains that rise so grandly to meet the glance of Morn, were surely not set there to flash back that glance from the bristling line of steel; the soft, luxuriant plains of Ceres and Flora were surely destined finally to some higher object than to be the battle-fields of Bellona and Mars. War, it

13*

must be allowed, is a relic of chaos and old night. But let us not imagine that this is the whole truth concerning it; its source leads us back to the unfathomable mysteries, but its history is not utterly inexplicable, and its actings are not by any means simply malign. Let it be granted that human history bears unquestionable evidence of some fearful taint, of some fatal curse; let it be recognized that the path of the generations has been over a burning marl, which would not become the pavement of heaven, and war becomes explicable. It has not been all in vain that the generations have ever marched to battle music: the car of *Civilization* has dripped with blood; those throes and throbbings which mark every new birth of society have been wars.

The great event which has given tone and color to the history of our time, and without a knowledge of which it is impossible to understand the nineteenth century, is the first French Revolution. It was the last great awakening of the European intellect; as every other such awakening, it was followed by wars: —

> "For all the past of Time reveals
> A bridal dawn of thunder peals
> Wherever Thought hath wedded Fact."

We venture the assertion, that the character of these wars has been very widely misconceived. Mr. Carlyle, alluding to them, and to Pitt as one of their chief movers, exclaims: — "The result of all which, what was it? Elderly men can remember the tar barrels burnt for success and thrice immortal victory in the business, and yet what result had we? The French Revolution, a Fact decreed in the Eternal Councils, could not be put down," etc. We shall not stay to ask how it came that the "Eternal Councils" ceased to act when Pitt came upon the stage, and allowed that singular puppet to cut the threads of destiny and play his part in independence of them; we shall merely remark, that, to our thinking, the Eternal Councils, or, as we shall prefer saying, the hand of the Christian God, was as manifest in the wars as in the revolution. The time was not yet come for democracy; it was destined that the fire which threatened to gird the world should, for the time, be quenched, and nature did not grudge a deep deluge of blood for the purpose. Were there no other end attained by these wars than to prove, in the groans and thunders of battle, that it was not the doctrine of Voltaire that was to renovate the world — that the light in which the nations were to rejoice was not to shine from the saloons of philosophism — it were enough to demonstrate their supervision and direction by the eye of Providence. To use a figure suggested by Shakspeare, the tree of humanity had to be lanced, and lanced fearfully, at least once more, ere it reached its final glory and beauty.

The lions of democracy arose in wild fury; they were then yoked in glad submission to the car of their emperor, and would have drawn him in triumph, like the god of old, around the world; but an instrument was raised up and duly fitted to dash him from his seat, and to send him to his lonely isle. Upon both of these from the first rested the eye of God. The name of the one was Napoleon: the other was that dauntless, calm, and stately hero, over whose tomb, with a tear of pride, and not of sorrow, Britannia now weeps.

Arthur Wellesley, the Duke of Wellington, was born in Ireland in the year 1769. Both the precise locality and the precise date of the event have been disputed; we think the writer of the biography which appeared in the *Times* has established that the month was April, and rendered it at least extremely probable that the place was Dublin. By original extraction he was English, but a naturalization of more than two centuries had rendered the family from which he sprung thoroughly Irish. In the same year which witnessed the arrival of Wellington in our world, there was another little boy born in Ajaccio; he was ushered into the world on a piece of tapestry, embroidered with scenes from the Iliad; they called him Napoleon. Arthur Wellesley received his military education at Angers, in France. In the year 1787, he received his commission as ensign in the 73d infantry regiment. In the boyhood of Wellington there occurred nothing deserving mention.

Strangely enough, it was in Belgium that Arthur Wellesley served his first campaign. There he received his first practical military lesson, in its rugged sternness, little dreaming that there lay the commencement of that training, which, on these very plains, was to result in his becoming the envy and admiration of the world. The campaign was extremely disastrous to Great Britain, and extremely profitable to her future hero. Of many great generals, and, with emphasis, of Napoleon himself, it might be said that victory is their ruin. The feeling of danger and the sounds of battle brace their nerves, and clear their intellectual vision; but the sound of a world's applause intoxicates and maddens them; thinking to shake the spheres, they suddenly find that they are mortal, and fall headlong. But of Wellington, and the whole class of generals which he represented, it may be truly said, that every mistake is worth a triumph, every defeat worth a victory. It was so in the case of Wellesley's first campaign. He saw there, in the most striking illustration, the combined action of defective organization, inefficient commissariat, and miserable equipment; he saw, in a word, the operation of all those errors and evils which are born of incapacity; and he witnessed their result — disgrace and destruction. Performing, in his subordinate position, all that clearness of vision and energetic action could effect; seizing every error or reverse, and making it "vassal unto" wisdom; he served a very valuable apprenticeship to his profession in this Belgium 'campaign which fell in the end of 1794 and the beginning of 1795.

In the beginning of the year 1797, Colonel Wellesley arrived at Calcutta; a short time afterwards, his brother, Lord Mornington, was placed at the head of the Indian government. The main features of his character were now distinctly perceptible. An intellect of uncommon clearness, comprehension, and vigor, was ruled and directed by a prevailing and ardent devotion to war; a calm but sleepless energy, in alliance with a penetrating intellect, searched every circumstance to its root, unravelled every complexity, and carefully stored every fragment of knowledge, which bore on the theory or practice of his profession; cheerfulness among friends, and reserve in general society, masked a soul whose power necessitated its internal working. In person, he is represented as having been handsome and soldier-like; the light in his eye was steady and piercing; an occasional abstraction and impatience indicated the fiery energy that was in want of a world to conquer. By accident or intention, he passed a few weeks at Madras, soon after his arrival in India; the period was short, but it was sufficient to enable him to acquire an accurate and comprehensive acquaintance with the affairs of the presidency, and the warlike capacities of the Carnatic. The time soon came when it was to avail him much.

Wellington's campaigns in India were three. The first

was against Tippoo Sultaun, the dreaded ruler of Mysore;
the second was the arduous, but somewhat amusing, chase
and destruction of Dhoondiah Waugh, the robber of the
Mahratta hills; the third was the glorious campaign of
Assaye, which rivalled the renown of Plassey, and continued one of the brightest blazons on the shield of Wellington. We shall concern ourselves but slightly with the first
two; Assaye deserves a longer notice.

The campaign against Tippoo, in which Wellesley served
in a subordinate capacity, ended with the capture of Ser-
ingapatam and the death of its former possessor.   This
took place in the summer of 1799. Colonel Wellesley was
appointed to the government of the place, and a very extensive jurisdiction assigned him. His discharge of the
duties thus imposed is strongly illustrative of his character,
and formed a very important part of that education which
produced the fortifier of Torres Vedras and the conqueror
of Waterloo. To our great general we may very emphatically apply the fine and pointed remark of Sallust concerning Jugurtha — " Sane, quod difficillimum in primis
est, et proelio strenuus erat, et bonus consilio " — his sound
and massive strength availed him alike in camp and cabinet.
Even at this early stage of his career, he displayed a comprehensiveness which could administer the affairs of provinces, and a minute accuracy which could investigate the
most intricate or insignificant detail of currency.   Into
every department of the administration he introduced
efficiency; the affairs of the provinces over which he ruled
soon wore an improved aspect; and the gratitude and
applause of those over whom his sway extended rewarded
his efforts.

The long chase which issued in the slaughter of Dhoondiah and the dispersion of his followers, is of too small

importance to detain us; but an incident which marked its close deserves notice. In the camp of the robber chieftain was found his little son, aged four years, and they brought him to Wellesley. He treated the child with tender kindness, protected him while he remained in India, and, on leaving for England, committed a considerable sum of money to the care of Colonel Symmonds for the use of the boy. The act was kindly and beautiful; it rests upon his early laurels like a sunbeam. The campaign against Dhoondiah took place in 1800; Wellesley was created major-general in 1802.

The battle of Assaye was one of the boldest and most brilliant ever fought by Wellington. The campaign originated in the antagonism of two great powers, between which lay the contest for the possession of India — the Mahrattas, of the west, and the British, whose territories lay principally to the north and east. The Mahrattas were a powerful and warlike people, who had successfully resisted the empire of the Great Mogul. Against the British power, three of their mightiest chiefs contended — Scindiah, Holcar, and the Rajah of Berar. Their force was formidable and imposing. By his experience in other campaigns, however, Wellesley knew well the conditions of an Indian war; of the country, in its every feature, he had the most intimate knowledge; and he had formed a correct idea of the power of the British soldier.

To comprehend clearly the various aspects and movements of the battle of Assaye, is not a very simple matter; what picture we have ourselves formed of it in our own mind, we shall endeavor to present to our readers.

The Kaitna, a small branch of the great Godavery river, which rises in the north-west of the peninsula of Hindostan and flows south-east, runs from west to east. On its north-

ern bank is the village of Assaye, and, some small distance
to the west of that place, the village or station of Bokerdun.
It was posted on the northern bank of this stream that
General Wellesley, advancing from the south, descried, on
the 23d of September, 1803, the combined forces of Scindiah
and the Rajar of Berar, in number about 50,000, with an
immense park of artillery. The British force did not number 5000 men. The right of the enemy's position was at
Bokerdun — it was occupied by cavalry; their left, consisting of infantry, extended along the banks of the stream
towards Assaye. Wellesley determined to attack the infantry. To accomplish this, he wheeled to the right, and
marched along the southern bank of the Kaitna, until he
passed their left. The enemy's cavalry came pouring from
its position on their right, and was opposed by the Mahratta
and Mysore horse in the British interest. His rear and
flanks thus protected, Wellesley succeeded in crossing the
river to the left of the enemy. He at once formed his men
into three lines, of which the last was cavalry; facing
towards the west, they advanced; the 78th Highlanders
were kept in reserve. The confederate Mahrattas had
watched these movements with an interest which may well
be conceived. They saw the British cross the stream
beyond their left flank, and perceived, with an apprehension
quickened by the sense of terrific danger, that their left
would be taken in flank, and rolled back in utter ruin.
Their position was untenable, and an instant alteration
was imperative. With a swiftness and regularity to be
imputed to French assistance, they effected it. They drew
their infantry from the banks of the Kaitna, and flung it
across the space between the stream and Assaye, with its
left strongly posted on the village; it once more looked
the British in the face. In this line, and in great strength

about Assaye, were the enemy's guns. As the British line advanced, they received a raking and murderous fire; the guns of Wellesley were at once silenced; and the 74th and the piquets of infantry on the right, advancing against the left of the enemy, were frightfully hewn up. It must have been a spectacle of fearful but dazzling splendor. Under the fervid Indian sun, those slender lines, the faint noise of whose artillery was swallowed in the tremendous roar of that of the enemy, advanced with determined step against the turbaned ranks, a hundred cannon emptying their Cerberean throats upon them, and vast multitudes of the foe before. In their guns there was no safety and no hope. What then remained? One stern hope was left — the word was given — "Fix bayonets!" At once, along the thin red lines, through the darkening smoke, the steel gleamed out. On swept the British in the teeth of the great guns; on to victory. The eye never opened on the plains of Bengal, or the Ghauts of Himmalaya, that could bide the glitter of the cold British steel; the vast masses were shattered and dissipated, and the horsemen of Berar, that had rushed on the torn infantry of our right, were dashed back, as a cloud by a tornado, by the British cavalry. The latter then advanced upon the broken infantry, trampling it down and scattering it abroad. The battle was won; but there still was danger. The numbers of the enemy were so great, that it was impossible for the small British force to face them all at once; the Mahratta gunners, moreover, when the British bayonets advanced, had in many instances lain down as if dead, by their guns; and as soon as the British, by continuing their advance, left the ground clear, they rose and reloaded their pieces. One large body of the enemy's infantry formed again; but Lieutenant-Colonel Maxwell charged with the horse, and broke their ranks; their whole army then dissipated, leaving ninety pieces of cannon in the hands of the British. One of the most brilliant victories in the annals of war was over.

The defeated chieftains gathered their squadrons once more on the plains of Argaum, but were totally routed.

In February, 1805, our general left India; after a career where swift energy and dauntless valor in the field, threw a rare and beautiful lustre over moderation, firmness, and wisdom in the cabinet; where his strong natural genius had been practised and ripened; where he had earned the admiration and esteem as well of the subjects of his administration, as of his brethren in the field; and whence he came, a Knight Companion of the Order of the Bath, after having received the thanks of both houses of parliament, and with the first wreath of victory about his brow. He had secured his country in possession of the richest and goodliest conquest under the sun; he came to establish her throne among the nations at home.

We shall not trace minutely the career of Wellington between the campaigns of India and those of the Peninsula. In November, 1805, he served as chief of brigade in Denmark; returning thence, he commanded for some time at Hastings; in April, 1807, he was named chief secretary for Ireland; in August of the same year, he served with distinction in the Copenhagen campaign; and, about the middle of 1808, he was appointed to command a force destined for the Peninsula.

The first campaign which Wellesley served in Portugal is extremely interesting. In it he acquired that knowledge of the affairs of the Peninsula which enabled him finally to conquer; in it he first demonstrated to the world that there were soldiers who could meet the bravest legions of the resistless emperor, and that there was a general who could lead them. He received the news of his appointment to the command with what, in him, we might almost call exultant delight, and wrote to Lord Hill, with whom he had formerly served, expressing the hope that they would have more to do than had been the case last time. His wakeful and minute circumspection was displayed in the arrangement, provisioning, and equipment of the troops; his energy struck life into the whole enterprise. Sailing before the fleet which contained his army, he instituted a series of investigations and conducted them with singular success. Every reader of the immortal despatches of Wellington must, we think, be struck with admiring astonishment, as he perceives with what rapidity their author, amid all the darkness and complexity of the subject, comprehended, at this time, and mastered his whole position. The possibilities of the contest and the conditions of success were at once before him. The French were strong in Portugal, and held Lisbon; but Lisbon might be snatched from their grasp, and if it were once secured, the kingdom of Portugal could be defended against them. To win Lisbon then was the object of his first campaign; he attained it by a display of valor and ability which even contradiction and stupidity could but partly obscure. He landed his forces at Mondego Bay, and marched southward.

A new page was opening in the history of the French. Hitherto, since their revolution, they had rushed hither and thither, like rolling fires over the prairie, blasting and blackening wherever they came; no troops in Europe had stood before them. But a different set of men, under a new general, now landed on the shore of Portugal. In their rude island prejudice, they had scarcely sufficient originality to conceive the idea of fearing the French; it was almost a part of their creed, that they could beat them, two or three to one. On the heights and in the defiles of Rolica they first met the veteran legions of Gaul, and swept them away; around Vimiero, though Junot, Leison, and De Laborde led on the French squadrons, they again hurled them back. In a few weeks the French army would have been destroyed, and Lisbon gloriously captured. But Wellesley had outrun his nation in knowledge, and the wisdom of his ideas could not be discerned. Sir Harry Burrard arrived to take the command; Sir Hew Dalrymple followed; instead of the ruin of the French army, there came the convention of Cintra. Such was the first campaign in the Peninsula. Sir Arthur soon returned home.

In his absence great and disastrous events took place. The little Corsican came himself into Spain. Gathering, by the swift might of his genius, the various divisions of his army into resistless bolts, he launched them at the various Spanish and British armies. The Spanish hosts were smitten into confusion and almost into annihilation, and the British, under Sir John Moore, who, whenever they crossed bayonets, vindicated their native valor, were driven back to their waves. The emperor appeared resistless; and though Lisbon was still in our hands, a deep feeling of hopelessness took possession of a large portion of the British nation. But all was not lost: Britain possessed one man who could command successfully in the Peninsula. He had already advanced far beyond his contemporaries in knowledge of the state of the seat of war and the circumstances of the enemy; the rare military genius with which nature had endowed him had been fully developed by experience, and had been oftentimes crowned with victory; he knew well the valor and strength of the British soldier; he was himself animated by that calm

dauntlessness which is born of deliberation and strength.
To him, as her last hope, Britain confided her army for the
conquest of the Peninsula. In the series of campaigns
upon which he entered, he proved himself superior in warlike genius to every one of the great French marshals, and
fitted himself to contend with him who was greater than
them all.

To detail the various operations of the Peninsula campaigns, is manifestly here impossible ; we must confine
ourselves to a glance at one or two of their most brilliant
passages of war. Ere proceeding to these, we shall endeavor, by a general survey of the difficulties with which
he had to contend, to set in a fair light the genius and
prowess of Wellington.

First of all, we must consider the foes he had to contend
with. There were in Spain and Portugal about two hundred thousand French soldiers ; men who had shaken
Europe by their tread, whose eagles seemed to have been
grasped by Victory and borne forward as her own. They
were commanded by leaders who had attained their stations
by force of military genius, and who had received their
batons from the hand of the great military emperor. The
fortresses of the kingdom were in their hands.

After these, the state of the Peninsula and of its inhabitants demands notice. The country was worn by long
war, and the difficulties of communication were extreme.
The condition of the inhabitants was deplorable. Concerning the Portuguese, some hope might be entertained.
They were poor, and they had been beaten into national
ague; but they were at heart brave, and were not quite
impregnable to reason. The Spaniards, on the other hand,
save by their irritating Guerilla warfare, were useless, or
worse. It was only with the greatest difficulty that they
14*

could be induced to sell provisions to the British; in the
day of battle, they were either too obstinate to come into
action, or too cowardly to stand their ground when once
engaged; sometimes, particularly when defeat was certain,
they flung away their armies with insane foolhardiness.
Before the battle of Talavera, for instance, a united blow
would have shattered a French army; but the Spaniards
were as immovable as the Rock of Gibraltar; the opportunity being once irrecoverably lost, they did as those curs
to which the English were once likened — rushed into the
iron jaws of the French armies, and had themselves crushed
like rotten apples. The sickening vexation and the substantial detriment which these Spaniards inflicted upon
Wellington were incredible. In his own army, most important reforms were absolutely necessary to the hopeful
prosecution of the war. The commissariat, especially, the
full efficiency of which he speedily discovered to be indispensable, was in great disorder, and it was only by the
utmost exertion of his organizing genius and his overwhelming energy that a change was effected.

But, in order to obtain a comprehensive view of the
difficulties and entangling annoyances against which the
British general had to contend, and over all which he rose
in adamantine calmness, we must image to ourselves the
strong opposition which had its seat at home. Like that
ancient faction, which, by its plausible oratory and slimy
serpentine malice, finally brought to the dust the great
Carthaginian conqueror, the British opposition bent its
energies, zealously and unremittingly, to thwart the conqueror of the Peninsula. They strove to cripple him by
insufficient reinforcements; they underrated and misrepre-
sented his victories; every retreat or temporary loss they
magnified into a rout. Valiant in the unassailable assurance

of perfect ignorance, and flippant as currish stupidity always is, they stood behind the shield of public liberty, and uttered their vociferous criticisms upon the general's movements: it was the course of nature reversed — the lion had become provider for the jackals, and they would not on any account abate their inane howling, and allow him to do the work in silence. We can but faintly picture to ourselves the speechless disdain which would curl the lip of Welles-ley, as he heard from afar the unmeasured condemnation of his most masterly movements by some atomic critic! When, under the guidance of an idea far beyond the utmost flight of critic wing, he marched toward the iron bulwarks of Torres Vedras, did the united howl of the opposing "we" produce only a smile, or did he burst into a regular guffaw? Had the howl been as uninfluential and harmless as it was foolish, it would assuredly have been the latter.

Let the reader calmly present to his mental gaze all this array of difficulties and hindrances, and form his judgment of their vanquisher accordingly. We must briefly note the conditions of the contest which rendered it at all hope-ful. Wellington's first and firmest consolation was an in-destructible and well-grounded reliance upon British steel. He soon learned, also, that the difficulty of maintaining communications, and the absence of any one commanding power, made it extremely difficult for the French to form great combinations. Portugal was defensible. He had the sea behind him securing provisions and promising reinforce-ments. It was early in the year 1809, that he again landed in Portugal.

Wellesley disembarked at Lisbon; he was enabled to head an army of about 25,000 men, including certain Portuguese forces under the command of Beresford. Into every part of the service fresh vigor was at once infused; the com-

missariat was put into efficient working condition; every
necessary arrangement was made, every appointment attended to: and the British army, at length in the hand of one
who could wield it, proceeded in ardor and confidence upon
its career of conquest. Wellesley at once commenced his
march to the north; took Oporto most brilliantly, and swiftly
drove Soult out of Portugal. Turning then south-eastward,
to act in Spain on the line of the Tagus, in co-operation with
the Spanish General Cuesta, he fought the fierce and bloody
battle of Talavera, against the combined forces of King Joseph and Marshal Victor. It was one of those battles of frequent occurrence in the Peninsula, in which, after a tremendous conflict, the enemy was beaten back, but where, from an
inferiority in numbers, or a want of cavalry, the British
were unable totally to dissipate them. As it was thus, so to
speak, the type of a class, as it seems to admit of very distinct
picturing, and as it illustrates well the glory and the sadness of war, we shall venture upon a brief description of it.

On the northern bank of the Tagus, in the Spanish province of New Castile, stands the town of Talavera; beyond
it, to the northward, is a rugged plain, and at the distance
of about two miles a hill, with a valley of some extent
beyond. This plain was that chosen by Wellesley on which
to post his army to oppose Victor; the hill, where his left
rested, was the most important point in his position. His
line looked towards the east, to face the French who advanced westward. On the right, resting on the town of
Talavera, and in a position so secured by natural defences
as to be almost unassailable, were posted the Spaniards;
no dependence whatsoever could be placed upon them; the
highest hope was, that they would not run, and might
charge a broken column. The rest of the line was occupied by the British, their extreme left resting on the hill

we have mentioned. This hill, the key to the whole position, was of course the object of Victor's principal efforts.

On the 27th of July, 1809, the fighting commenced. It extended along the whole British line, but was severest on the left. At one moment here, on account of a temporary weakness, the flank was turned, and the French gained the summit of the ridge. But the valiant and true-hearted Hill rushed to the rescue with fresh troops, searched the ranks of the enemy with a withering volley, and then charged with the bayonet. The foe was hurled down the ridges, to return no more while the sun was above the horizon. The shadows fell over the Spanish hills, and the British lay down by their arms to wait for the morning. But Victor knew it to be of vital importance that he should win that hill. A feint attack was made upon another part of the British line, and, under cover of the darkness, the French advanced. Their very bravest came; but a foe as brave was awake and ready for them. Their dim lines drew nearer and nearer, until their eyes could be seen sparkling through the darkness by the silent British; then suddenly the stillness of the hills was broken by the echoing rattle of the British musketry, and the red tongues of flame, lighting up the lines of bayonets, fringed the skirts of Night with fire. Again and again did the French columns attempt to gain and hold the level ground on the top of the ridge, but the mangling hail came ever in ceaseless volleys from the unflinching British, and at length the levelled bayonet drove them down the hill-side. The French drew off, and both hosts snatched an hour or two of troubled repose; by five in the morning they were at the dread work again. The roar of cannon commenced at daybreak. The hill on the left was still the object of the enemy. Column after column advanced to the attack, and still with the same result.

They ascended the hill with that tried and disciplined valor
which had won them so many fields; the British, in their
immovable lines, eyed them as they advanced with calm,
savage sternness; just as the enemy reached the ridge,
they poured in their fire, and advancing with the bayonet,
forced them back. So it continued until half-past eight
in the morning, when the heat of the sun compelled the
weary combatants to desist. Then occurred a most touching scene. There flowed a small stream towards the Tagus,
along the British front, separating the armies. Thither, to
draw water, the soldiers of both armies came. Ceasing
for a moment to be teeth of the dragon War, they became
individuals and brothers; they flung aside their warlike
implements, chatted in friendly terms, lent each other what
little aids could be administered, and mutually succored
the wounded. In a few minutes the bugles called them to
their ranks, they shook hands like friends, grasped the
musket and the bayonet, and the only word between them
was death. It was a strange and most melancholy, yet
wildly beautiful spectacle.

The sternest fight of all followed. The main attack
now was upon the centre; it was met, and most gallantly
repulsed. But the guards, in an excess of ardor, advanced
in slight disorder. The perfect discipline of the French
enabled them at once to perceive and take advantage of
the circumstance. They charged again; the guards were
compelled to retire; the French batteries tore up their
flanks as they drew back; and the German battalion, which
occupied the ground to the left, was wavering. The victory
seemed within the grasp of the French; but there was an
eye beholding the whole from that hill on the left, an eye
that seldom failed to discern the moment of necessity, and
the mode of relief, the eye of Wellesley. He instantly

ordered up a regiment of infantry and a squadron of light cavalry, to charge the advancing French. With matchless valor and coolness, the difficult operation was executed; the foe was checked; the guards formed again behind, and charged with a cheer. An Irish regiment took up the huzza, and it went rolling to right and left along the British line. The islanders must have appeared somewhat incomprehensible to the French: shattered, mown down, fearfully thinned, they yet were in spirit to cheer; to tame them might well appear a hopeless task. The enemy retreated, and Talavera was won.

Wellesley, perhaps, equalled any general of ancient or modern times in the choice of positions. In care, in accuracy, in activity, he was a Fabius or a Scipio. He could detect, with a glance as swift as thought, the error of an opponent, as at Salamanca. These faculties are displayed in every part of the Peninsula campaigns; but on no occasion were the whole attributes of his genius called into such striking operation, or displayed in such imposing colors, as in the campaign of 1810, and the retreat on Torres Vedras. It was toward the end of this year, that Lord Wellington (for such he had been since Talavera), with the slow and stately motion of one who had counted every step, commenced his retreat towards Lisbon, before the overpowering columns of Massena. He had masked his great operation so skilfully, that the French marshal had no correct idea of the extent of the fortifications to which he was retreating, and boasted, with his nation's magniloquence, that he was to drive the English into the sea. It was proper to teach him, that the march was of quite a different nature from a flight. On the heights of Busaco, the British lion calmly faced about, refreshed himself with a deep draught of French blood, and then, proudly arising, moved, with regal tread, towards his lair. Massena still vaunted. On he came over the muddy roads, now drenched by the rains, and through a country which had been stripped of everything by the strict command of Wellington. This clearing the country of all means of support for an army, was an essential part of the idea of the campaign; its purpose is obvious, and the object of Wellington would have been attained sooner than was the case, if the command had been duly obeyed. At length Massena came to a dead halt; the bulwarks of Torres Vedras were before him. He saw, to his utter astonishment, a fortified line extending from the Tagus to the ocean; mountains scarped, valleys spanned, inundations prepared; the whole bristling with cannon. He gazed and gazed, in blank amazement, for three days; he found the lines impregnable. Had he forced the first, there was a second, and even a third, to be surmounted. At length, in savage, sardonic calmness, the British lion had lain down, backed by his native ocean, and gazed grimly over the vast squadrons. His growl would now be given through the throats of six hundred cannon. "You were to drive me into the sea, I think, — Come on!"

In due time Wellington left his lines, Massena rolling back before him. The French and their emperor now began distinctly to perceive, that once the British general had laid his iron grasp upon Portugal, there was no might of theirs which could make him relax it. We shall not follow him in his path of struggle and victory. The campaign of 1811 was signalized by the fierce but glorious fighting of Fuentes d'Onoro; that of 1812 was particularly rich, boasting both the celebrated sieges of Ciudad Rodrigo and Badajos, and the tremendous blow of Salamanca; at length, in 1813, he totally dissipated the French forces at

Vittoria, and encountered Soult among the Pyrenees. In 1814, after the magnificent accomplishment of the great task which had once appeared hopeless, he sheathed his sword at Toulouse. All that array of difficulties and toils had been smitten and subdued by the might of his valor and genius; those proud armies had been humbled; in no single battle had he been vanquished; and, dazzled by the beams of his glory, even his factious detractors had been silenced.

We now draw towards the end of that great martial drama which we have been briefly contemplating. While Wellington was marching upon France, with the armies of Napoleon in retreat before him, the nations of the north were closing in upon their great master. When the ducal coronet had been placed upon Wellington's brow and the marshal's baton put into his hand, after the great triumph of Vittoria, the contest in the north was still doubtful, although the scale of Napoleon seemed steadily rising; when the last blow was dealt at Toulouse, the sceptre and the sword had fallen from his grasp. They sent him to Elba, and Europe snatched a few moments of restless repose, while huge armies, not yet disbanded, lay like nightmares on its troubled bosom. But the end had not yet come; the thunders were to awake once more, ere the azure of peace was to smile over Europe. Suddenly it was awakened, as by a red bolt of fire passing across the sky: Napoleon had burst his chains, and was again at the head of his armies. And now the two extraordinary men, who had been born in the same year, and who had, from the first, been destined to meet, were finally to close in the wrestle of death. Once more the wild Celtic vehemence and valor, under a leader of mighty but kindred genius, were to come into conflict with the still, indomitable

strength of the Teutons, under a leader whose overwhelming powers were all masked in calmness. We must omit
all preliminaries, and endeavor to gaze upon the great contest itself.

After various passages of war, the two hosts lay facing
each other on the heights of Waterloo; the French were
posted on one ridge, the British on another, and there were
several important posts of defence between them. The dim
morning of the memorable 18th of June, 1815, looked down
upon the British squares on the one hill-side, and the vast
masses of French cavalry and infantry on the opposing
heights; in the valley between them, Summer had spread
out a rye-field: ere evening, it was to be trodden flat, and
welded together by human gore.

It is a common enough remark in the present day, that
the modern battle lacks the interest and sublimity of the
ancient one: mechanically, it is said, you shoot, and mechanically you are shot at; the wild fire that lit the eye of
an Achilles can gleam no more; the shattering sway of the
one strong arm has ceased to be of account in the day of
battle; give us the fiery melee of the olden time, in which
a Hector could mingle, and of which a Homer could sing.
Is it, then, so superlatively and exclusively noble and difficult, to deal the stern blow, when the nerves are strung by
the animal excitement of the combat, and the enthusiasm
is raised by the presence and justling of the foe? And is
it nothing to gaze, unflinching, upon the slow, steady advance of the column, from which the eye of Death is calmly
glaring? Is that deliberate determination of small account,
by which death, whether it comes in the shattering cannon
ball, or the tearing musket bullet, or the cold bayonet stab,
is chosen before flight or surrender? We declare, without
hesitation, that the modern battle is a grander spectacle

than was the ancient: around no Homeric battle was there
ever such a terrific sublimity as there hung around the
field of Waterloo. Napoleon did not, with bared arm,
rush into the midst of the combatants, trusting to his single
prowess. Wellington did not, heading with musket and
bayonet the onward charge, expose his bosom to the steel.
But did ever an Achilles or an Attila avail so much in the
day of battle, as that dark-browed Corsican, or that calm,
clear-eyed Briton? Each remained apart, wielding the
tremendous mechanism of war, mightier than the very
gods of Homer. And had the valor which they wielded
become mechanism, had human heroism no place in that
field? Let us look upon it, and see. Under the fitting
drapery of jagged and trailing clouds, which seemed weeping over the fearful scene, stood a certain number of little
squares, ranged on the slope of a valley; toil-worn they
were, drenched with rain, and few in number, on the bleak
hill-side. On the ridges to which, with dauntless eye, they
looked, were ranged three hundred cannon; from all their
throats, through the long and weary hours, was poured
forth the shower of iron, tearing and shattering those little
squares, winnowing their ranks with a tempest of death.
And whenever the mangling shot had done its work, and
a gap yawned, on dashed the lancers or cuirassiers, as the
ocean dashes on the rock riven of the thunderbolt. Yet
it was all in vain. The roar of death from those three
hundred cannon-throats they heard undismayed; the gleam
of the lances and the glittering of the cuirasses, as the
horsemen dashed out from the cloudy smoke, with Death
upon their plumes, they eyed unswerving. Hour after
hour rolled heavily away, and the patient Earth, with all
her summer burden, wheeled on to the east. The squares
dwindled. and several united into one; the arm was grow-

ing heavy, the scent of blood filled the air, the ground was fattening with human gore; yet they yielded not. In silence they closed up their ranks, as brother after brother fell, a mangled corpse; with the earnest prayer of agony, they implored to be led against the foe: but yield they never would; the car of Death might crush them into the ground, but it was only so that a path could be made. Sterner or nobler valor never fought round windy Troy.

> "O proud Death,
> What feast was toward in thine eternal cell!"

From noon until eve those cannon had roared, and squadron after squadron of horsemen had poured upon those squares; and now, as the shades of a gloomy evening were beginning to fall, the fight was ever becoming the sterner, and the light in that dark fiery eye, which directed the French columns, the more wild and agitated. Once more as if by a tremendous effort to wrest the sceptre from Destiny, an attempt was to be made by Napoleon. His old guard yet remained. They loved him as children love their father; they had received from his hand the wreaths of honor and victory; some of them had followed him to the flames of Moscow; on some of them had risen the sun of Austerlitz: and now for that dear master they were to go against those unconquerable squares. Beyond them lay fame, and honor, and victory; to yield a foot was destruction and despair. Slowly, under the rolling smoke of those great guns, they advanced, with the firm tread of men whose nerves had long been strung to the music of battle: we shall not liken them to tornado or thunder cloud; there is no spectacle so fearful to man as the calm, determined advance of thousands of his brothers to the strife of death. Let the brave have their due! The old guard advanced most gallantly;

but they were ploughed up, as they approached, by the British artillery, and a murderous fire from the unquivering British arm searched their ranks as they endeavored to deploy; valiantly did they attempt it, but it was in vain. Torn and mangled by that terrible fire, they wavered; in a moment the British horsemen dashed into their ranks, and rolled them backwards in wild confusion. All was won on the one side, and all was lost on the other. Who can tell the feeling of serene and complete satisfaction which then filled the breast of Wellington! And, ah! who can image to himself the dread moment when thick clouds rushed over the fire of that imperial eye, whose lightnings were to smite the towers of Earth no more! Lo! mid the thickening dusk, while the cheer of another host comes on the gale, the shattered squares have opened into line. At last, the bayonets glittering afar in the cloudy air, they sweep down the ridges to victory. For a moment Napoleon saw the long line, as it came on like the rolling simoom; Shakspeare could not have voiced his emotions at the sight. And he passed away to his lonely rock in the sea, to exhibit the sublimest spectacle of modern times, whose deathless sorrow could be sung by no harp but that of the melancholy ocean.

Now was the time when the genuine and lofty manhood of our mighty Wellington displayed itself. He had reached the highest pinnacle of fame, the eye of Europe was fixed upon him, and his grateful country exhausted in his behoof her storehouse of honor and reward. It is such moments that try men. The towering Andes, with the serene air of the upper heavens about their brows, present us with two phenomena: to those solitudes of the pathless sky, by the force of wind and the tumults of the lower atmosphere, are borne the smallest insects; in those serene solitudes,

15*

in the full flood of the undimmed sunshine, floats the condor. The difference between the two is marked. The
insects, borne aloft by external, and not by internal strength,
are tossed hither and thither in the thin air, with their
little pinions tattered, and their little senses bewildered;
the condor, with outspread fans, rests upon the liquid ether
as his native element, whither nature had designed him to
ascend. The phenomena are replete with meaning to the eye
of wisdom. By popular applause, by confusion and tur-
moil, the human insect is often borne for a time aloft, to
be dashed about and to fall; the man who, rising far over
his fellows, and basking in the full beams of glory and victory, rests there placid and immovable as the condor, is a
true and mighty son of nature. His strength is from within.
So, most emphatically, it was with Wellington; the world's
applause did not quicken a pulse in his frame, or flutter,
for a moment, his calm and manly intellect.

In connection with this part of the career of Wellington,
there is one name which we cannot pass over; if not an
actual spot in the sun of his glory, it is at least a faint mist
which has obscured it. That name is Ney. We must confess a very strong wish that Wellington had done his
utmost to save Ney. To say he was not required to do it
by justice, or even by honor, is probably to assert a fact;
but it is virtually to admit the absence of a satisfactory
plea. Why talk of the iron rod of justice or the cold code
of honor here; hath mercy no golden sceptre to extend to
the vanquished? How beautiful, as he returned resistless
from the field, would this trait of human kindness have
shown; as a sunbeam on the wings of a proud eagle, that
at eventide, seeks his island-eyrie, after having vanquished
all that resisted! He had stilled the tempests of Europe
as the wise and kind Magician stilled the elements and the

demons; and when, like him, he was to lay his terrors aside, would not the spectacle have been still more noble and sublime, if, like Prospero, he had closed all with a strain of mercy's music? We shall not say that the affair left a blot on the duke's escutcheon; we can imagine that, with his rigid habits of adherence to form, his unwillingness in any particulars to overstep his powers or prerogatives, and the natural reserve of his character, he might not feel himself called upon directly to interfere; but, had he for once cast all such feelings aside, and striven energetically to save Ney, it would have cast such an enhancing light over all his glories, that we cannot but regret its absence.

We shall not follow the Duke of Wellington in the remaining portion of his career. As a statesman, he displayed the same decision and the same intellectual perspicacity which had marked him as a soldier; he had a deep sympathy with that old Conservatism which has now been so severely battered by Free-traders and Manchester schools, but which numbered in its ranks much of the highest and the noblest blood in Britain; when the trumpet of advancement spoke so clearly and so loud that it could be neither mistaken nor resisted, he advanced. It was when he was at the head of the government, in 1829, that the famous measure for the emancipation of the Roman Catholics was passed.

We seem to see him, after the pacification of Europe, taking up his abode, in calm majesty, in the island round which he had built such a battlement of strength and of glory. We shall apply to him the superb thought of Tennyson: —

"With his hand against the hilt,
He paced the troubled land, like Peace."

We trust that some portraiture of the character of the

Duke of Wellington has been presented to the reader in
the foregoing paragraphs. It well became us to trust for
such portraiture to his mighty deeds rather than to our
puny words. But we deem a few supplementary remarks
necessary for the general summing up of his character. His
radical characteristics were calmness, clearness, strength;
they are easily read, and it is not difficult to refer to their
action every portion of his career. We see them everywhere: in the unerring but silent care with which he gained
a comprehensive knowledge of the conditions of every
contest in which he was engaged; in the piercing and certain glance by which he detected the error of an opponent;
in the sedate and massive composure of his despatches,
where clearness of vision produces pictures rivalling the
efforts of art; in the marble stillness and strength of his
firm cheek and unwrinkled forehead. We trace the same
characteristics in his valor. He has been called cautious
and hesitating; after the charges of Assaye, the passage
of the Douro, and the eagle swoop of Salamanca! The
accusation has been founded on a simple mistake. We
have been told, and with sufficient truth, that the word
impossible is a word of ill omen; the scrupulous, hesitating
ideologist who fears to take a step lest the earth yawn, is
little worth. Yet the power to discern the impossible is
but the necessary complement of the power to discern the
possible. A thousandfold clamor declares that such a thing
cannot be done, but the man of commanding intellect distinctly hears the voice of nature saying it can, and does it;
he is declared valiant, fiery, and so forth: a similar clamor
pronounces such a thing to be possible, but the man of
mind still hears the voice of nature whispering — "No,"
and abstains from doing it; he is called cautious, phleg-
matic, or cowardly. Both clamors have been heard in the

case of Wellington; and it were a question which was the more inane. Few eyes ever looked upon a battle-field with a surer perception of the possible and the impossible than his; he would not draw his sword to hew rocks, but when he did draw it, it went through.

Much has been said concerning the coldness of Wellington's emotions, and his alleged want of kindliness. In this portion of his character, too, we find the traits we have specified. He possessed a kindliness all his own. It must be granted that he never exhibited that strange fascination of genius which has been so powerful in many instances — in a Mirabeau, a Napoleon, a Hannibal. Yet a manly kindliness was his, which comported well with the massive strength of his character. He loved, if 'we may so say, in the mass; his kindness was that of calm, considerate reason, and borrowed no flash from passion. In India he used no small arts to secure attachment; he was encircled, and he wished to be so, by the dignity of a highborn British gentleman. Yet his rule was felt to be kindly and beneficent, and the inhabitants of the wide provinces whose affairs he administered blessed him in their hearts. He might not, with sentimental sigh, lament over the individual loss or destruction; but the general prosperity, the happiness of the people as a whole, lay near his heart: he did not care to dispense those small personal favors whence are born kind words and smiles, but he spread his blessings, as from a great cornucopia, over the land. It was so, also, in his military career. If we may say that he did not love each soldier, we must yet assert that no general ever loved his army better. If the individual soldier had to be sacrificed for the good of the army, he hesitated not; but, since the efficiency of the army required the comfort and safety of the individual soldier, the British private could not pos-

sibly have sustained fewer hardships in Spain than he experienced under Wellington. In a word, and in all cases,
those under our great chief experienced that security and
assured joy which weakness always finds under the shield
of strength. We might appeal to the case of the captive son
of Dhoondiah, to prove that kindness lay deep in his nature;
it was this which, uniting with his powerful faculties, naturally produced the considerate beneficence which we assert to
have distinguished him. We cannot believe that he looked
upon his army merely as a machine, and that all his care
for it arose from simple calculation; but he was content,
if he *deserved* his soldiers' love by maintaining their general comfort, to be without it rather than abstain from
sacrificing one for the good of all. Of all theatricality he
was singularly void, and his emotions were always under
the strict guidance of reason.

There have been countless historical parallels instituted
between Wellington and other great generals. He has
been very ably compared to Cromwell, and in some respects
he resembled that astonishing man. The same piercing
vision, the same swift energy, the same organizing genius,
distinguished both. But the parallel fails in a most important point: the conditions of the time made it morally impossible for a Cromwell to be produced in the last great
European outburst of intellect. In the great Puritan awakening, the infinite elements of religion and of duty had the
most prominent and pervading influence: the Puritan felt
himself fighting under the banner of Jehovah; the Earth was
to him a little desert, bordered by the celestial mountains,
and what mattered it though he fought and toiled here, if
he saw the crown awaiting him yonder. A time which
produced its highest literary impersonation in Milton, might
have, as its great martial impersonation, Cromwell. But

in that mighty shaking of the nations which is still going on, the infinite elements of our nature have probably had less direct influence upon the minds of men than was ever the case before. The highest idea of the philosophism from which it sprung, was, that man should conquer the elements, assert his freedom, and carpet for himself the earth with the flowers of paradise. Science was put into the place of God; the light of earth was deemed to have utterly eclipsed the light from heaven. Never, perhaps, did the world so minutely answer to the idea of a stage, where puppet philosophers and puppet armies played their parts in the most profound unconsciousness that God held the wires; never was the Divinity, who was silently shaping the ends so totally invisible to those who were rough-hewing them. Of the distinctive opinions of this era, we regard Shelley as the greatest literary impersonation; its two greatest martial impersonations were Napoleon and Wellington. It is but a partial resemblance that there can be between the great Puritan general and the conqueror of Waterloo; a more correct parallel would be between the Dukes of Wellington and of Albemarle.

We think we find a singularly close parallel to the career of Napoleon and Wellington in that of Hannibal and Scipio. The first of these ancient generals is pretty generally recognized as the greatest military genius that ever lived. He ran his course from victory to victory, until a general arose to oppose him, whose attention was sleepless, whose accuracy was unfailing, whose intellectual vision was penetrating, whose valor was dauntless, and who could bring troops into the field which no African levies could match. They met on the plains of Zama; fame has not failed to record that the generalship of Hannibal at least equalled that of Scipo; but victory fled forever to the

Roman eagles. Wellington belonged to the class of generals represented by Scipio; Napoleon to that represented by Hannibal. The wild force of genius has oft been fated by nature to be finally overcome by quiet strength, and never was it more signally so, than in the case of Napoleon and Wellington. The volcano sends up its red bolt with terrific force, as if it would strike the stars; but the calm, resistless hand of gravitation seizes it, and brings it to the earth.

We look upon the late duke as one of the soundest and stateliest men that Great Britain has produced; one of those embodied forces which are sent by God to perform important parts in the history of the world, and around which their respective generations are seen to cluster. The memory of such men is a sacred treasure. The men of Elis did well in appointing the descendants of Phidias to preserve from spot or from detriment their grand statue of gold and ivory; it had been produced in one generation, it was much if following generations kept it whole and untarnished. Our great Wellington has just been placed in the Temple of the Past, to sit there with the heroes of other times, and to witness that among us too, in the nineteenth century, a mighty man arose: it is the duty of us and of our children, to see that no blot abide upon his massive and majestic statue.

VI.

NAPOLEON BONAPARTE.

The figure of Napoleon Bonaparte first emerges into the view of history at the seige of Toulon, towards the end of the year 1793.

The revolutionary storm, in which the evening of the last century went down over France, was at its wildest working. Those fierce, irregular forces, which, in the world of mind are scientifically correspondent to the tornado, the earthquake, the fever, the volcano, in the world of external nature, and which seem retained for seasons of crisis and emergency, were performing their terrible ministry. The statical balance of society had been disturbed: the normal forces, the forces of calmness, of growth, of persistence, required to be re-adjusted. The untamed, primeval powers, which always underlie the surface of civilization, like old Titans under quiet hills and wooded plains, had broken their confinement; the solid framework of capacity and anthority, by which they had been compressed, had crumbled down in mere impotence and imbecility; and they now went raving and uncommanded over France. Fear, fury, hot enthusiasm, fanaticism, ferocity, the courage of the wildcat, the cruelty of the tiger, hope to the measure of frenzy, suspicion to the measure of disease, spread confusion through all the borders of the country. At Toulon the general confusion was forcibly represented, though but in miniature. The town, defended by a motley crew of British, Spaniards, Neapolitans, and insurgent French, was besieged, on behalf of the convention, by two armies. These weltered wildly round it, strong in numbers, in valor, in zeal, in stubbornness, but rendered powerless through want of control and direction. Here, as universally over France, the gravitation by which faculty comes into the place of command had not had time to act. Cartaux, the general, strutted about in gold-lace, self-satisfied in his ignorance of the position of affairs, bold in his unconsciousness of danger. Representatives of the people, empowered to intermeddle on all occasions, swaggered here and there in the camp, storming, babbling, urging everything to feverish haste, making progress anywhere impossible. Noise, distraction, fussy impotence: such was the spectacle presented on all hands.

Then appeared, to take the command of the artillery, the young Corsican officer, Napoleon Bonaparte. Though very young, just completing his twenty fourth year, he had a look of singular composure, taciturnity, and resolution. Short and slim, but well knit and active, his figure and port were expressive at once of alertness and self-possession; his eye very quiet and very clear. It would hardly have struck a casual observer that *here* was the commanding and irresistible mind, which was to introduce order, the highest, perhaps, of which they were capable, among the tumultuous forces of the French Revolution.

Looking steadily and silently into the matter, the secret of success at once revealed itself to Napoleon. The troops and artillery had been scattered and dissipated. Yonder was the keystone of the arch; it was an endless business to batter upon each stone in the structure; concentrate the fire upon that one point, bring down that one stone, and the whole must fall. The town and harbor of Toulon lay here to the north; the channel by which both communicated with the Mediterranean stretched yonder towards the south: and that promontory, at some distance from the town, its strong fortifications giving it the name of Little Gibraltar and indicating the importance attached to it, commanded this channel. If, therefore, Little Gibraltar was won, you could sweep the gateway of the harbor in such a manner that the British fleet would be shy of remaining; and the British fleet once withdrawn, Toulon could offer no resistance. Thus clear and definite was Napoleon's thought, and it was to be proved whether he could as skilfully convert it into action. In action he seemed thought personified; thought made alive, and armed with the sword of the lightning. The wild valor of enthusiasm had been nothing to this directed courage; the dogged obstinacy of fanatic rage had been weak in comparison with this calm resolution; the haste and fieriness of Celtic ardor had been tardy to this imperturbable swiftness. Day and night, sleeping only for a few hours in his cloak by the guns, he toils at his batteries, collecting cannon, devising feints, turning the very blunders of incompetence into occasions of advantage; no stupidity, no envy, no obstacle can ruffle his composure or daunt his courage; no fatigue can blunt his alertness, or cause a nerve to flutter in that slight but steelly frame. At last all is prepared. Suddenly there bursts upon Little Gibraltar an overwhelming fire. Eight thousand bombs are poured on it over night: in the morning, the troops surge in, victorious, through the shattered walls, and Little Gibraltar is taken. Toulon then falls; and Napoleon Bonaparte is a marked man.

During the spring and summer of 1794, he was variously

employed; surveying the Mediterranean fortresses, fighting
in the Maritime Alps, always doing the work in hand speedily, quietly, well. Hitherto he professed Jacobin principles,
and had used his pen on behalf of the extreme revolutionary party. He was now intimate with the younger Robespierre. While engaged in the Maritime Alps, he was
urged by the latter to accept the command of the national
guard of Paris. Had he done so, had Napoleon instead of
Henriot commanded for Robespierre on the 10th of Ther-
midor 1794, how strangely the destinies of France and of
Europe might have been modified! But his Jacobinism
was never too fervent for the control of an austere, calcu-
lating, most practical judgment: and it seems likely that
already, not distinctly seen, but gradually clearing itself
of obscuring vapors, his own star, serene, steady, cold, was
beginning to concentrate all the energies of his soul into
one intense passion of devotion to self. He decisively re-
fused. Augustin Robespierre was, indeed, an "honorable
man," manageable enough, doubtless; but he had discerned
Robespierre the elder to be "no trifler." The iron Napoleon knew the iron Robespierre, and instinctively recoiled
from one whom he knew he could not bend. Events were
left to their course. The sword of the Terror, held only
by the giddy, flustered Henriot, was shivered into fragments. Robespierre and his party were overthrown, the
Jacobins dispersed, and the current of the Revolution
turned into new channels. The reaction set in with extreme violence; and Napoleon, at first perhaps seriously
endangered by his connection with the Robespierres, came
to Paris and fell out of employment.

The reaction from the principles of the Reign of Terror
was violent: but strong as it was, the inhabitants of the
capital, not the mere mob, but the sober and weighty por-

tion of the population, were not disposed to forego the greatest of those prizes for which they had so long and so desperately contended. This sacrifice the Convention, by the constitution of 1795, definitely and beyond question required of them. In the beginning of October of that year the sections of Paris rose in arms. Barras, whose eye had fallen on Napoleon at Toulon, pointed him out to the Convention as a man on whom reliance could be placed. On the night of the third of October he was offered the command of the forces available for the suppression of the insurrection, Barras being nominally his chief. He was in the gallery of the Convention when the proposal for his appointment was made. He retired to deliberate. What thoughts passed through his mind in the interval can never be known: but at the end of half an hour, he had bidden adieu to his Jacobinism forever. To what extent he had been disgusted by the excesses of the Jacobins, to what extent a close observation of that in practice which had looked so beautiful in theory, had intensified or developed the radical skepticism and cynicism of his mind, need not be conjectured; but whatever faintly roseate hues of romance linger about the youth of Napoleon, from his outspoken and ardent devotion to the revolution, here finally fade away. That man cannot be called the soldier of democracy, who deliberately made himself the instrument of bridling democracy, and subjecting it, before he was himself its sovereign, to a selfish and contracted oligarchy.

But a piece of work was now to be done, and the Napoleon of Toulon became recognizable. There were fifty guns at the neighboring camp of Sablons. These guns were the Little Gibraltar of Vendemiare. Self-possessed, calm, but with that swiftness which startled and bewildered an opponent, like the flash of a meteor out of a dark and

silent sky, he ordered Murat, a man to be depended upon
for swiftness, to bring in the pieces. They were clutched
almost from under the eyes of the sectionaries. The Convention held its meetings at this time in the Palace of the
Tuileries; on this point the attack of the insurgents was
directed, and around this point Napoleon marshalled his
defences. On every bridge and quay communicating with
the palace, sweeping every street and open space, he posted
cannon. In the centre of the bristling circle he stood,
quiet, composed, as one at home. It was the fourth of
October, 1795. In the early part of the afternoon the
Parisians advanced to the attack, numbering about forty
thousand. Habituated to street-fighting by six years of
revolution, and flushed by some apparent successes of the
preceding day, the sectionaries poured furiously along the
streets towards the Tuileries. It was not the first time
that the citizens of Paris, familiar with the conquering of
their King and of their Parliaments, had flooded those
avenues. On the famous tenth of June and twentieth of
August, 1792, for instance, they had come on in wild flood,
and a monarchy had gone down before them. But they
were now encountered by a thing new in those years. The
unfixed gaze and maudlin good-heartedness of Louis, always
ready to parley, unwilling to shed a drop of blood though
to save a torrent, terrible only to his friends, had given
place to the compressed lips, dark brows, and unflinching
eye of Napoleon. Betrayed, uncommanded body-guards
were here no longer; but in their place an army in position,
strung to exertion in every nerve, as a muscular arm is
strung by a determined will. Napoleon would do *his*
parleying through the throats of fifty pieces of cannon.
The sectionaries, sweeping on fiercely, were torn up
by cannon-ball and grape-shot. The tumultuous mass

recoiled; sobered suddenly, as a blustering bully is sobered by the buffet of a brawny arm. The guns continued to play; the ranks under the command of Napoleon advanced; in a few hours the sectionaries were driven to their homes and disarmed. The piece of work was done.

Napoleon had now stepped fairly beyond the sphere of private life. His marriage with Josephine, for whom he seems to have entertained no slight affection, soon took place. He was appointed to the command of the army of Italy, and in the spring of 1796 reached the head-quarters at Nice.

Of all the periods in the life of Napoleon, the mind is apt to rest with most enthusiasm upon that of his early campaigns in Italy. His fame may be said to have been as yet unsullied; even that apparent defection from the principles of liberty, which a severe investigation of his conduct reveals, admits not unreasonably of being traced to a soldierly love of order. And he had won his exalted position through so honest and unmistakable a display of intellectual power! Unfriended among the myriads of revolutionary France, and at first scowled upon by envious incompetence, he had approved himself a man of indubitable and overpowering capacity, who could think, who could act, whom it would clearly be advantageous to obey. One cannot but experience a thrill of emotion as the imagination pictures him in his first appearance among the soldiers of Italy. Of all warrior-faces Napoleon's is the finest. Not only has it that clearness of line, that strength and firmness of chiselling, which gives a nobleness to the faces of all great soldiers; there is in it, in the eye especially, a depth of thought and reflection which belongs peculiarly to itself, and suggests not merely the soldier but the sovereign. And perhaps the face of Napoleon never looked so nobly, as when first an army worthy of his powers waited his commands, the calm assurance of absolute self-reliance giving a statue-like stillness to his brows and temples on which still shone the brightness of youth, the light of a fame now to be all his own kindling that intense and steadfast eye, and his gaze turned towards the fields of Italy. Cannot one fancy his glance going along the ranks, lighting a gleam in every eye, as he presented himself to his troops? "Soldiers," thus ran his proclamation, "you are almost naked, half-starved: the government owes you much and can give you nothing. Your patience, your courage, in the midst of these rocks, have been admirable, but they reflect no splendor on your arms. I am about to conduct you into the most fertile plains of the earth. Rich provinces, opulent cities, will soon be in your power: there you will find abundant harvests, honor and glory. Soldiers of Italy, will you fail in courage?" In a moment he had established between himself and his soldiers that understanding by which, more than by cannon or bayonet, victories are won. Privates and commanders at once felt that this was the man to follow.

Then commenced that marvellous series of campaigns which makes the year 1796 an era in the history of warfare, in the development of civilization; in which the fiery energies, unchained by the French Revolution, were first directed by supreme military genius against the standing institutions of Europe to their overthrow and subversion; in which the eye of the world was first fixed in wondering gaze on the fully unveiled face of Napoleon. Not merely to the soldier are these campaigns interesting and profitable. It is for all men instructive to mark the achievements of pure capacity, to watch the wondrous spirit-element controlling and effecting, dazzling difficulty from its steady march, causing lions to cower aside in its sovereign presence. We are so constituted, besides, that we cannot behold energy, perseverance, courage, resolution, without a thrill of emulous sympathy. As we note the progress of that intrepid, indomitable Corsican, from victory to victory, we kindle with those emotions which animated the troops of Napoleon; which sent the grenadiers through the grape-shot sweeping like snow-drift along the bridge of Lodi; which renewed and renewed the bloody struggle on the dykes of Arcola; which made the French columns scorn rest and delay, forget the limit placed to human endurance, rise over the faintness of fatigue and crush down the gnawing of hunger, march through mountain paths all night and spring exultant on the foe at break of dawn, if only the way was led by *him*.

A review of these campaigns, even of the most cursory description, is here impossible, and would be superfluous. All men may be supposed to have a somewhat familiar acquaintance with one of the most brilliant passages of modern history, and to be capable of taking the same point of view which must be occupied in order to cast the eye along their course, as illustrating the character of Napoleon.

The Italian campaigns seem specially adapted to demonstrate a military capacity at once indubitable, many-sided, and supreme. They exhibit not only the fiery spring that has so often caught the smile of fortune, but the cool calculation and patient resolution which seem to compel it. They show the victor crowned, not once, or twice, or thrice, not under this favoring circumstance of to-day or through that happy thought of to-morrow, but so often that the possibility of fortuitous success is eliminated, and under circumstances of disadvantage, so manifold and so varied, that even envy, unless aided by crotchet, stupidity or fixed idea, must own that this is beyond all question, the inscrutable and irresistible power of mind.   The first fierce onslaught by which Sardinia, bleeding and prostrate, was snatched from the Austrian alliance, by which the gates of Italy were thrown open, and by which Europe was startled, as at three successive thunder peals, by the victories of Montenotte, Millesimo and Mondovi, all in the space of a month, might, at least possibly, have been the result of youthful daring and the valor of the Republican army. But the defeats of Colli, the Sardinian, were succeeded by those of Beaulieu, the Austrian; the defeats of Beaulieu were succeeded by the defeats in two campaigns of the well-supported and resolute Wurmser; the defeats of Wurmser were succeeded by the defeats, in two campaigns more, of Alvinzi, also furnished with overpowering numbers; and when Archduke Charles advanced to re-conquer a thoroughly subjugated Lombardy, he too was met and driven back.   There were six distinct campaigns; and when Napoleon, at their close, dictated, in 1797, the treaty of Campo Formio, he remained indisputably the first warrior in Europe.

A great deal has been said of the change introduced by Napoleon in these campaigns, into military tactics. He broke through, it is said, all the rules and etiquette of war, poured his forces always on single points, was now in his enemy's front, now in his rear, and, on the whole, introduced a new system of warfare. That he introduced a change in the mode of carrying on hostilities, among the generals of Europe, does not admit of doubt. The system of warfare by which Napoleon was overthrown, put in operation by men who had marched under his banner, was indeed a more rapid and fearful thing than that over which he won his first triumphs. But it seems as little doubtful, that the change was nothing more than that natural one which is inevitable in any art or science where consummate genius displays itself. His generalship was essentially that of all the greatest generals. To form combinations with such invention and accuracy, and execute them with such celerity, as will bring an overpowering force to bear upon a single point, had been the object of generals from Luxemburgh to Dumouriez; and had been effected, by the former against William of Orange and by the latter against Brunswick, with a skill and celerity not unworthy of Napoleon. Wellington studied war among the Ghauts of Himalaya, yet the ablest combinations and the most impetuous attacks of the best Marshals trained in the school of Bonaparte were unable to baffle him. In our own time we have seen war settle back to that laggard habit, into which it had fallen in the hands of the Austrians before the revolutionary campaigns. The advent of military genius of the first order might have introduced precisely such a change of tactics under the walls of Sebastopol, as Napoleon introduced on the plains of Lombardy. He did not provide himself with a new horse; but he was the man to put Bucephalus to his speed.

The quickness and clearness with which, in these campaigns, he apprehended the features of every position, and the necessities of every situation, are amazing. The reports of spies, the vague hints of rumor, became clear before him. As if by second sight, he saw in the far distance every disposition of his enemy. With the pieces before him on a chess-board, it would have required discrimination and decision, to estimate or anticipate every move of his adversary, and instantly to adapt his own force to thwart it. But with armies overwhelming in number, approaching over wide spaces of country, with only the reports of spies

or traitors to depend upon for intelligence, with a thousand
openings for mishap in the very transmission of orders,
with the certainty that a slip might be ruin, to have the
whole spread out as clear as the starry spheres before his tel-
escopic eye, and again and again, by swift perception and
decision, to launch the bolt just where it was needed: —
this indeed demanded a master mind. And he effected
these things so often and so variously! First, as we said,
D'Argenteau was overpowered in Piedmont, the French
army concentrating itself into a wedge and breaking through
the centre of the Allies. Then came the brilliant fighting
of Lodi and the investment of Mantua. Wurmser and
Quasdonowich were next to be overthrown. They were
near each other at the bottom of the Lago di Garda, and
could they have united, resistance might have been vain.
But swift as lightning Quasdonowich was shattered and
flung back on this hand, and the whole flood, wheeling
round like a heady current, turned to sweep Wurmser
away on that. Wurmser, tough and valiant, retreated for
a time, and then advanced again on Mantua, leaving Davidowich with a strong army to defend Trient and the passes
of the Tyrol. Suddenly, while Wurmser was looking out
for the French along his front, he was startled by the intelligence that, far in the rear, Davidowich had been utterly
routed. In a moment, this spirit-like Napoleon was down,
irresistible, upon himself. The eye of a civilian may not
deserve much confidence; but this overthrow of Davidowich *first*, and advance thereupon on Wurmser, with all
his Austrian communications broken, and not improbably
in some slight bewilderment, assuredly *looks* one of the
finest bits of work to be met with in the annals of war.
It is needless to multiply instances. Such was Napoleon's
mode of carrying on hostilities.

The amplitude of comprehension with which he embraced every circumstance of the war, appearing to have the end as distinctly before him as the beginning, and the remote as visibly present as the near, baffles description. Consider that single instance of his first passage of the Po. He has in a month laid Sardinia prostrate at his feet; he has taken eighty guns, twenty-one standards, and two great fortresses; he has slain or captured twenty-five thousand of the enemy; he is twenty-six years of age; and now, as he concludes the treaty with the king of Sardinia, Europe is looking on him with wonder and admiration. His treaty is signed. Among other stipulations, he is careful to have it specified that it will be permitted to the French army to cross the Po at Valenza. Beaulieu takes the alarm; spares no pains to make his position at Valenza sure. He is looking eagerly for the French columns, when lo! he is informed that Napoleon has already crossed at Placenza, fifty miles down, and that he, Beaulieu, must face about, fast enough if he would prevent an entrance into Milan. The veteran of twenty-six! With the first laurels on his brow, the plaudits of Europe in his ears, and a monarch accepting a treaty from his dictation, he had closed his eye at once to the past, saw only the future, and in the very council chambers remembered that he was in the field. There was nothing very brilliant, certainly nothing chivalrous here: but what could escape a coolness, a presence of mind, a power of vision like this?

That forwardness of look, that instant forgetfulness of the past, was one of the most remarkable characteristics of this greatest worker of modern times. Other soldiers look to victory for rest; Napoleon's might have looked upon it with apprehensiveness, as the unfailing herald of new toil. He indulged himself in no raptures over his battle-fields; not a look did he take: was the work over, or could it be confided to inferior hands, he was away on the instant, to front battle on some distant field. At Rivoli, his exertions were overpowering. He had three horses shot under him. At nightfall, one would have said that, without repose, flesh and blood could hold out no longer. But not a moment's rest did he take. The victory could now be completed by Massena and others; and he set out on the instant for Mantua, marching first all night and then all day. He arrives at Mantua. Any creature in the form of man, were he a mere incarnated spirit, would surely now seek repose. But Napoleon does not seek it. His soldiers, indeed, are unable to hold out any longer, but not he. He passes the night in walking about the outposts. "At one of these," says Lockhart in his own clear, admirable way, "he found a grenadier asleep by the root of a tree; and taking his gun, without wakening him, performed a sentinel's duty in his place for about half an hour; when the man, starting from his slumbers, perceived with terror and despair the countenance and occupation of his general. He fell on his knees before him. "My friend," said Napoleon, "here is your musket. You had fought hard, and marched long, and your sleep is excusable : but a moment's inattention might at present ruin the army. I happened to be awake, and have held your post for you. You will be more careful another time." He happened to be awake! Mr. Emerson might well say that this was a man of stone and iron.

But in truth, in these campaigns, he showed himself armed at all points. He could manage the Directory just as well as the Austrians. Barras had recommended him for Vendemiare, as a man who would not stand upon ceremony; and now he found it was perhaps too true. The

Directory, professing unbounded admiration, would have divided the Italian army, giving part to Napoleon, part to Kellermann; thus, in all calculable certainty, ruining Napoleon, subverting his conquests, and bringing an Austrian army upon France through the Sardinian Passes. He saw through their design and defeated it in an instant, by simply throwing up his command, and compelling them, afraid of public opinion, to reinstate him. For every emergency, he had its own requirement. At Lodi, a furious charge, a display of dauntless valor, was necessary. So he seized a standard and rushed into the tempest of grape. At Arcola, the battle was won by a sudden thought, a clever trick, which could, however, have occurred only to a mind absolutely imperturbable and perfectly clear. At Tagliamento, he conquered by a stratagem which reminds one very much of the ancient generals. In the thinking and the acting part of his profession, he was equally at home. You may say of him, that never did any one more notably diminish the interval between the tardiness of thought and the swiftness of action. As he himself said in after years, his head and his hand were in immediate connection.

Such was the Napoleon whom we might have discerned at the conferences of Formio, in October, 1797. Ere that time he had observably altered his demeanor with friends and dependants. He appreciated, with his usual clear, cold accuracy, his position; he was the head of a triumphant army, the unbounded favorite of the French people, now fairly kindled into a passion for military glory, and the subject of so feeble a government as the Directory. He said afterwards that his ambition was strong but of a cold nature: it would have been more strictly correct to say that it was of a practical nature, that it never passed the limits of the possible, that, like every other quality and characteristic of his mind, it was of a sternly realistic nature. It admits of no doubt that schemes of empire were already beginning to dawn upon him.

It must be added that, at the date of the treaty of Campo Formio, another aspect of Napoleon's character had become manifest. In his dealings with the Lombard peasantry and with the Grand Duke of Tuscany, he had shown himself thoroughly unscrupulous in the means he used to effect his ends. He crushed the Lombard insurrection with cruel severity, showing an utter disregard to the effusion of blood. "It is the nature," he said, "of the giant to squeeze." It is doubtless a general characteristic of strong and rugged minds to allow the end a large power of justifying the means, especially if they have been accustomed to carnage as the instrument of their purposes. Cromwell's mind seems to have been originally by no means rugged, but rather kindly and affectionate; yet his words about the "knocking on the head" at Drogheda make one feel somewhat chill. At all events, Napoleon had now shown that there might easily be a stronger necessity with him than the necessity of sparing a brother's life.

In the beginning of 1798, we find him again in Paris. He knew himself to be the most popular man in France, but made a show of retiring into a private station. He lost no opportunity, however, of ingratiating himself with the people, and observed carefully the weakness of government. But he discerned that his day of opportunity had not yet arrived. He in vain attempted to gain peaceably a seat in the government, and, as his Italian army was no longer around him, he had no sword in hand to cut his way to one. With that ambition of a cold nature, he could bide his time.

Having been appointed to the command of the army

destined for the invasion of England, and discovering that such an invasion was then at least impracticable, he procured the assent of the Directory to a descent upon Egypt. He sailed in May, 1798.

There are but two circumstances demanding notice in connection with the Egyptian campaign.

The first is the new and striking instance it afforded of Napoleon's personal endurance. In the burning heat of an Egyptian July, the army set out from Alexandria, to march along the Nile and bring the Mamelukes to an engagement. The enemy had cleared the country of every living and every green thing. The sand threw up its burning glare, as if in concert with the flaming sun above. The air swarmed with noxious insects. There was little water, and that nauseous. In one word, all those torments and agonies pressed upon the French hosts, with the description of which we have now become so familiar. The soldiers became mutinous in their torture; the fiery spirits of Murat and Lannes were driven almost to madness; they trod their tri-colors in the dust. But Napoleon suffered nothing. He would not even sleep in the middle of the day. He "wore his uniform buttoned up as at Paris; never showed one bead of sweat on his brow; nor thought of repose except to lie down in his cloak the last at night, and start up first in the morning." Really the forty centuries that looked down upon him from the pyramids had seldom seen so remarkable a being.

The second circumstance in this Egyptian campaign which seems deserving of special observation is the institution, on the part of Napoleon, of a series of improvements in the condition of Egypt, of which the beneficial effects have not ceased in our own day. This, for the first time, brings into prominent view a phase of Napoleon's character

17*

not suggested by his warlike exploits. The power of destruction was but half his capacity; nor would it seem to have been that part which he most highly prized or most willingly indulged. He too, with the right instinct of an imperial mind, loved to see the world grow greener round him. The savans whom he had taken with him to Egypt, examined, in obedience to his orders, the "long-smothered traces of many an ancient device for improving the agriculture of the country. Canals that had been shut up for centuries were re-opened: the waters of the Nile flowed once more where they had been guided by the skill of the Pharaohs or the Ptolemies. Cultivation was extended; property secured; and" adds our authority, "it cannot be doubted that the signal improvements since introduced in Egypt, are attributable mainly to the wise example of the French administration."

But, on the whole, the Egyptian expedition did not turn out precisely in accordance with the expectations of Napoleon. His progress eastward was arrested at Acre. The dreams of oriental dominion, which, for a brief space, had fascinated. or amused his imagination, faded away forever. He became aware that, in his absence, great events, disastrous to France, but which might prove propitious to his ambition, had taken place in Europe. He quitted Egypt without apprizing his soldiers of his departure; and in October, 1799, was once more in Paris.

The incompetence and corruption of the Directory had ere now disgusted all parties, and the reverses which had been sustained by the French arms, in Holland, Belgium, and Italy, had prepared the people of Paris to welcome back the victorious young general. He brought with him tidings of the victory of Aboukir; earnest that the old

Italian glory might still be recalled. He was received with enthusiasm.

Circumstances, he soon discovered, were favorable to his views. A sword was ready for him and he did not scruple to grasp the hilt. Three regiments of dragoons solicited the honor of being reviewed by him, and a large proportion of the military men in Paris requested permission to wait upon him with congratulations. These all were directed to present themselves at his house at six o'clock on the morning of the 18th Brumaire, 10th of November. Meanwhile measures were taken by the supporters of Napoleon, Sieyes and others, to turn their presence to advantage. The legislative power was at that time lodged in the Council of Ancients and the Council of Five Hundred. The former was convoked in the Tuileries at seven o'clock on the morning of the 18th, at the moment when ·Napoleon was surrounded by the chief military force of Paris. Two decrees were proposed and passed: first, that the meetings of the legislative bodies should be transferred to St. Cloud; second, that Napoleon should be named commandant of the troops and National Guard of Paris. The object of the first was to remove the Council of Five hundred from Parisian support, in the prospect of its subversion; the second armed Napoleon with that weapon which it was necessary at least to brandish over the heads of the defenders and representatives of French freedom, and which he was henceforth to retain as sceptre. These decrees were passed. Napoleon was invested with his new command in the midst of the officers assembled round him; and the nomination was hailed by the soldiery with acclamations.

Nothing further of importance occurred on that day. The two councils met next day at St. Cloud. Napoleon had already surrounded the chateau in which they were to assemble by a body of soldiers under Murat; by this act alone putting the character of the following proceedings beyond doubt. It is painful to trace what followed. One hurries over it as a scene of despicable mock-tragedy, scandalous to all parties. The Council of Ancients proved subservient. The Council of Five Hundred assumed a different tone and attitude; the hall echoed with heroic, death-defiant eloquence; a patriotic oath was sworn, even Lucien the President, though Napoleon's brother, being compelled to take part in it. The legislators of France were to die at their posts. The presence of Napoleon in the hall served only to endanger his own life, and to raise to height of still nobler temper the loquacious heroes. Then entered grenadiers, with ruthless look, and naked, level bayonets: and the legislators of France, the patriotic oath still hot on their lips, scampered off by door and window! Had Louis the sixteenth, on the 23d of June, 1789, sent a similar force of grenadiers, say under Captain D'Agoust, into the Hall of the Third Estate, would the result have been *this* ?

It was now decreed, by such remnant of the French legislature as gave itself wholly to the purposes of Napoleon, that the two councils should be adjourned until February, and that the government should be lodged provisionally in the hands of three consuls, of whom the first was Napoleon. Sieyes coming, with Ducos his brother consul, next day, to transact business, and thinking, sure enough, Napoleon would consent to remain the mere military man, leaving civil and diplomatic affairs to be regulated by his own incomparable capacity, discovered that he was mistaken. "Bonaparte," he said in the evening, "can do, and will do, everything himself." The Abbé and his colleague felt themselves unceremoniously converted into tools. Napoleon was ruler of France.

The first act of the Napoleon drama was now approaching its completion. In order to obtain for Bonaparte the name of Emperor, and to consolidate power in his hands, two things still remained to be done. It was necessary first, that he should, by a firm and sagacious internal government, demonstrate his capacity to secure to France that calmness and stability, which had so long been wanting to the distracted country, and without which the operations of industry could not be sustained: and second, that he should, by some brilliant exploit of foreign warfare, encircle his government with that glory which, in the eyes of Frenchmen, hides innumerable faults, and which might render him certain of the enthusiastic support of the army. The achievement of these two objects may be considered as filling up the period between the 19th Brumaire, 1799, and the coronation, in December, 1804.

The campaign of Marengo was peculiarly adapted to excite the military enthusiasm of the nation, and to silence any Republican murmurs against the rule of the First Consul which might linger in the army. The skill with which the intention of Napoleon was masked, and the originality of the whole conception of the campaign, might be exhibited and dwelt upon, as demonstrative of military genius; but the most remarkable circumstance connected with this campaign seems after all to have been its magnificent daring. Suspicions have been thrown out, to all appearance groundless, as to the personal bravery of Napoleon in later years; but in all the early part of his career, his courage was not only dauntless but fiery. If in any respect the massiveness and adamantine strength of his character could be said to partake of French vehemence and Italian excitability, it was in the recklessness with which he rushed into fire, as at Lodi, or confronted perilous risks, as in crossing and re-crossing the Mediterranean with a Nelson on his track. And the Italian campaign of 1800, with its passage of the Alps and victory of Marengo, could have been ventured upon only by a man whose mind rested on a basis of utter soldierly fearlessness. The prize for which he played was indeed splendid; but the alternative of success was absolute, instant, irretrievable ruin: yet his hand never shook, his eye never once filmed or quivered, as he staked all on one dread throw. It may indeed be fairly questioned whether, in this campaign, Napoleon's daring did not approach the character of foolhardiness; whether it can perfectly vindicate its claim to the character of that high valor, whose seeming recklessness advances steadily under the shield of foresight, whose most startling swiftness is but the laggard step of material energy following the geometry of mind. In the case of any other man save Napoleon, the assertion could be made without hesitation that it did. But much could be risked by an intellect so vigilant, a readiness and presence of mind so reliable, and a resolution so inflexible, as Napoleon's. "I think this is a battle lost," said Dessaix, coming up on the evening of Marengo and seeing the French columns all broken and retreating. "I think it is a battle won," answered Napoleon; and in an hour he had added to the roll of his fame one of the most brilliant victories he ever gained. A man who could thus depend on himself in execution could be very daring in conception. Be this as it may, the battle was won; the French conquests in Italy were almost entirely restored; and Napoleon returned to Paris, dearer than ever to the French army, the boast and darling of the nation, and with the hopes of his opponents smitten into the dust.

The internal government of the First Consul was the gradual development of the system of the Empire, and the elaboration of those ceremonies and grandeurs, by which the French people were to be studiously reminded of Charlemagne. It would be inappropriate or impossible to view it separately. Suffice it here to say, that a tranquil and acquiescing, if not in any degree enthusiastic France beheld Napoleon, on the 2nd of December, 1804, set upon his head that diadem, which he had already encircled with a legion of honor and a brilliant constellation of marshals.

The empire of Napoleon is one of the most remarkable phenomena of modern times, and one fraught with deep and varied instruction. It will doubtless form a subject for investigation and discussion during centuries to come; and more than one may elapse before its character is accurately explained, or its place in the scheme of Providence discerned. But enough has already been done to render it possible to ascertain and define with something of scientific precision its essential feature. To do this will prove synonymous with discovering the radical character of him who was the founder and impersonation of that empire.

It is safe to permit one's enthusiasm large scope in contemplating Napoleon as emperor of France. The structure he erected was truly imperial in its dimensions; stable, many-sided, imposing; and the mind of which it was the image was the most variously and magnificently endowed that has exercised sovereignty for many centuries; if, indeed, in these ages, there has appeared any man who can on the whole be pronounced intellectually greater than Napoleon. No sooner did he become First Consul than

every department of the administration acquired a firmness
of tone altogether new. It was not the formalized rigidness
of the old regimé, nor was it the fierce tension of the Ter-
rorist rule: the one was the regularity of decrepitude, the
other the overstrung activity of fever: here method and
energy were combined. It is curious that he, whose career,
contemplated in a general way, has so brilliant, sudden,
meteoric an aspect, should have been called, and called
truly, the most methodic of mankind. It is not impossible
that Soult, Massena, or Moreau, would have defended
France from external enemies nearly as effectually as Napoleon. But as every one of his marshals fell even here
behind the great leader, so, in all the qualities which belong
to the sovereign as distinguished from the soldier, he was
incomparably superior to them all. To develop the material resources of the country; to extend mental cultivation
and encourage mental activity, to the utmost limit consistent with the security of despotism; to adorn France with
great works; to preserve national morality and love of
order, so far at least as was essential to national stability;
and to provide a uniform and equitable system of laws for
the nation: — such were the objects he set before him.
And he worked in the closet as he worked in the field.
Every department of the administration was under his eye.
No technical details could repel him; nay every sort of
practical endeavor, every science, every economic and industrial art, enlisted his ardent sympathy. In every department his suggestions were valuable: he seems to have
been as much at home with the jurists engaged on the
Code Napoleon, as in directing the organization of the
forces.

It is affecting to observe how this noblest aspect of the
character of Napoleon, his profound and comprehensive

sympathy with the works of peace, his instinct, deeper than all his warlike tendencies, that peace is greater than war, comes out in St. Helena. He boasts, with real warmth of exultation, that he would have made the French populace the best educated in Europe : and the emotion with which he thought of Austerlitz was languid in comparison of that with which he recurred to the Code. His general mode of alluding to his victories, indeed, evinced a sagacity and soundness of mind, little less wonderful than the powers displayed in their achievement. They were quite ordinary matters; nothing mysterious or very great about them; dependent on an observance of the value of minutes, on quickness, coolness, presence of mind, and mere work-a-day, matter-of-fact qualities, on a committal of *fewer* blunders than your adversary, on fortuitous circumstances which did you no honor. But the thought was really dear to him that his influence might live in the ways of French existence as a peaceful and benignant presence; that somewhat of the orderliness and prosperity of citizen life would be traceable to him; that he would go down to posterity with the fame of a law-giver.

It would almost appear to be an inseparable characteristic of the mode in which mankind is educated, that truth after truth is lodged in the general mind in an extreme and one-sided form. For the last five and twenty years, the literary world of Britain and America has rung with denunciation of hearsay, of tradition, of system. Mirabeau was a man not of systems but "with an eye;" Danton, the same; Napoleon it would be loudly exclaimed, the same. But no magnificence of rhetoric can in the smallest degree affect the simple scientific fact, that men and nations work by system, that the inventions and methods of genius can be in great measure stereotyped and made the property of

the race, that parchments, laws, constitutions, are the ultimate fruits of political civilization. To discover the principles of such, to construct and establish them, is the work
of genius; they are effective precisely in proportion as they
are put in operation by ability and energy: but it is an
error, precisely co-ordinate with the error of misconceiving
the corresponding functions of genius, to represent them
as in themselves of no value. And in no case does the
mind of Napoleon exhibit a greatness so truly and calmly
imperial, as in the earnest endeavor to give perpetuity to
what otherwise would have been fleeting; to leave its
stamp on the institutions of the nation; to breathe its
ethereal spirit into the framework of system. Genius is
the vital sap pouring from the root and stem; it is the glory
of civilization to conduct and disseminate it through a
thousand branches, twigs, and leaves, that fair fruits may
ripen season after season, and that common hands may
pluck them. Genius is the electric fire of heaven, mysterious, inscrutable; institutions, laws, formulas, systems, are
the terrestrial wires, along which it may penetrate to every
town and village, bearing the words of ordinary mortals.
By overlooking this two-fold fact, by exaggerating either
of its sides, you throw all human history into confusion.
Look only to the regulation, and you become the apologist
of solecisms, the admirer of mechanism, the defender of
form without spirit, the believer in men that are mummies
and in armor that is rust. Look only to the force, and your
philosophy becomes one not of man but of men. You learn
to palliate that sin against the human race by which in all
ages national freedom has been crushed under individual
strength. You sympathize with expulsions of parliaments
and Reigns of Terror. You formalize your fatal your blasting error, and proclaim it as a truth, under the name of

hero-worship. Napoleon, as may presently appear, can vindicate no claim to have, in his public capacity, wholly and disinterestedly devoted himself to serve France in this best and broadest manner. But as seen by posterity, bearing in the one hand that sword which blazed so fearfully, so irresistibly over Europe, and with the other resting on the Code Napoleon, he will continue to afford a sublime testimony to the two-fold truth, whose practical evolution is the evolution of civilization, that the great man works for his race and that the race must work together.

The Napoleonic empire was one of great advantage to France. That must be allowed at once and emphatically. Napoleon speedily brought all the factions by which the land had been kept in a state of distraction to work harmoniously under his orders, to own the strong gravitation of his genius. "My principle was," he said in St. Helena, "*la carrière ouverte aux talens.*" It is the principle of all prosperous enterprise; and his magnificent success was the natural result of the ability and determination with which he carred it out. Capacity was the one thing he looked for, and the comprehensiveness of perception with which he detected it was marvellous. His soldiers, his marshals, his ministers, were masters of their work; pretence, dreaming, verbiage, he could not tolerate for a moment. He did not himself shrink from labor. His toil was such as makes us amazed at the powers of the human mind and body. While in the field, while directing the motions of large armies on extended lines, while forming combinations that required exact geometric calculation, devising expedients possible only to a mind acting with the most free and tranquil energy, executing movements and operations which demanded exhausting physical endurance, he yet continued to scrutinize every department of the domestic administra-

tion. He placed his crown on a gloomy brow, where
thought and care rather than exultation learned to rest;
and his seat on the throne of France was not what you
would call an easy one.   There is a pathos in these words,
made use of to O'Meara in St. Helena: — "The happiest
days of my life were from sixteen to twenty, during the
semestres, when I used to go about, as I have told you I
should wish to do, from one *restaurateur* to another, living
moderately, and having a lodging, for which I paid three
louis a month. They were the happiest days of my life.
I was always so much occupied, that I may say I never
was truly happy upon the throne." Thus he worked, and
made all work who owned his authority. The government
in every part was a model of industry and energy. The
foreign enemies of France trembled before a power, at
once fiery in its intensity and perfect in its organization.
The subjects of the empire found themselves stimulated,
in whatever direction their capacities lay, by the prospect
of civic honor. The private soldier, the marshal, the man
of art, of science, of industry — every one could gain a
place in the legion of honor, if only his excellence in his
department were pre-eminent. The treasures of science
and the monuments of art enriched and adorned the empire.
Well might Frenchmen regard with pride, and the world
contemplate with awe and wonder, this consistent and
stable structure. From amid the volcanic heavings of the
Revolution, it had risen in its strength and massiveness,
like a granite mountain, buttressed about with rocks, re-
pressing into submission and silence the fires on which it
was based, and beating back proudly the tempests by which
it was surrounded.

But there is a negative side to all this, which must be
fairly brought into view, before the distinctive feature of the

Napoleonic empire can be defined, or the character of Napoleon accurately determined.

The Napoleonic empire was a despotism. To say so may seem the utterance of a truism; but even if it is so, the truism must be put conspicuously forward. The fair and free development of the human mind in France was interfered with, impeded, constrained. Only such expansion was permitted to the national intellect, only such action allowed to the national will, as were consistent with the purposes of one man. Whatever mind submitted itself or devoted itself to Napoleon might work and prosper; but the sun, moon, and stars of intellect had to leave their natural orbits and do obeisance to him.

Further, the imperial system of Napoleon was specially vitiated by its peculiar adaptation to the purposes of war. It has been said that Napoleon's profoundest instincts acknowledged the paramount nobleness of peace; and this is true. But it has not been alleged that he gave his instincts full play; and the fact is certain, that the whole organization of French imperialism takes the aspect of a martial apparatus. Countless inducements tempted youth into the army. The whole system of education was adapted to the cultivation of military qualities. The conscription compelled all men to regard themselves in the light of possible soldiers. It is not a beautiful spectacle. The very influences which are by their nature pre-eminently pacific, the knowledge and culture whose natural office it is to elevate, to expand, to humanize the mind, brought into the service of hatred, of ferocity, of war: the rain and sunlight not left to fertilize the field and clothe the forest, but set to ripen one vast harvest of dragons' teeth.

This glance at the Napoleonic empire sends us back to
18*

look with more searching scrutiny into the character of its founder.

It has been exceedingly common, of late years, to speak of the intellectual and moral nature as identical, to confound intellect, feeling, and conscience in one unity of power. But it is not advisable to reject truth, solely because it is very certain; to rush to paradox, merely because men in general acknowledge plain fact. So manifest is it that conscience, reason, and emotion are not synonymous, — so explicit is the testimony to the possibility of a disturbed balance among these, borne by the Jugurthas, the Syllas, the Borgias, of history — that one cannot but suspect, when their necessarily proportionate soundness and development are insisted on, that the asserter has permitted himself to be deceived by some process of more or less subtle logical legerdemain. It is certain that an infraction of any moral law can be brought out as a negative quantity by the calculation of reason; every crime, be it granted, is a mistake. But this does not justify the assertion, that a powerful intellectual capacity is inconsistent with infraction of the moral law. Mistake may be unconsciously committed under the form of crime, when, were it known or thought of as mistake, it would have been avoided. The whole meaning and point of the common distinction is, that moral defect or delinquency prevents the reason from coming into free and perfect action: that selfishness clogs it, and lets it not gain that high, pure pinnacle, whence it could have swept a sufficiently wide horizon; that impotence of conscience seals its eye, and permits it not to see the chariots of fire, the horsemen, and the spearmen, the unsuspected, unnoticed difficulties and dangers, with which seemingly innoxious crime is filling the air around it. No refining will remove from human nature this possibility, from human history this fact. As well attempt to prove that, the higher you ascend the Alps, the more broad and luxuriant are the cornfields, the softer and brighter the roses. Jura and Mont Blanc are high and strong; but their lofty precipices are very bare, and they are covered with unmelted snow. This, as well as most other phenomena of nature's scenery, has its analogue in the world of man.

The intellect of Napoleon Bonaparte was of a supreme order; but the moral and emotional nature, conscience and feeling, were not in proportionate power. This mal-adjustment was the essential feature of his character, and wrought his ruin. It found its natural counterpart in his imperial system.

After the conclusive handling the subject has received from Mr. Carlyle, and especially from Mr. Emerson, it will hardly now be maintained that there was not some dark and baneful taint in the character of Napoleon. It may be exhibited with precision under one or two particulars.

It is impossible, first of all, to acquit him of a guilt for which it were difficult to find another name but murder. Explanation might suffice in one or two cases. But the savage extermination of the later Italian campaigns; the deliberate order that thirteen hundred Arab prisoners who had received quarter should be shot; the slaughter of D'Enghien and Palm: these are things which cannot be explained away. Those hands will never wash white.

After murder may be ranked blasphemy. A great many superfine things have been said about Napoleon's fatalism, and his rejection of the materialistic logic which argued that there was no God. But really his fatalism was little more than a kind of thunder behind the scenes; less for use than effect. He did not let fate fight his battles for him. He did not commit himself very trustfully to fate, in that early campaign, which lasted seven days, in which he flew along the ridges of the Tyrol and the banks of the Italian rivers like fire glittering and darting among the clouds, and during which he destroyed forty thousand Austrians without taking off his boots! Fate seemed to have agreed with Dessaix that Marengo was a battle lost; but Napoleon took the liberty to believe that it was a battle won. If he did not use many precautions to secure his person against assassination, it was not, however he might assert it, because of any confidence in the disposi- tions of fate: it was simply because he considered the omission of such precautions as safe as their observance. In St. Helena, he put off the doctors, having no confidence in medicine, with reference to fate: but he was careful that the state of his stomach should be communicated to his son. Had fate forgotten *him?* Napoleon did not whimper, or betray a weak surprise, when overtaken by disaster; but that had far more to do with trust in himself, and gen- eral strength of character, than with trust in fate. His belief in the existence of God may mean more or less. It probably comes to little more than an attestation to the fundamental human instinct that the First Cause of the Universe is mind. In any view it cannot be alleged in his commendation. Belief in a God without either trembling or worshipping, is a reasonable condition for no finite being.

"There are so many different religions or modifications of them," remarked Napoleon, seemingly in a light and careless mood, in St. Helena, "that it is difficult to know which to choose. If one religion had existed from the beginning of the world, I should think that to be the true one." Not in that way was the bridge of Lodi passed: not in that way was the sword of Austerlitz or of Jena bared and sheathed. By close, earnest, self-subduing study, by indomitable, sleepless attention, did he perfect himself in the science, and master the art, of war. Strange, that he should have thought a question of which the mere statement involved infinitudes of consequence, might be so lightly shuffled aside, while the concerns of the poor three-score years. and ten rose into immeasurable importance, shutting out the heavenly constellations, and sternly concentrating within their narrow space his whole immortal energies! The words may be remembered, with those of Tacitus and Suetonius, as showing how utterly limitless is the possibility, even for great minds, to mistake the nature and relative importance of things. Contemplated from the stillness of eternity, will it not seem *reasonable*, that Napoleon should have bent his giant intellect to solve that great problem which thus flitted faintly and momentarily before him, and passed away forever? In other things, he was so little of a skeptic! A thousand blunders and disasters in war did not conceal from him the possibility of its once more becoming defined and successful, through determination and capacity. Spectacles of poltroonery, corruption, falsehood, unprecedented, perhaps, since the fall of the Roman empire, did not make him skeptical of building up a great, compact, commanding empire. But here he let a whiff of air blow him from the firm land, to drift off on a dark and shoreless sea. Apply his rule generally, and you put a stop to all work, you paralyze the right hand of humanity. All truth comes with difference of opinion; all success is rescued from failure. Generalize from error, and you will believe in no truth: generalize from failure, and you will never stir from the spot on which you stand. But the power of rejecting the generalization of skepticism is the mark of a great practical man; the believer, the hoper, is the man who advances the standard of the race; and this is well enough recognized; only in the case of religion are men apt to accept the skeptical generalization at a glance. Napoleon did not think it worth his while to look: and so it was not given him to catch sight of that one religion, which *does*, like a thread of celestial, imperishable gold, lie along the whole vista of human history.

Levity, however, in passing by this great enquiry, though beyond question indicative of a mind in which the authority of conscience was not duly acknowledged, is not the crime with which it is intended chiefly to charge Napoleon. It is in another application that use is made of the word blasphemy. He was the first potentate who, deliberately disbelieving the Christian religion, yet deliberately took it and made it a stool on which, while seated on his throne, to set his foot. For state purposes, he deliberately and with perfect heedfulness, put into the hand of Christ a sceptre which was but a reed, and set on Him a royal robe recognized as a mockery. Hitherto the Christian religion had not been used as a Cagliostro might use a spectral illusion, or a mystery of sulphur and saltpetre, purely as a sham, entirely for effect. The door of the apartment in which Napoleon worked would be thrown open of a Sunday for a few minutes, while in a farther room, a mass was being said or sung. Next morning, all the papers had it that the emperor had attended divine service. It was an insult to God and man: a lie to earth, a lie to heaven. The practically atheistic character has adhered to the Bonapartist dynasty. That prayer, offered up on occasion of the baptism of the present imperial prince, in which Louis Napoleon and Eugenie, representing magnanimity and charity, were recommended to God as furnishing the model of a perfect character for the scion of the race, was a marvel-

lous intensification of blasphemy; an improvement even on
the stage mass. But is it not a fact to strike one dumb, that
men calling themselves Christian priests have been found
in our time to lend themselves to these performances?

There may be men bold enough, blind enough, or bad
enough, to extenuate or deny Napoleon's guilty unconcern
in the shedding of blood: and to accuse any modern monarch or statesman of blasphemy, in enslaving or insulting
Christianity and its ordinances, has in these days almost
an antiquated look; but no denial or palliation is to be
apprehended in relation to the third great charge to be
brought against Napoleon, that he unhesitatingly and systematically made use of falsehood, that he habitually told
lies. To prove this is entirely superfluous. Its recognition, even in France, is embodied in the phrase, false as a
bulletin; and to exhibit it in the comprehensiveness with
which it applied to all parts of his existence and activity,
to his government, to his war, to his conversation, would
be to pass his whole history in review. He deliberately
took falsehood into his service; he enrolled, as nearly as
possible, the devil in his legion of honor. The central
virtue, the keystone of the moral arch, is truth. The Christian God is the God of truth; and the devil is primarily
and emphatically the father of lies. To say, therefore, that
a man is a liar, is to say that the banner has been in his
case taken from the hand of God's standard-bearer on earth,
conscience, that his moral nature is in anarchy. Mr. Carlyle expressly affirms that Napoleon was a liar; he also
asserts the necessary conformity, nay, the identity, of the
moral and intellectual natures: was Napoleon, then, a fool?
Our literature has gone too far in the direction of paradox
and puzzle.

Such is the result of an inquiry into the character of

Napoleon, keeping specially in view the region presided over by conscience. But the emotional nature is capable of distinction, from the province of conscience on the one hand, and from that of pure intellect on the other. To know, to worship, to love; reason, conscience, charity: these may be said to exhaust the capacities and qualities of man; the will being looked upon as the generalissimo which marshals all the powers of the mind, and brings them out to battle. Napoleon lacked the right imperial mantle, charity.

This is clearly exhibited in the mode in which he extended his conquests over Europe; specially in the way in which he treated prostrate antagonists and nations. So early even as in his Italian campaigns, he had exhibited a dark and perilous implacability in his dealings with Venice. To offend or insult him was, during his whole career, to incur destruction. His wrath might tarry, but that was only because he had a consciousness that it could not cool. His conduct to the Duke of Brunswick and the kingdom of Prussia was that of a nature too stern, cold, unloving. His breast was not wide enough or warm enough for a nobly philanthropic scheme of empire: you would say he rather loved to see the victim writhing under his heel. It may be argued that it was beyond his power really to do anything for Poland: but at all events, faithfully as the Poles served him, no quickening warmth fell over Poland from the cold glimmering of that solitary star.

The bareness of Napoleon's nature, his steelly indifference to the melting touches of human sympathy, is suggested, in a very painful and melancholy manner, by several of his conversations in St. Helena. His declarations that he had loved no one may go for little; perhaps they tell on the other side. But it is appalling to mark how all interest and importance seem to him to concentrate in

himself: how the principal point of eulogy to be conferred
on his very mother appears to be the entireness of her
devotion to him. "Never yet, I believe," he said, "has
there been such devotion shown by soldiers as mine have
manifested for me. In all my misfortunes, never has the
soldier, even when expiring, been wanting to me — never
has man been served more faithfully by his troops. With
the last drop of blood gushing out of their veins, they
exclaimed, *Vive l'Empereur!*" Yet there never seems to
have escaped him a single sentiment of pity for all those
myriads that had died for him. One can imagine, on some
still, sleepless midnight, when the moan of the Atlantic
made the silence seem more deep and melancholy, the soldiers that had died for Napoleon, that had followed him so
faithfully from Montenotte to Beresina, rising before him
for a last review, trooping past in their millions, pale and
shadowy, and casting on him, from those eyes in which
eternity had written its earnestness, an amazed, upbraiding
look. But there is no evidence that he ever conceived
such a look as possible. It seemed right, appropriate, quite
in the order of things, that men and nations should bleed
for him. Humanity recoils from such ghastly self-deifica-
tion. The snow-clad mountain stands alone.

Napoleon was not naturally of an evil nature: nay, when
you glance over his youth, with its manly frankness, its
democratic ardor, its touches of romance, you feel that
naturally he was nobler than all save a few men of that
time. But the greatest and truest nature cannot escape
the influences by which it is surrounded; and the youth
and early manhood of Napoleon were encompassed by
influences that might have chilled the heart of an angel,
and turned to cynicism the openness of a celestial brow.
It was the time when materialistic philosophy and senti-

SECOND SERIES. 19

mental morality had brought out, in fullest manifestation, their dire brood, lust and lies. It is doubtful whether, in any age of paganism, Napoleon would not have met with more to exalt him above self and the present, and to inform him that the world of sight is not, as those vain babblers, singularly satirizing themselves, used to call it, the universe. Everything he saw in public life, except the mere valor of his soldiers in the field, combined to impress him with a contempt for human nature. Traitors, hypocrites, embezzlers, liars, scoundrels — such were the men by whom he knew himself to be surrounded, and whom he yoked to his car of empire with about as much respect as he would have felt for a team of wolves. Barras, by whom he rose, he knew to be utterly dishonest, a coward, a thief; Fouché was, in his own words, "a miscreant of all colors;" from Talleyrand and Sieyes down to Barrere, there was no man, or hardly one, whom he could esteem. With the whole spiritual universe representing itself to him as a doubt, a triviality, a matter to be laughed at or sniffed lightly aside, and with the world of man awakening only his contempt, was it so much to be wondered at that his nature cased itself in ice, that he became the friendless, unloving being, who saw in men only his tools, and for whom there was no God but his star?

The most cursory glance at the leading events which preceded and accompanied the fall of Napoleon, will show that it was this incompleteness, this bareness of strength, this self-worship, which was the radical cause of his ruin. But it must not be forgotten that his rule brought with it benefits. It did so, not merely to France but to Europe. Capacity is always of a value, of a beneficence, which may be pronounced incalculable. The man of power has an instinctive pleasure in doing work well and seeing it well done; apart from obstructing influences, it is natural for intellect to produce ᵗthoroughness and excellence, as it is natural for the stream to bear the barge, or the wind to purify the atmosphere; and in spite of opposing selfishness both the instinct and the fact were illustrated in the history of Napoleon. It is a circumstance, not to be too profoundly pondered, that France was in a more discontented, turbulent, poverty-stricken, every way miserable condition, under the innocent Louis XVI, than under Napoleon. And but a few months since, Count Cavour informed Europe, that the Italian provinces of Napoleon had, under his rule, enjoyed an equality of law, and a general prosperity, such as they have not enjoyed under Austria. There may be an infinite remove between the best despotism and a low species of freedom; but the despotism of imbecility is the most woeful calamity that can fall upon the human race. Colossal intellectual power, unaided by love, unguarded by virtue, was the essential characteristic both of Napoleon and his empire; it was not good, yet not the worst.

The coronation took place in the close of 1804. The power and glory of Bonaparte had not, however, culminated. His ambition was only awakening.

In 1805, after overthrowing Mack, at Ulm, he advanced towards the north with the armies of Austria in flight before him. Vienna opened her gates. Massena drove the Archduke Charles from Italy. In the month of November, Napoleon was drawing towards Austerlitz, where the emperors of Austria and Russia, with their combined army, dared at last to await him. The story of the wily Carthaginian, opposing the invisible might of his genius, to the vast material power, and blundering courage of the Roman, and luring him on to the tremendous catastrophe of Cannæ, must occur to one who marks Napoleon, leading on the emperors towards the fearful snare of Austerlitz. And is it not the Napoleon of Italy we see, as that figure passes on horseback along the lines at midnight, to see that all is ready for the morning, an hour's sleep by a watch-fire having first refreshed the imperial soldier?

The victory of Austerlitz laid Austria prostrate before Napoleon; and when he returned to France, vassal thrones, filled by the Napoleon kindred, had begun to twinkle here and there over Europe.

The year 1806 saw another nation overcome. It was against Prussia that the flight of the irresistible eagles was this time directed. Bewildering the Prussian king and his generals, by the novelty and rashness of his combinations, by the breathless speed of his assaults, Napoleon brought the force of the kingdom finally to bay at Jena; and shattered it to fragments. Here again, we have a glimpse of the incomparable, indomitable worker, whose brain neither victory nor ambition seemed able to heat. His heavy train had not arrived, and the battle was to take place next morning. But the eye of Napoleon, seeing what it brought with it the power of seeing, fell upon a rocky plateau, on which no one had ever thought of placing guns, but on which even a few would have an extraordinary effect. He became in a moment the artillery officer of Toulon. He set his men to cut a road for the guns through the rocks, encouraged them by the offer of large sums of gold for every piece brought into position, and spent the whole night among them superintending the work. The victory of Jena was the reward. This " child of fortune " was of that petulant, overbearing kind, which force the fickle mother to take them in her arms.

Two circumstances of evil omen have to be noticed at this point.

The first is that display of imperiousness, insolence, and cruelty, exhibited towards the royal family and the people of Prussia, as well as every one who dared to counteract his projects, which at this time instilled into the breast of the German race that exasperation, that rage, that sense of injustice and insult, with which it came fixedly to regard Napoleon, and which, bursting at length into flame, proved unquenchable.

The second is the promulgation of the Berlin decrees, which took place during his short residence at Berlin in 1806, and corresponded with that of the decrees of Milan. These famous edicts instituted the continental system of Napoleon, one of his darling schemes, and illustrating, even though based in an erroneous idea, the decision and comprehensiveness of that extraordinary mind. With that piercing sagacity which distinguished him, he had seen into the fact, that the only European power which presented to him a front really and wholly unassailable, was Great Britain. By one of those magnificent strokes in which the drama of nature surpasses, in boldness of contrast and gorgeousness of decoration, the drama of fiction, Napoleon was made aware almost at the same moment, of the victory of Austerlitz and the defeat of Trafalgar. It was as if the sun had risen full and bright, touching his diadem with brighter gold; and on the instant, from the opposite quarter of the heavens, the levin brand had leapt out, and scorched half his crown into blackness. He perceived that England could not be attacked by sea. The only hope was to attack her by land. And the mode in which he concluded this was to be done was determined by his conception of the cause of British greatness.

He imagined the power and wealth of Britain to depend wholly on the sea; that she resembled Tyre, Carthage,

Venice, and the other maritime powers.   This was a mistake.   Tyre, Carthage, and Venice became great through
mercantile talent and advantage of situation.   They possessed, within themselves, no other natural centres of wealth
and population.   Their position, therefore, was precarious.
But Great Britain is *by nature* a rich country, and would
remain thickly peopled though the rest of the world were
ocean or desert.   It possesses within it more rich and
varied sources of natural wealth, more numerous centres
of population, than perhaps any equal space on the face of
the earth.   A fruitful soil, iron, coal, wood: these make
her independent of other lands.   She strikes her huge tap-
roots among the iron and coal, far beneath the surface of
the sea.   Of this Napoleon had no idea.   He believed that
if he ruined her commerce, he ruined herself.   And how
did he propose to ruin her commerce?   By a method which
might certainly have checked a portion of her export trade;
but which flung back civilization itself on the continent of
Europe; and inflicted intolerable hardship on the European
nations.   He proposed to close every continental market
against British produce.   In order to weaken the mercantile navy of Great Britain, and produce some clamors among
her people, for no more than this could he effect, he demanded the sacrifice of nearly the whole commercial navies
of the continent, and brought upon the populations of the
several countries extreme distress.   It seems never to have
dawned upon him that there is in trade a precise equation,
a geometrical balance, which it is absurd even in imagination to suppose unequal.   *Why* does nation trade with
nation?   Because *each* is advantaged.   Buyer and seller
are, and must be, convertible terms.   The buyer wants, and
comes where he can find; the seller has, and sells; by degrees the seller brings the goods which are wanted to the

door of the buyer; and that is an export trade. Napoleon
made war upon the sellers of England; but most of these
could go elsewhere, or have their goods consumed at home;
he made war also and equally upon the buyers of Europe;
which brought such oppression and calamity over the various countries, that they groaned under his shadow as under
the shadow of death. History does not show a more express or instructive exhibition, of the bearing of one kind
of knowledge upon another, of the danger in great practical undertakings, or the formation of great theories, of
ignorance of the great fundamental laws which govern *any*
province of human affairs.

The year 1808 is signalized, in the history of Napoleon,
by the opening of what he himself named the Spanish
ulcer. In spite of the objections which were to be urged,
on grounds of political expediency, to an interference in
Spanish affairs, objections which did not escape Fouché
and Talleyrand, it may be considered doubtful, whether to
mere intellectual perception, the impolicy of the measure
was obvious. It was of the highest importance to Napoleon to reduce to utter humiliation every branch of the
house of Bourbon. His views on England required the
command of the whole sea-coast of Europe. The heroic
resistance of the Spanish people could hardly have been
anticipated. Most important of all, no sign had appeared
on the horizon, unless, indeed, Napoleon had happened to
turn his eye on Assaye in the far East, to indicate that
Britain possessed a general able to contend with the imperial marshals; while the irresolution and incapacity of the
British administration of the war made it natural to conclude that, except on one element, its opposition could not
be formidable. Historical fact corresponds with this view
of the case. The Spanish conquest might be considered

complete, when Wellington appeared with untrammelled powers, on the scene. It was with great difficulty that the latter managed to work his way to free and resolute action, through the terror of military superiors, overawed, seemingly, like all Europe, by the fame of the French troops, and through the apprehensions of London aldermen, who thought this fiery and reckless young general was going to ruin everything. As soon as it became evident that Britain too possessed one of the select warriors of human history, the Spanish ulcer became indeed a serious matter. But this was hidden in the future. Meanwhile one thing only was evident; — that the treachery and usurpation of Napoleon's dealings with Spain were an infraction of the eternal laws of conscience and of mercy, a deliberate and stupendous sin. He did not *see* how this should work his woe; he did not *perceive* that he was sowing the wind; intellect was wide awake; but there came no word from conscience to hint that this was baleful seed: it was sown; and the unexpected whirlwind came.

The affairs of Spain seeming in a prosperous condition, Napoleon turned again northwards. In the spring of 1809, Austria declared war. The campaign which followed was attended with the same success as had marked all Napoleon's wars with the house of Hapsburg. Never did the genius of the great soldier shine forth more conspicuously. War was declared on the sixth of April. Napoleon's armies were comparatively few, and lying dangerously apart. But as if at the waving of a magician's wand, they came together, and bore down upon the enemy. On the twentieth of the month, there was one defeat; on the twenty-first, another; on the twenty-second, the army of the Archduke Charles, 100,000 strong, was utterly broken and routed. This was the victory of Eckmühl. The conqueror again entered Vienna. On the sixth of July was won the crowning victory of Wagram. War had been declared precisely three months before; and now the great Austrian monarchy lay once more, powerless and gasping, at the feet of the terrible soldier. Prussia and the whole German land had heard the sound of war on the Danube, with a listening and surmise, of awe and apprehension not unmingled with hope. As a victim in the swoon of death, catching sounds of attempted rescue, might show a heaving of the breast and a quivering of muscle, the nation gave here and there a sign of life and awakening: but as that victim, at the sight of the murderer's knife, reeking with new gore, and in the glance of his eye lit with new triumph, might sink back into stupor, so it drew one deep sigh and settled back into submission. The conviction sank deep into the mind of Europe that this Napoleon was actually invincible.

Nor can this result excite surprise. If you follow the career of this wonderful man, from Montenotte to Wagram, if you watch the flight of his eagles from the pyramids to the Niemen, if you estimate the genius displayed in the campaign of Marengo, in the campaign of Austerlitz, in the campaign of Jena, in the campaign of Friedland, in the campaign of Wagram, you pause in awe and astonishment at the unexampled spectacle. In these ages there has been no such display of the strange and magnificent energy of mind vanquishing material difficulty.

The greatness and glory of Napoleon now reached their point of culmination. Allied to the royal house of Austria, with none north of the Pyrenees daring to lift up a hand against him, with vassal kings on this hand and on that, an army habituated to conquer at his absolute command, and a king of Rome slumbering on his knee, he seemed placed be-

yond the shafts of fortune, on the last glittering peak of
human attainment. This was in 1810. Fifteen years before,
he had been the unnoticed artillery officer, his idea of happiness, a decent house in Paris and a cabriolet, with only
here and there a piercing eye to discern that under the
soiled uniform there lurked one of the immortals.

But his fall was sudden, headlong, irretrievable.

Napoleon had begun himself to be the prey of that fierce
passion, that intense steady-burning ambition, which had
already made so fair a portion of the world its prey. He
had not hitherto found empire the pledge of happiness.
As his ambition strengthened, his brow had darkened and
his eye filled with a more stern and anxious earnestness.
He was not now that Napoleon who had addressed the
army of Italy, his eye clear and bright, hope and victory
on his crest. Ambition and empire had marked themselves
on his brow in lines of care. It seems one of nature's
grand appointments, that all wild, distempered things take
a garment of gloom, of sadness; that peace, health, and
beauty dwell together. The light announces its presence
in a smile diffused over the whole face of nature: but the
samiel wraps itself in the purple mist of the desert: and
it is in the lurid cloud that the electric spark lies hid. Napoleon's ambition had passed all healthy stages; at each
draught of the maddening chalice, his thirst had become
greater; and now, beneath his imperial diadem, his eye
cast a troubled and ominous glare. It seems probable that,
at this time, the thought of universal dominion actually
had hold upon his mind. At all events, there was still one
thorn which pierced him to the heart. Britain still defied
him. One power remained which had never trembled at
his name or done him the least obeisance. The bitterness
of the pang which this knowledge occasioned was rendered

more intense by a slight but galling mixture of apprehension. He could not feel his very throne secure, until this enemy, of boundless wealth, of indomitable pertinacity, and whose supreme maritime dominion made it impossible for him with all his power to do so much as throw ten thousand men from Italy to Sicily, was effectually humbled. In one last continental struggle, he would overwhelm Russia, and then, having crippled Great Britain by the operation of the Berlin and Milan decrees, he would bring all the fleets and armies of Europe, to annihilate, at one fell swoop, the power and independence of the contumacious Island.

Russia was ready for war. The Austrian match had damped the cordiality which had long subsisted between the Czar and the Emperor. The continental system was becoming intolerable. The gradual confirmation and extension of the power of Napoleon on the Polish territory was looked upon with apprehension. Enough: the Czar was prepared for hostilities. In the summer of 1812, Napoleon concentrated his armies for the great Russian expedition.

Much has been said, and perhaps somewhat vaguely, on the subject of the Russian campaign, and the particular error committed by Napoleon in engaging in it or carrying it on. He trusted presumptuously in fate; he entered into conflict with the elements; and so on. Not at all. He looked as cautiously after the helping of fate now, as he had done at Friedland, or Eckmühl. "I was," he said to O'Meara in St. Helena, "a few days too late — I had made a calculation of the weather for fifty years before, and the extreme cold had never commenced until about the 20th of December, twenty days later than it began this time." That man left nothing to fate. His intellect was still clear. This early setting in of the cold was the first great cause, in his own belief, of the failure of the Russian attempt; the second was the burning of Moscow. Human prescience could have anticipated neither.

The truth is, Napoleon committed one great error in this Russian expedition, and, so far as appears, but one. He did not preserve his rear; he did not secure his retreat. If you look closely into his former campaigns, you find, with the exception, perhaps, of Marengo, no battle which does not exhibit the most cautious circumspection in securing a retreat. He fell back instantly, though seemingly on the way to victory, if, as at Aspern, his communications in the rear were broken. He always made it a grand object to cut off the retreat of his antagonist; once he had his enemy in a position where defeat was ruin, he attacked with confidence as one sure of an outwitted prey. In St. Helena, he charged the Duke of Wellington with defective generalship at Waterloo, because, as he alleged, the allied army had no means of retreat. But now his own retreat was insecure: defeat was destruction. He passed across Europe towards the north, accompanied not by the blessings and good wishes, but by the suppressed indignation and muttered curses, of its peoples. Fear and amazement guarded his throne, not love and seemly reverence. No human being is strong enough to despise these. Men now watched him with eyes of menace, and with right hands on the hilt. Disaffection had spread deep and far. His imperiousness, his insolent haughtiness, had turned against him even Bernadotte to whom he had given his baton, even Lucien who had served him so well, even the vassal kings on whom he conferred a humiliating grandeur. France was becoming weary and sick at heart; even glory became cold in its glittering, when there seemed to be no end of war, and when it might almost be said that in every house there was one dead. He took with him, too, his Grand Army, his old invincibles, that would so proudly die for him; and who could never be replaced. To all or almost all this, he was blinded. The greatest and most important part of it arose from moral causes and *so* escaped him.

The story of the Russian campaign is the most solemn and tragic in the annals of modern warfare, if not in the whole history of war. No poet of these times, so far as one may judge, has possessed a power necessary to its poetic delineation. Perhaps in their very highest moments, Coleridge, Shelley, or Byron might have caught certain of its tints of gloom and grandeur; now and then, a tone of melody from Mrs. Browning's harp may reach the epic height of its sublimity. But he who depicted the woe of Othello and the madness of Lear, and he who described the march of the rebel angels to the north along the plains of heaven, might have joined their powers to bring out, in right poetic representation, the whole aspects of the Russian campaign. Perhaps it may lie among those subjects for which common life affords no precedent, and common language no words. And, indeed, no description seems necessary. The poetry of nature, in its weird colors and deep, dark, rhythmic harmonies, is already there ; we have but to open our eyes and contemplate it. Those brave soldiers, those dauntless, devoted veterans, those children of victory, swift as eagles, fearless as lions, who had charged on the dikes of Arcola, and hailed the sun of Austerlitz, who were the very embodiment of wild southern valor, following Napoleon, the son of the lightning, beneath the dim vault of the northern winter, there to lay their fire-hearts under that still, pale winding-sheet of snow, the northern blast singing over them its song of stern and melancholy triumph : what could be more sublime poetry than that? It is simple fact. Then, how grandly is the darkness broken, as those flames touch all the clouds with angry crimson, and a great people, thrilling with a heroic emotion, lays in ashes its ancient cities rather than yield them up to an invader. Worthy flowers to be cast by a nation in the way of that emperor! "It was the spectacle," said Napoleon in St. Helena, alluding to the conflagration of Moscow, "It was the spectacle of a sea and billows of fire, a sky and clouds of flame ; mountains of red rolling flames, like immense waves of the sea, alternately bursting forth and elevating themselves to skies of fire, and then sinking into the ocean of flame below. Oh, it was the most grand, the most sublime and the most terrific sight the world ever beheld !" A sublime sight indeed ; it were difficult to name one more sublime : unless it were the sight of *him* describing it, a hopeless captive in that lonely isle.

It is needless to linger on the closing scenes of the imperial drama. The events of the campaigns of 1813 and 1814 have been already fore-shadowed. Europe rose upon Napoleon, like a bristling lion, gnashing its teeth in fury and hatred. Men who had followed him in the field, or had acted under his order, who had learned to guess, not at any particular kind of tactics, but at the working of his mind, were arrayed against him. Bernadotte and Moreau did more to vanquish him than all the generals of the coalition. His combinations and designs were anticipated, and only by combinations could he hope to contend against those overwhelming odds. France beheld his disaster with the indifference of exhaustion. It was a case in which no conceivable power of intellect or resolution could have availed him. Yet in his whole career there is no period in

which his genius and character were more strikingly displayed, in which our wonder and admiration more constantly attend him.   Even the hosts that were overpowering him paid him the most expressive tribute.   They feared
to meet himself.   The conviction was immovable, that
some mystic character of invincibility attached to him individually.   Nor was the belief unreasonable ; in hardly
any case did he actually come into collision with his foes,
without their retiring, bleeding and discomfited, from his
terrible gripe.   But even victory was fatal to him; his
antagonists could afford more blood in defeat than he in
victory.   And wherever he was not himself present, they
were victorious.

Napoleon has been severely reprehended for the blind
and dogged obstinacy with which he clung to empire and
prolonged a hopeless conflict.   It were difficult to obviate
these reprehensions.   And yet is it easy to resist a feeling
of sympathy with that unconquerable spirit, as those enemies, whom, severally, he had so often vanquished, bore
down upon him together ?   It was an epic ending.   So
dauntless, so indomitable did he·stand, firm as adamant to
the last :—

> Like a statue thunder-struck,
> Which, though quivering, seems to look
> Right against the thunder-place.

Of Elba, and the brief meteoric gleam of the hundred
days, it is needless to speak.   Napoleon had fallen, and, in
the Europe of 1815, it was impossible to rise.

So he was borne over the ocean to St. Helena.   There
he remained; on his death-bed: for he died day by day,
during those weary and mournful years.   Sad it is to mark
that royal mind preying on itself, the old irresistible ener-

gies eating away their own case. One could weep for the
hero of Toulon and Lodi, the victor of Rivoli and Wagram,
the mightiest emperor since Charlemagne, bickering there
about names and shadows with Sir Hudson Lowe. But
sympathy must not degenerate into sentimentality; a reasonable compassion will buttress itself on the strength of
fact. Napoleon's idea of empire was behind the age; not
Christian; outraging those instincts, which, even with Christianity abjured in name, cannot wholly leave the hearts of
once Christian nations.   That old conception of Atlas, one
stupendous giant upholding the earth, was not the highest:
the world is sustained by the chains of gravitation, wrap-
ping it all around, and more invisible than the sunbeams.
The progress of humanity is *from* the pyramid; towards
the cottage.

Of the general result of the Napoleonic wars, and the
bearing of the first empire on the progress of civilization,
there is not much to be said. Regarding the course of
determined opposition taken, throughout, by Great Britain,
and at last adopted by the government, and far more nobly
by the people of Russia, a fair and deliberate investigation
leaves no room for two opinions.   That men should court
platform effect, by ringing changes on the expenditure in-
curred by Great Britain in the restoration of the Bourbons,
that men, not desirous of producing any such effect, but
biassed by particular opinions, should yield assent to the
same view, this is conceivable and natural enough; but
that men professedly despising popular opinion, men of
piercing insight and accurate knowledge, should give in to
so empty a common-place, should speak of Britain as struggling, during those years, to suppress the French revolution,
or any "fact" of the kind, is truly wonderful. Britain
made peace with a revolutionary government: that is a

fact; and it settles the question. England would all along have been too glad to cultivate pacific relations with any cabinet in Paris, which did not threaten the total overturn of European relations and its own national existence. The Bourbons were not restored at the peace of Amiens: it was not for their restoration that Britain again took arms and fought on till the peace of Vienna. Britain made war against that great enemy, the inmost desire of whose soul was her subjugation. Warring for nothing, warring for the suppression of the French Revolution, designed in whatsoever councils! The coasts of France were lined with armies ready to land on Britain; the bays of France were covered with vessels to bring them across: and to the last day of his life, it was the deliberate belief of Napoleon, that the attack might have been successful. Great Britain played in those years a noble part, and one from which it would have been cowardice and infatuation to shrink: it is not seemly for the next generation after that which fought the long, stern battle, to begin to sneer! Since the wars of Marlborough, there has been no such epic period in the history of England. And in the magnificent prosperity which has attended her since, there may be found the natural reward of her constancy and courage.

It is not so easy, it seems, indeed, impossible, to discern how the Napoleonic empire has aided in the evolution of right civilization, what place it occupies in the scheme of a beneficent Providence. The cycles of the world are slow. Divine purposes may come to light after many days, which for the present are shrouded in darkness. But hitherto there appears to be little result from all that bloodshed; the battle-field of Europe has not yet grown green. Grant that the fetters of caste have been broken, that a certain social equality has been realized on the continent, that the

20*

French Revolution occasioned and the power of Napoleon
secured these things. Is not, nevertheless, the aspect of
European civilization, nay in some respects the aspect of
universal civilization, gloomy and discouraging? Despotism, dark, strong, humiliating despotism, reigning on the
continent; the brain of Europe, its free intellectual and
moral power, smitten by that baleful enchantment, the arm
of Europe, its industrial energy, fettered and constrained:
Jesuitism, following Despotism, shedding pestilence where
there already is night : — such is the literal spectacle
presented by the continent.   Freedom is indeed still in
vigor, nay, in nascent vigor, in Britain and America.   But
do these great peoples fully understand and accept their
mission?   Do they unite to proclaim to mankind the blessing and the glory of that liberty by which they are distinguished?   Do their mutual intelligence, their sympathy,
their brave co-operation, woven together into one bow of
peace, striding from shore to shore of the Atlantic, write
in characters of power and beauty the vindication of freedom?   The answer cannot be wholly affirmative.

VII.

PLATO.

CASTING a rapid glance over the generations of mankind, in their path over the stage of time to the stillness of eternity, we discern, for the most part, but a general, confused company, marching steadily on, undistinguishable save in the mass; as when we see a host in the distance, the individuals are lost in the general body, and we can discern with distinctness only a few, the leaders and standard-bearers of the army; round these, the various battalions are ranged, and march under their banners. One of the greatest of these standard-bearers we mean at present, for a brief space, to contemplate.

The assertion that history and biography are one, we must pronounce an error. That history is the condensation or essence of countless biographies, we must also, whatever Mr. Emerson says, declare erroneous. Biography treats of the individual; history treats of the mass; and the laws which govern each are diverse. This we can at present stay neither to prove at length, nor to unfold in detail; but remark that there is, in the oft-repeated observation touching the identity of history and biography, such an approach to truth, as to account for, and render plausible, the error. Biography and history are intimately, all but inextricably, intertwined. There can be no doubt that

every great thought which has struck new life into the
veins of universal man has been uttered by some individual man; that, in the case of the unfolding of every banner
round which the nations have clustered and marched, the
proud honor of having upreared it can be claimed by some
one among the sons of men. Biography in each case asks,
"What was it which the individual did?" History in each
case asks, "How was the mass of men affected by his
thought or action?" Individual great men are to history
representative ciphers, by which she denotes certain moving
powers of thought or action; national movements are to
biography certain great expressive hieroglyphics, by which
she calculates the force of her individual great men. If
philosophical precision is to be sought at all, they must be
kept distinct. Intimately connected truly they are; twin
sisters, looking on each other with the kindliest smile, both
feeding the lamp of knowledge, but pouring their pure oil
from different vessels.

The task we propose to ourselves at present partakes
both of history and of biography: we desire approximately
to ascertain the distinctive characteristics of the man we
survey, and to trace his influence upon mankind; to appre-
hend, in a general way, both the mass and momentum of
the force which first caused commotion in the stream of
time, and to trace the widening ripples it occasioned.

In the widest distinction, men may be divided into thinkers and actors. Not that thought does not swiftly array
itself in armor, and grasp the weapons of action; and not
that action is ever effective without a viewless steam power
of thought, setting the mechanism in motion; but that the
two great classes of men — whom we represent, on the one
side, by the Platos, the Homers, the Solons, the Shakspeares,
the Newtons; and, on the other, by the Alexanders, the

Cæsars, the Charlemagnes, the Cromwells, and the Napoleons — are set in marked contrast to each other, and present themselves in very different aspects to the eye of the biographer or historian. Nay more, their effects upon the destinies of men are different and distinct in certain grand characteristics. And we may, in passing, hazard the remark, that in our day, while the effect of great thinkers upon human history has been most ably and eloquently exhibited, the effect of great actors has been exhibited with far less adequacy and correctness.

There is but one other remark which we deem it necessary to make, ere proceeding to our subject; namely, that our space utterly prohibits anything like detail or minute portraiture. Our treatment of the questions which we may pass in review must be general. We trust that it shall not, therefore, be vague or valueless; the widest truths are always the most general, and are useless only where they have not their roots soundly imbedded in the particular, and so cease to be truths.

Plato was the greatest thinker of antiquity; he was probably the greatest reflective thinker of all time. Opinions have varied exceedingly regarding him, and, save in great leading characteristics, the student of his works will find difficulty in discerning the features of his philosophy; but all men regard him as the grandest embodiment which the ages have afforded, of one great phase of human thought, and recognize him likewise as the culminating point of that historical epoch in which this phase of the human mind found, perhaps, its most imposing development, the era of Greek philosophy. Plato and Aristotle are the two sages who lead the two great divisions of philosophic thinkers through all time. But Aristotle was the pupil of Plato, and the critic of his system; and even while we accord all

honor to the Stagyrite, we can say that Plato was the centre
figure of Greek speculation, that he made all who went before his teachers, and that all who came after were, with more
or less of intelligence and originality, his pupils. And this
fact at once and directly leads us to our proper mode of
procedure on the present occasion; our task shapes itself
into the discussion of two questions, the one biographic,
the other historic. Respecting Plato himself we ask, What
were the distinguishing characteristics of his mind and of
his thought? Respecting the philosophy he represented
— the distinctive Platonic, as distinguished from the Aris-
totelian phase of Grecian philosophy — we ask, What was
the part it played in human history, and in what light are
we now to regard it as a prospective agency?

Plato was born 430 B. C., in Ægina, an island in the
Saronic Gulf, between Attica and Argolis; or in Athens,
for there is a diversity of opinion. His father's name was
Ariston, his mother's Perictione, and his own Aristocles.
He obtained a Greek education. This is saying much. It
implies that every faculty of the intellect, every emotion
of the heart, and every capacity of the physical frame, was
duly exercised. He excelled in gymnastics; he wrote poetry
in his youth, of which some fragments yet remain; and is
reported to have composed an epic, which he committed
to the flames, on seeing its inferiority to the work of Homer.
He studied rhetoric and music.

But the light which was to rivet his eye unchangeably
had not yet dawned upon him. He was still a young man,
not above twenty, when he heard Socrates; but his destiny, both for himself and for mankind, was thereby and
at once fixed. He devoted himself to the search after
truth.

The effect of the teaching of Socrates upon the philosophic mind of Greece is clearly definable. Cousin pronounces him to have given it an irresistible impulse in the direction of reflection; he turned it inward: he made thought the king of the world and philosophy subjective. This is true, and perhaps the whole truth; but we neglect a very important element in the Socratic influence, if we overlook the tremendous earnestness with which Socrates sought for truth, the rapt religious devotion with which he sacrificed everything at her shrine, the elevating moral influence he exerted. By the joint endeavors of Grote and Lewes, we may presume that we have now reached the truth concerning the sophists: they were the public, and of course paid educators of Greece, and they were the embodiment of what may be called the morality of polite Greek society. Higher than this they did not go; lower than this it were unfair to place them. But Socrates came forth to voice the holier and intrinsically the more powerful, although too truly the ever-obstructed sympathy, which burns in the human breast, for truth itself, truth pure and abstract, truth arrayed in the unsullied white of heaven, and alluring by no spangle or gold of earth. Truth, he proclaimed, was to be sought for its own sake; and the method by which it was to be sought, was what in its widest sense may be embraced in the term conversation. This conversation, dialectic, might be either audible or inaudible; it might proceed either in the public school-room or in the private chambers of the soul; in either case it proceeded by definition and division, by searching scrutiny and discrimination of the true from the false or irrelevant. The great soul of Plato was at once charmed by the words of Socrates; under the rugged, repulsive form of the dogged, irresistible arguer, he discerned the hallowed and searching fire that is immortally noble, and irresistibly attractive to

the noble: as if his past life had been but a dream or a
May-game, he abandoned everything for philosophy, for
truth. Not that anything became excluded, but that everything attained a new relation. The sun was set in his
system, a retinue of worlds might circle round it, but every
one that could not be bound and regulated by its influence
must fly away.

For ten years Plato was the disciple of Socrates. At
the death of his master, whom he vainly endeavored to
save, he travelled into various lands, and investigated the
doctrines of many philosophers: he abode first for a time
in Megara, passed thence to Cyrene, thence to Egypt, and,
after accumulating what may in general terms be called the
whole knowledge of his time, returned to Greece. He
opened his school of philosophy in the immortal Academy.
He was then about forty years of age. He visited Syracuse three times; on returning from the first visit, he was
sold for a slave, but bought by Annicus of Cyrene, and set
free: he died at the age of eighty-three, and continued
writing, it is said, to the very last.

On the subject of the travels of Plato, there has been
much exaggeration and misrepresentation: for our own
part, we cannot regard it as anywise improbable that he
should push his researches in the east; and the remark of
Numenius the Pythagorean, quoted by the writer on Plato
in the "Encyclopædia Britannica," "What is Plato but
Moses in Attic Greek?" is certainly a strange one: but
we deem the subject of slight importance, since the great
fact is unquestioned, that Plato embraced in his own mind
all that previous or contemporary philosophers could afford
him.

And this unfolds to us one great aspect of the mind of
Plato, conveying an important lesson to all men of all ages,

and perhaps with special emphasis to the men of this hasty, feverish time. For ten years, between the age of twenty and thirty, he sat at the feet of Socrates; for what we may, speaking roundly, call other ten years, he walked over the world, seeking knowledge wherever it was to be found; and then, with a majesty, becoming one to whom all generations were to listen, he returned to Athens, and opened his mouth under the plane-trees of the grove of Academus. This power of waiting, this silent, dauntless search, not after originality but after truth, showed the intrinsic soundness and strength of the soul of Plato. The grandest originality, too, is thus always won: it takes the arms of a giant, a Titan giant, to bear unswerving a world; our own Milton never staggered under his learning, and Plato bore all his with the calmness of commanding strength.

He is recorded to have been very-melancholy. "Plato," says Lewes, whose notice in his "History of Philosophy" is a good introduction, though only such, to the study of the great philosopher — "Plato was intensely melancholy. That great, broad brow, which gave him his surname, was wrinkled and sombre. Those brawny shoulders were bent with thought, as only those of thinkers are bent. A smile was the utmost that ever played over 'his lips; he never laughed. 'As sad as Plato,' became a phrase with the comic dramatists." This melancholy is suggestive of much. Plato had looked abroad over mankind, had grappled with the problems of thought, had witnessed the degraded, prostrate state of the world. He found the intellect of man weak, he saw the majority of men wretched, he beheld passion, often almost brutalized, ruling men. While, therefore, he fixed his eye upon truth and immortality, that eye was shaded by a cloud of sorrow and of doubt. It was no misanthropic egotism that made Plato sad; like the crowned

sage of Israel, he saw that all around him was vanity, and
that men would pursue only vanity. He discerned clearly,
though it might be that he could not give definite expression to that under a sense of which he labored, the fallen
state of humanity. This will appear more obviously in the
sequel, but of the fact we are perfectly assured. That is a
most striking and suggestive passage in the "Republic,"
where he speaks of the sowing of virtue in an unkindly
soil, and the corruption, by malignant influences, of what
is best in human nature into what is worst: it seems to us
pointedly and mournfully applicable, as we may be permitted with a slight anticipation to remark, to his whole philosophy. It is not enough that truth be sown by the hand of
man or angel upon our bleak, ungenial world; there is not
depth or richness of soil to nourish its roots, there is not
purity or balminess of atmosphere to bring gently out into
fulness of beauty its heavenly blossoms. The hand of
"some god" must guard it. So Plato felt; so Christianity
says. Well enough to talk of the beauty of truth and the
resistless charm that dwells in her eye: truth is a light that
shines through a cloudy atmosphere, and the hand of God
must be stretched out from heaven to put the clouds aside,
ere men can fully or clearly see it. Nay, even when they
see it, their weak eyeballs, as Plato magnificently says in
his myth of the cave, cannot look upon it fixedly. In fact,
Plato saw the great struggle that goes on in the history
and heart of man: there is a sympathy and a profound one
for the true, the good, the beautiful, and so there is truth
in the assertion, that if men saw virtue, they would fall
down and worship it: but there are also other sympathies,
which supplement the former, and compel us to admit the
humiliating fact, that men cannot look upon pure truth or
pure virtue undazzled. Plato discerned both facts and

the unaided human intellect could do no more : a greater
than Plato was required to cast more light upon the subject.

Plato was, in person, a strong man, but had a weak voice.
He was never married. He lived in a region above not
only the popular morality and mythology of the age, but
above the vast majority of men in all ages. With tremendous strength of will, he bent his mind to the continual
contemplation of truth. Below him rolled the turbid
streams of mundane passion 'and endeavor. As he dwelt
alone in that lofty and silent dwelling of thought,

> " Far off he seem'd to hear the dully sound
> Of human footsteps fall."

In his youth, his bosom had been filled with human sympathies, which had voiced themselves in passionate melody,
and, with all his remorseless dialectics, we believe his mind
to have been radically of the poetic type; but his eye
caught the gleam of truth, and, irresistibly fascinated by
the sight, he compelled his buoyant, exuberant genius to

> " Braid his golden locks by Wisdom's side,"

and walk submissively through life, as her humble servant.
All else he scorned with the true philosophic pride. Di-
onysius, who had caused him to be sold as a slave, trembling for his miserable reputation, hoped Plato would not
speak ill of him; Plato "had not leisure to think of Diony-
sius." Yet sadness, as we said, descended on his brow;
for the state of man was melancholy, and he himself could
not but discern that philosophy could not scale the walls
of mystery which girdle humanity: gazing ever upward
with wistful eye, he still saw

" The sacred morning spread,
The silent summit overhead,"

and felt, however indistinctly, that he was not

" Nearer to the light
Because the scale is infinite."

He looked to death as the gate of entrance to the abode
of pure truth, and life was valuable only as it was used by
reason in unveiling the realities which lay shrouded under
phenomena.

The grand characteristics of Plato's system of thought
can be discriminated with sufficient accuracy, and it is to
these we must restrict ourselves. We obtain insight into
the whole, by considering his idea of knowledge, and the
method by which that knowledge was to be attained.

The knowledge of sensation is varying, and not to be
relied on; sensation gives us the many, and philosophers
must seek the one; there is a " type of perfect in his
mind," which man can find nowhere in visible nature; the
knowledge of sense is phenomenal, spectral, merely representative; for true knowledge we must turn to reason : so
said Plato.   Hence arose his world-famous theory of ideas.
These ideas were the original perfect types of things, existing, whether independent of God or not, in a region
superior to this world.   Lewes, with a very happy and
exquisite ingenuity, supposes the objective existence of
ideas to have been merely the exercise, in the province of
philosophy, of the strong tendency of the Greek mind to
project its conceptions into realities; that general terms
were formed by Plato, as by all other philosophers and
men, and that their independent existence was simply an
act of creative imagination.   Be this as it may, the fact

is certain, that Plato distinctly enunciates the separate existence of the ideal types of which things are copies; and that this is the central point of his whole philosophy. Knowledge, then, with Plato, meant the perception, in whatever way, of ideas, of the perfect and unchanging types which phenomena bodied forth. To use the words of a very able writer on the subject, "Plato, like a writer of our own time, regarded philosophy as an undressing of the world, as the means of discovering the certainty and the eternity, which are in this world hidden and wrapped up in the garb of the mutable and the temporal."

Such being the theory of knowledge entertained by Plato, how was this knowledge to be attained? The question at once introduces us to his doctrine of reminiscence. The human soul, in a previous state of existence, visited the region of ideas, and the whole object of philosophy is to recall the images seen there. And how can this be done? By reason, aided by sense, or, more strictly, acting upon the information afforded by sense. The phenomena of sense convey somewhat of truth, but, by their multiplicity, diversity, and deviation from the original type, are apt to mislead: sense must submit to reason; dialectic, the exercise of thought by the scrutinizing philosopher, leads to true knowledge. Plato excluded poets from his "Republic," but we imagine he would have listened to the following words of our great reflective poet: —

> "Our birth is but a sleep and a forgetting:
> The soul that rises with us, our life's star,
> Hath had elsewhere its setting,
> And cometh from afar:
> Not in entire forgetfulness,
> And not in utter nakedness,
> But trailing clouds of glory do we come,
> From God who is our home."

21*

The God of Plato is the universal architect of ideas: he created first the types, and then the world as a copy of them; or (for his opinion varies in various works) ideas were created from all eternity, and independent of God, who merely shaped the world after their model.

We must beware lest we fail utterly to discern the sublimity of this Platonic region of ideas, or the truth it does, after all, embody. Plato saw that nothing was perfect here. Justice never lifted up her voice among men without being obstructed and half silenced by the discordant noises of fraud, and vile cunning, and adverse circumstances. Men, with half-idiotic listlessness, knew virtue to be fair, and good, and heaven-born, and sunk into the harlot-arms of vice. The visage of truth was dimmed by the mists of earth, or, to use the image of Milton, her form was cut into shreds, and the philosopher could only go searching after her members, and endeavor to arrange them into "an immortal feature of loveliness and perfection." Plato imagined a land where all this was changed; where truth reigned in undimmed splendor, surrounded by justice, and temperance, and love, and all the celestial train. Thence he had come when he arrived upon this world of semblance and shadow; thither, while sojourning here, he would steadfastly look, unheeding the joys or the afflictions of earth; and thither, when death opened the eternal gates, would he return. The truth in all this is the great truth on which Christianity is founded. Thus did the grandest intellect of antiquity, unconsciously to itself, look back to Eden, and forward to Heaven.

We shall glance at one or two phases of Plato's general system.

We have heard much of Platonic love; and, meeting it in the sentimental novel, one is tempted to unite with

Byron in his exclamation, which seems to touch the very
sublimity of impudence—

> " O Plato, Plato, you're a bore ! "

But the idea was, and is, a sublime one. It meant the
union of two individuals by that sympathy which results
from, as it occasions, unity of aim, when that aim is the
highest to which they can aspire, namely, pure truth.   In
the soul, Plato saw two motive powers, which he represented under the emblem of two steeds: the one of altogether celestial mettle, snow-white, shapely, mild, swift,
and requiring neither whip nor spur: the other of dark hue,
of fierce, unkindly temper, and scarcely to be urged on, by
Reason the charioteer, with whip or spur; like the steeds
of the respective horsemen that joined the wild huntsman
of Bürger.   These typified, respectively, the sensual, the
earthly, the passionate,— and the intellectual, the celestial
portions of the soul of man.   The noble courser strove
ever towards what was holy and high; the base horse
sought the excitements of earthly passion.   When two
individuals agreed mutually to restrain the black steed, and
to turn constantly and resolutely the head of the snowy
courser to the abodes of truth, a Platonic friendship or love
was formed.   We think that, when well understood, there
is but one nobler idea attainable by man than Platonic love,
and that is Christian love; wherein every celestial element
of the Platonic flame is embraced, and a truer humanity
blended therewith.   We imagine the poem of Christian
love has not been yet exactly written; we venture the
assertion, that the poem of Christian love has not yet been
even faintly prefigured; we know not that it has been so
much as attempted.

Plato's views of politics are very interesting, and closely

characterize his system. In that very singular and clever
medley, written by Mr. Emerson, and headed "Plato,"
which contains about as comical a mixture of truth and
absurdity as was ever concocted by genius and eccentricity,
Plato is pronounced a man of balanced mind. He was a
man who could see two sides of a thing; he combined the
imagination of Asia with the precision of "result-loving,
machine-making Europe." We have afterwards the rather
startling intimation contained in the following sentence:
"As the poet, too, he is only contemplative." And, glancing onwards, we meet the following: "He did not, like
Pythagoras, break himself with an institution. All his
painting in the 'Republic' must be esteemed mythical,
with intent to bring out, sometimes in violent colors, his
thought." We do not deny a poetic element in the mind
of Plato; his mind was probably of the Miltonic type, and
his great projection of the ideal world we have already
characterized in accordance with this theory. But how
could a man be only contemplative, who is the fiercest,
most searching arguer and analyzer? Imagination, we
doubt not, exerted a very strong unconscious influence over
his system, but it was allowed to intrude for a moment only
as the humble handmaid of truth; and even then, so to
speak, it had to take the disguise of dialectic. As to the
republic, we utterly repudiate the notion that it was mythical: it was not, indeed, brought to the test of experiment,
but, if the voice of history is to be credited, that was simply
because Plato could not prevail upon the reigning powers
of Syracuse to permit the attempt. The whole tone of
the work in which his views are expounded, seems to us
absolutely demonstrative of the fact, that Plato was in stern
earnest, and would have risked his life for his scheme.
Taking this for granted, we remark, that, as to Plato being

a man who possessed a balanced mind, and so forth, the
observations of Mr. Emerson have certainly some truth,
but convey an utterly inadequate and vague idea. In a
sense, nothing was too little for the attention of Plato,
because everything, however insignificant, might awaken
some remembrance of the former residence of the soul,
might afford some glimpse of the essential truth of an idea.
But, in order at all to conceive the true position of Plato
among the thinkers of the world, we must contrast him
with Aristotle, and Bacon, and all that other great class
which they represent; and we then discern that his distinctive character was, that he did not, so much as Aristotle,
or by any means so much as Bacon, embrace that great
side of things, which is the actual as distinguished from
the ideal, the present as distinguished from the past and
the future, the finite as contrasted with the infinite. If
this great distinction is to be maintained; if the one class
is that which subjects nature to reason, and the other that
which subjects reason to nature; if there is a difference
between the ideal construction of a world from the copies
of ideas, and the humble examination of a world by the
interpreter of nature; if Coleridge's remark, that all men
are born followers either of Plato or of Aristotle, is other
than sheer unmixed absurdity, then Plato was not a man
who, in this sense, saw both sides of the matter, but the
embodiment of *one* great phase of the human mind. Clearing away every notion of that mythical theory of Mr. Emerson's, let us see how Plato constructs his state, as contrasted with the manner in which we may suppose Bacon
to have gone about a similar undertaking.

Bacon at once opens his great embracing eye upon nature.
He listens to the voices of history. He hears every exclamation of the mob, and watches the gleam in every eye.

He enters the senate-house; he attends the criminal and
civil court; he follows the host to the battle-field.   He
studies man in the mass; the great national aggregations
into which humanity has been grouped; the minor movements of united masses, bound together by some tie of
religious or political motive, as the Assassins, the orders of
monkery and knighthood, the Jesuits; the influence of
churches and superstitions.   He studies man most carefully
in the family; the tree of which the national forest `s com-
posed, and the healthfulness of the whole determined.   He
looks scrutinizingly at man as an individual; he asks how
individual and national motives act and re-act upon each
other; he weighs the force of patriotism against interest,
of private affection against public good.   He regards everything as already virtually determined for him; his grand
problem is to produce harmonious action among elements
already existing; he turns reverently to nature, as to the
manifested power of God, and says, Thou hast determined
— tell me how.   Every passion in the human breast is
taken as a calculated force, not to be extinguished, but
partly to be regulated, and partly to be provided for or
against.   And, when he has done all, he proceeds with fear
and trembling, lest at any moment the forces which have
escaped his calculation awake, and blow up his fabric.

    Plato has to construct a republic.   He looks at once to
reason, and turns from phenomena to ideas.   He asks,
What is the ideal of perfection in a man?   He assumes
this to be the ideal of. perfection in a state, and proceeds
to develop it accordingly.   The grand distinction between
the two constructors becomes at the outset obvious.   Bacon
took the initiative from nature: Plato takes the initiative
from reason, and endeavors to chain nature down on his
procrustean bed: but the giant will not be bound.   Nature

points to the family relation as coëval with history — the holy, personal, tender, beautiful tie between man and wife. Plato can distinctly show that it will be promotive of public felicity to disregard it. Nature says, I have appointed the family circle for the rearing of men: my way is to "turn the heart of the fathers unto the children, and the heart of the children to their fathers." Plato has abundant arguments to prove that a set of public nurses will manage the matter better. Nature says, I approve a distribution of labor, and have gifted men diversely. Plato says, I am happy to agree with you here — in this case, be my servant. In every instance, Plato judges; and the fact of his following nature, in certain cases, is no more proof that he submits to her dictation, than the fact that a man allows his horse to pursue the way homewards when he knows it, is proof that he would not turn his head if he found him going off the road. Nature, in a word, is Plato's bondmaid, not his queen.

This, we think, indicates both the extent and the source of Mr. Emerson's inaccuracy. The problem of problems, which has tried and baffled the intellect of man in all ages, is to unite the ideal of his soul with the determinations of nature. The Platonist, the utopian poet, the socialist dreamer, shapes his ideal such as it may be; scrimp, spare, and hungry-looking, like the angular ideals of certain dismal modern improvers, youthfully fresh and arrayed in the hues of morning, as that which was to convert the banks of the Susquehanna into a pantisocratic garden of Eden, or glittering in all the gorgeous beauty which Shelley hung around his pile in the "Revolt of Islam." He then brings it forth, begilded and bedizened, and proclaims, huskily or musically, that it is to stand forever. Nature arises, and sweeps it away, blowing it all into the air by the link of some treacherous Guy Fawkes, or summarily wrecking it in blood. The Baconist reads nature, and is on the right way, but has as yet, we suspect, been reading but the half of man; for he must include the ideal in his scrutiny, or make a fatal omission. The man who can and will unite both, will renew the world: or, rather, let us plainly say, that no man will unite both, but that Almighty God, in the evolution of human history, will bring it about by what means — almost certainly, indeed, human — are most in accordance with his high will.

On the various subdivisions of Plato's political state we cannot enter. They corresponded to the capacities and feelings of the human being. Philosophers, answering to wisdom, ruled; the army, corresponding to courage and the irascible propensity in man, defended the state; crafts-men of various sorts, representing temperance, plied their various avocations for the benefit of all; justice pervaded all classes. The family relation was to be destroyed; all things were to be had in common.

Respecting the general tendency of Plato's philosophy, viewed morally, the testimony is uniform and unwavering. Speaking of his works, Sir James Macintosh remarks:— "The vein of thought which runs through them is always visible. The object is to inspire the love of truth, of wis-dom, of beauty, especially of goodness, the highest beauty; and of that supreme and eternal mind, which contains all truth and wisdom, all beauty and goodness." "When," says Ritter, "we review all these doctrines of Plato, it is impossible to deny that they are pervaded with a grand and sublime view of life and the universe. This is the noble thought which inspires him to say, 'God is the con-stant and immutable good; the world is good in a state of becoming, and the human soul that in and through which

the good of the world is to be consummated.' In this sublime conception we recognize the worthy disciple of Socrates; to illustrate it, was the object and design of his
whole philosophy." "The secret," says Mr. Emerson, "of
his popular success, is the moral aim which endeared him
to mankind." And to the same effect are all testimonies.
This it is, truly, which explains the earnest fascination with
which all great souls in after generations looked back to
Plato: here was one man who could deliberately prefer the
unseen to the seen, who could snap asunder and cast aside
from his giant arms the fetters of sense and of passion, and
ascend, though alone, to the serene solitudes of truth.
Hence it is that the hallowed light, streaming from his
serene, passionless eye, has touched the heads of so many
generations, and lies, like a pillar of tremulous radiance,
along the stream of time: hence it is that, while his separate dogmas pass away, while the outward frame of his
system, like a body once arrayed in beauty and buoyant
with life, dies and moulders away, the spirit that dwelt
within it, the celestial ardor that impelled him towards the
holy, the beautiful, and the true, never dies.

To trace, in its grand lineaments, the influence of Plato
on mankind, is a task which might occupy much space, but
which may, we think, be disposed of, with considerable
adequacy, in even a few paragraphs. That influence soon
connected itself with Christianity, and has to be discussed
in that relation. Were we to discuss at length the inviting
and momentous questions, What is the relation of philosophy in general to Christianity? and What is the precise
influence which Platonism has exerted in connection with
the latter? we would manifestly be led into wide fields of
discussion. But it is often remarkable into how small a
compass the essentials of a great subject may be compressed;

and we trust that, avoiding the first question, we may give somewhat of a response to the second.

The whole course of ancient philosophical discussion, after the time of Plato, was, as we have said, directed by the tremendous force of his impression. From Greek philosophy arose Roman philosophy; it was a faint echo, but that echo was mainly of Platonism. Cicero was a great admirer of Plato.

But a new and altogether singular power now arose in the world. It was strangely allied and strangely opposed to Platonism and all philosophy. It was strangely allied: the conceptions which the gifted mind of Plato had but dimly formed were brought forth in complete development and unsulled radiance; whatever was true in his system, was re-proclaimed "with authority." It was strangely dissevered from Platonism: its essential idea, its starting-point, its object, were different from those of philosophy. Men were not to *discover* God, and then worship, if so be that their reason approved the same; God was revealed, and men were to look — God commanded, and men were to obey. We shall borrow an illustration from the geological history of our globe. There was a stage, certain theorists have maintained, in the adaptation of our world to be the residence of man, when it was encompassed by a dense and humid atmosphere, suffused with a faint spectral radiance. Behind this mantle of luminous haze, the sun shone in his own beauty and strength, but no eye on our planet could see him. Now, suppose a physical philosopher to have awakened under the veiling mist, and to have commenced a series of observations regarding the origin of light. We can imagine him, after long gazing and careful reasoning, arriving at the conclusion that, since the light seemed stronger in one part of his sphere of vision than elsewhere, and somewhat more gathered round a centre, there was probably one great luminary from which it radiated; we can imagine him settling dubiously the position of the sun, and arguing about its form; but doubt would still perplex him: until that glorious morning came when God said, "Let there be light," and the mist, opening its cloudy folds, and rolling swiftly away to east and west, the sun-rays triumphantly streaming along its wreathing gorges, revealed the whole lower world as the recipient of light and heat from one great source, one great sun. That physical philosopher seems to us to emblem well the position of mental philosophy, as represented by Plato, in relation to God. Dim streaks of a celestial fire, faint gleams of a celestial light, suffused, with feeble radiance, the atmosphere of earth: Plato, gazing long and considering earnestly, pronounced that they came from one God, but his tongue faltered, and, like Schlegel, he may be said to have died with the word "but" on his lips. Christianity revealed the union of goodness and God; the one the light of the universe, the other the eye from which it streamed. Such was the difference between philosophy and Christianity, the great essential difference; the one with piercing gaze looked from earth to heaven, the other descended from heaven to earth; the one endeavored to discover God, the other revealed him. There were many more. Christianity was in its essence more human than philosophy. The noble, and dauntless, and untiring Plato had climbed the heights of philosophy, to attain a region of serenity, but of coldness; he ascended the mountain to near the stars, but he reached the dwelling of eternal snow; his banner was inscribed "Excelsior," but the light was still at infinite distance above him, when he had to wind that banner around him and die. "Plato the man was almost completely absorbed in

Plato the dialectician;" a sublime melancholy shaded his brow. Christianity hallowed humanity, and gathered round itself, as in a queenly robe, every noble and home-like emotion of the heart. Christianity was in its means diverse from philosophy. From the midst of a downtrodden and depraved people, in a wild mountain-land, Christianity shone forth upon the world; poor mechanics were its missionaries. Hear the grand words of Milton, in speaking of God's way of acting in the case:—"It had been a small mastery for him to have drawn out his legions into array, and flanked them with his thunder; therefore he sent foolishness to confute wisdom, weakness to bind strength, despisedness to vanquish pride; and this is the great mystery of the gospel made good in Christ himself, who, as he testifies, came not to be ministered to, but to minister," etc. It was not the accumulation of the learning of the past and present, and some addition thereto by human originality: it was light from heaven, or it was nothing.

With this great and mysterious power philosophy came into collision, and the philosophy which so came was chiefly Platonism. For several centuries, the grand struggle continued. The combatants on the side of philosophy were the members of the famed Alexandrian school. The struggle took two forms — that of direct antagonism, and that of proposed amalgamation by one of the parties. We can trace neither process. Philosophy, in the hands of such men as Proclus and Porphyry, was directly opposed to Christianity; professing a wide and enlightened tolerance for other religions, and endeavoring, by exposition and eclecticism, to interpret their symbols in accordance with truth, these men turned a deaf ear to Christianity. Their hostile attempt was vain. Plotinus, on the other hand, and his followers, with the whole Gnostic school, and, we suppose it must be added, certain of the Christian fathers, built up, or endeavored to build, a motley, though magnificent edifice on the twin foundations of philosophy and faith. They, too, failed. Philosophy at last sunk into silence, or withdrew into the cloister with the monk. There, century after century, Platonism continued to maintain a feeble existence, along with the more generally honored system of Aristotle. During the middle ages, took place the famous dispute between the realists and nominalists; the former asserting the real existence of general terms, the source of the Platonic ideas, and the other asserting general terms to be but marks of general classes, and mere abstractions. In the fifteenth century, about the time of the diffusion of Greek literature over Europe, on the occasion of the reduction of Constantinople by the Turks, the study of Plato revived under the patronage of the celebrated Cosmo de Medicis. The great mover in the matter was Gemistius Pletho, by whose suggestion Cosmo established a Platonic school at Florence. Marsilius Ficinus, son of Cosmo's physician, was educated, for the purpose of translating Plato into Latin, which he did, together with certain of the works of the later Platonists. Since the Reformation, the works of Plato have been known to all the learned, and his influence has been very deep: the "divine Plato" is a household word in literature.

All strictly speculative philosophy may be said to be Platonic. Plato might be called the eye of humanity looking towards the infinite. The questions which agitated him have never been solved, and perhaps never will be, yet we can nowise agree with the advocates of an exclusively positive science, that the attempts of philosophers to solve them have been merely a kind of sublime crotchets: we recognize the long struggle, as the grandest fact, except Christianity, in the history of man.

Even late German philosophy, with its swiftly-changing phantasmagoria of systems, is greatly respectable to us, as another embodiment, and it may be the last, of man's endeavors to scale the universe by himself. We cannot, however, look upon this philosophy, or any other, which dissevers itself from Christianity, as so illustrious as was philosophy in Greece in the days of Plato. A moment's reflection upon the contrast between the mythology of Greece and the religion of Christ, will show our reason for so speaking. And, if we might venture one dubious glance into the future, we would institute a certain parallel between the stage at which modern philosophy has now arrived, and that at which ancient philosophy had arrived at the time of the Alexandrians. Ancient philosophy had striven to stand alone; when Christianity appeared, it made the twofold attempt to oppose, and to buttress itself upon it: both attempts failed, and the evolution of modern civilization commenced. For several centuries, modern philosophy has struggled dubiously, and seems at length to have died amid the Morphean mists of Germany, or at least to have reached that stage at which all the questions have been asked, and none satisfactorily answered. Christianity still lives, and the union of Christianity and philosophy is the grandest problem at present before the human mind. With philosophy as opponent, Christianity will stand; an amalgamation is opposed essentially to the genius of both. Shall philosophy, entering the temple, become, with nobler auspices than in the middle ages, the handmaid of Christianity?

VIII.

CHARACTERISTICS OF CHRISTIAN CIVILIZATION.*

A celebrated German author of the last century entitled one of his works *Christianity, or, Europe.* The words express his emphatic conviction of the inseparable connection between modern civilization and the Christian religion; and this conviction has been entertained by all the most profound thinkers who have directed their attention to the subject. Christianity has been recognized as the original spring, and pervading life of modern existence. Whether it has been looked upon with the eye of reason or of faith, whether it has been regarded as springing wholly from earth or as having come down from Heaven, no one has been able to contemplate modern history at all, without earnestly and deliberately contemplating *it.* In the eye of Gibbon, there was no answering gleam of faith or hope, as he looked towards that star which rose in the East, and ascended, in tranquil majesty, over the wild sea, strewed with the wrecks of empire, in which went down the sun of Rome. Yet even he could not pass Christianity by, as an ordinary phenomenon. Were it only as a philosophic wonder, he could not but pause to consider that "pure and humble religion" which "gently insinuated itself into

* A lecture delivered in Manchester and Liverpool, England, Oct. 1856.

the minds oi men, grew up in silence and obscurity, derived new vigor from opposition, and finally erected the
triumphant banner of the Cross on the ruins of the Capi-
tol;" and which, "after a revolution of thirteen or fourteen
centuries," was "still preferred by the nations of Europe,
the most distinguished portion of human kind in arts and
learning, as well as in arms." Goethe, a far profounder
man than Gibbon, and fitly representing a loftier form of
that rationalism, of which, in its French manifestation, no
better representative could be found than Gibbon, has
spoken of Christianity with deep reverence, as the greatest
moral fact of human history, as a point of attainment from
which the race cannot recede, consequently as an influence
which cannot die. Baron Humboldt finds Christianity re-
moulding men's conception of the physical universe, and
breathing the influence of a deeper and softer humanity
over nations. M. Guizot points to the Church as "the
great connecting link — the principle of civilization — between the Roman and the barbarian world." Lord Lind-
say and Mr. Ruskin tell us that Christianity is at tne heart
of all that is truest and best, most nobly human and most
purely spiritual, in modern art. If we turn to writers who
have more expressly considered the relation of Christianity
to human history, we find the attestation still more explicit, the unanimity still more complete. Frederick von
Schlegel, the very able author of *The Philosophy of History*, discovers in Christianity "the new words of a new
life, and new light and moral and divine science, that was
to unfold new views of the world, introduce a new organization of society, and give a new form to human existence."
Neander, a more powerful and healthful thinker than Schlegel, agreed with him here, and devoted his life to exhibit
the progress already made by the spirit of Christianity, in

pervading and fashioning the life of mankind. "The great Founder of Christianity," says Philip Schaff, one of the most recent, but, it may prove, one of the greatest of Church historians, "The great Founder of Christianity is the vital principle and the guide, the centre and turning-point, and at the same time the key, of all history. . . . In ancient history, what is most remarkable and significant is the preparation for Christianity by the divine revelation in Israel, and by the longing of the benighted heathen. As to late history, Christianity is the very pulse of its life, its heart's blood, its central stream."

But I must pause. To do more than indicate the abundance of testimony on this point is forbidden by the comprehensiveness of my subject and the proportionate shortness of my time. I shall consider it beyond dispute that Christianity has been the vital spirit of the modern time, and it will be our endeavor, this evening, to attain some definite and distinct apprehension of those principles which it introduced into civilization, and of their mode of manifestation in the several epochs of European history. The task is one of difficulty, and only with extreme inaccuracy can it be now performed; but its performance with even partial success will amply reward effort. No subject of contemplation could be more august than that of the celestial influence of Christianity, searching the depths of the human spirit, and evolving its powers in the broadest, the most varied, the most profoundly moral and spiritual, of civilizations. No intellectual exercise could be more invigorating or profitable, than that of penetrating the essence, or embracing the grand manifestations, of that influence. The point we desire to reach is high; but it is not necessary that our prospect be indefinite. Apt as we British are to boast of our practical talent, and our power to appreciate individual facts, there are other nations which might, perhaps, read us a lesson in the art of taking broad views, of reducing the multiplicity of phenomena to the unity of principle, of marshalling facts by law. A traveller, if such may be imagined, passing along the ridge of the Andes, would come upon the sources of the great South American rivers, Orinoco, La Plata, Amazon. As he saw the fountain, bubbling from the hill-side, or trickling down the ice-crag, and as he marked its silver thread winding away on the boundless plain, would· no more be revealed to him than the few drops by his side or the thin streak below? Would not his mind's eye, reaching far beyond his physical vision, behold the stately river, rolling on, in the pomp of its gathered waters, hollowing out valleys for the abode of nations, with forests and savannahs green around it, and cities resting on its banks? Would he not read the geography of a continent in the trickling fountain and the slender thread?

Thus it is that certain facts do not end in themselves. They are suggestive or representative of a thousand others. And of such representative facts are we in quest this evening. Nay more. An illustration is, indeed, but an illustration, and we shall seek not only to discover the fountains, but also, more or less, to trace the streams, of Christian influence in modern times; but with this premised, we may find the position of our supposed traveller closely similar to that we are to occupy. The centuries which witnessed the spread of Christianity, we found ourselves entitled to regard as the moral, intellectual, social, and political watershed, bounding the whole continent of modern life. Those streams of influence then commenced their course, which have ever since continued to flow. At times, they may have been slow and turbid; at times, their windings may have been so circuitous that the attainment of the goal seemed impossible; at times, they may have rushed on in wild haste and tumult, as of the torrent and cataract; at times they may have disappeared altogether, like rivers running under ground. Yet to them, the grand conformations of national life were always owing; from the most circuitous winding, there was always a return; and even though they should in some quarters seem to be lost, and in some others to be turbid or obstructed, the experience of the past combines with faith in Divine Providence to assure us, that they will ultimately work themselves clear, draw towards them new tributaries, and irrigate with their healing waters all the provinces of human life.

It will promote perspicuity to keep distinctly in mind that I begin by offering a succinct view of the new influences or principles originally introduced by Christianity into civilization; and shall then proceed to trace their action in the various epochs of European history.

Christianity, then, first of all, introduced a new *moral* influence, of mighty power, or rather, a series of new moral influences, into civilization.

It is not a very safe exercise to exhibit, even on a broad and general scale, how much better we are than other men; and I most cordially sympathize with that broad and generous philosophy, which scorns to add a glory to truth and righteousness by darkening, beyond what is necessary, error and vice.   Christianity need not shrink from acknowledging that God did not leave himself without witness among the heathen nations.   "Beneath the ashes of Pagan superstition," says Schaff, "there glowed a feeble spark of faith in the unknown God."   "The nations," said Edward Irving, and his words have of late been substantially and unanswerably confirmed by Archbishop Whately, "The nations are but the apostacy of the Patriarchal religion, as the ten tribes were of the Jewish, and the Papacy is of the Christian." Many of the Greek philosophers, with their Roman followers, sincerely pursued truth, and propounded elevated and inspiring doctrines. The death of Socrates has been for two thousand years a lesson of magnanimity and of placid courage, and an attestation of the fact that, if conscience and reason are honestly listened to, they may, in the individual case, give such assurance of the immortality of the soul, as will render a man calm and satisfied in death. If, lastly, it is noble to rise superior to the pleasures of sense, and to gird up the mind to pursue the wise, the beautiful, and the true, then may we still learn something from Plato's majestic control of passion and passionate devotion to truth.

But such men as Neander, Schaff, Whately, to mention no others, have now put it beyond all reasonable doubt that, the moral system of the Pagan world was sapped in its very foundations, and full of irreparable flaws from top to bottom. Philosophy, indeed, pierced at intervals into the region of pure moral truth; but in no case was the ethical system of any philosopher entirely correct; principles destructive of the very essence of virtue were maintained in not a few of the schools; and, most important of all, the multitude was scorned by all the philosophers. The teaching was not perfect for those who enjoyed it, and the mass of mankind could not enjoy it at all. The philosophy of Socrates, indeed, seems to have been intended for the household and the market place; but if from Plato it derived the advantage of mature elaboration and scientific form, it was forever raised by him beyond the sphere of common life. The accepted fashion with philosophers was to approve the superstitions of the vulgar as received by them; to regard the popular mythologies as mechanical appliances for the preservation of order; and to be serenely indifferent whether men in general believed their own doctrines or not. The reasonings of philosophy were to practical morality as a theory of rain is to the fructifying shower. When we turn to the mythologies themselves, matters are still worse. They were pervaded by that profoundly manichean character, which, I venture to assert, must attach to all religions framed by the unaided human mind — framed negatively, I mean, by the gradual loss of truth anciently revealed, and substitution of human falsehood — and unpurified by the direct inspiration of the Almighty. The torch of natural conscience, blown upon by the tempest of passion and the strong side winds of error, will always toss flickering from side to side, unless steadied by the hand of God. So it was in Greece and Rome. The good and the bad were alike inpersonated in divinities, and alike worshipped. Precepts of virtue alternated with examples of vice. The well-disposed Greek might strive after wisdom, self-restraint, gentle fortitude, and valor, on the model of Minerva; but why should he not also cultivate brutal ferocity with Mars, whose soul, as has been said, was in the butcher's knife? The sovereign of Olympus, venerable Jove himself, furnished him with a history, not unworthy, — perhaps I should say not worthy, — of the Newgate calendar. One mock divinity would back him when he stole, another when he was unchaste, another when he lied. Of the immortality of the soul, he could not be assured. Death was to him a thought of utter woe. The happiest among the dead were not so happy as the living, and the many were miserable. All that related to a future, or a spiritual existence, was to him a faint forecast, a vaguely hinted mystery, a wavering haze, a mere dream. The two ghastly negations of essential manicheism pressed upon his life: he could not be assured that the good is infinitely better than the bad; and he could not be assured that happiness in this universe is, on the whole, triumphant over misery.

Great, in all respects, was the change wrought by Christianity. It did no dishonor to the efforts of reason to scale the precipices of truth and virtue: but for the first time, it let down from Heaven the ladder of faith, on which the way-faring man could ascend to meet the angels and to know his God. It thus assumed a radically different position from that of philosophy. On the other hand, all the impersonated vagaries of heathen mythology were taken up and annihilated in the one God of revelation. The effect on the moral and intellectual state, the influence in bracing up the whole nature and unifying the conception of the moral and physical universe, of the simple belief in one God, instead of many, it is perhaps impossible to exaggerate. Manicheism, in its very essence, was now as good as extinguished. It might re-appear in flickering gleams, but it could never more reach the heart or brain of Christian nations. "God is light;" these words proclaimed the eternal and infinite superiority of holiness to wickedness: "God is love;" these words proclaimed the essential triumph of happiness over misery. This was indeed a Gospel to mankind. There is something very melancholy in that essential manicheism of unrevealed religions. It seems to me the deepest wail, — the most lorn and dreary cry, — that has proceeded from the sad heart of humanity. There was good in the world, indeed, the early and the latter rain, the smiling, opulent summer, the palm trees and fountains, the broad harvest fields, the warm home-affections. There must be a divine Giver of all this; so the rejoicing heart believed in Orumzd, the preserver; in Apollo, the God of light and music; in the benignant strength of Thor. But was joy the prevailing thing in the world? Did not long drought burn up the corn, and turn the bounty of summer into famine and pestilence? Did not the weary traveller, after long journeying, sustained by hope, over the desert sand, find often, as he came to the remembered well, that its waters were dried up, and he had only to lie down and die? Did not treachery, falsehood, cruelty, intrude even into the domestic circle, and might not mortal hatred lurk behind the smile of friendship? These questions could not be put aside. They were answered by the rising in the soul of a great agony and a mighty fear. Some power, stupendous as that of the beneficent Deity, must have it as its special attribute to torment and destroy mankind. So Ahriman, the god of darkness and destruction, rose up in eternal defiance against Ormuzd, the preserver; the arrows of Apollo shot blight and plague, as well as summer warmth; and Thor and the good divinities had to wage endless and internecine war with the giant demons of the northern mythology. So it always was. Man escaped from the sorrow of the world, only by casting the shadow of it over the whole face of Heaven, to spread over him one infinite vault of starless night. He could not dare to set Ormuzd above Ahriman; nay, might it not be that the beneficent Ormuzd ·would not be swift to punish; and was it not better, more wise, more prudent, if one must choose, to attend chiefly to the worship of Ahriman, to propitiate the destroyer? So the simple, sorrowful heart sank down literally to the worship of devils. But Christianity gave at last the sublime assurance to man, that love, that light, that beneficence, hold eternal sway in this universe; that in hating and defying evil and all its supporters in earth and hell there is safety, victory, peace; that God, the Creator and Preserver, has smitten the devil and his angels into eternal confusion

by the mere breath of his indignation. Christianity showed
the shadow of human sin falling over the face of Heaven;
but there it did not settle in the blackness of despair;
it brought out the ever-burning celestial lights of divine
mercy and redeeming love. And no night can blacken
those stars!

All those truths of spiritual order, at which Paganism
vaguely guessed, were now put beyond doubt. The immortality of the soul was distinctly affirmed. The spiritual nature of man and his present and future spiritual existence
were opened up. Time was made to rest on eternity.

Virtues which contradicted the whole genius of ancient
life and morals, but which, once propounded, awakened a
response in man's deepest nature, were proclaimed by Christianity. Gentleness, mercy, humility,— all those virtues
which are antithetically opposed to the central virtue of
the old world, pride, were preached to the nations in the
words of the Saviour. Self-negation came in the place of
self-assertion; trust came for determination; revenge passed
into forgiveness; hate became love; war became peace.
To subdue another and reign over him was no longer the
sublimest conception, the loftiest ideal, of men and nations.
Archbishop Whately rightly recognizes it as a grand distinguishing characteristic of Christianity, that it sent men
to learn of little children.

And all this ethical perfection was, I must repeat, no possession of a select few, attained by the method of reason;
it was a free gift from God, bestowed in His Son upon all
men, and to be received by faith. "Antiquity," says Neander, "was destitute of any independent means, adapted
alike to all stages of human enlightenment, for satisfying
man's religious needs." This all-sufficing and all-suiting
means was now found; faith did for the multitude what

reasoning could never do ; and the magnitude of the result in relation to the moral life of mankind cannot possibly be over-estimated. The exception became the rule. The change was as that from the wintry scene, with, indeed, here and there an icicle fallen, here and there the snow melted from a spire or house-top, here and there sun-beams clustering about the mountain side, but- the general scene all wrapt in snow, and the landscape of summer, where the light rests conspicuously. on no single points, and that just *because* it floods the whole prospect.

Another change, of a practical nature, bearing relation to the ethical teaching of the world, was introduced by Christianity, too important to be overlooked, even in this brief summary. That mature scholar and profound, if somewhat desultory thinker, Thomas De Quincey, has brought prominently into notice the fact that Paganism had nothing, or next to nothing, to show corresponding to the moral and doctrinal instructions of a Christian ministry. Archbishop Whately, too, in his work on the peculiarities of the Christian religion, has not failed to specify that it alone, of all religions, has no priesthood, no specially privileged class, who can lift moral responsibility from the shoulders of their fellow men, or mechanically open for them the gates of Heaven. The circumstances commented on by these acute writers, though not identical, are closely allied. The fact that no priest comes between the Christian and his God leaves in its untrammelled might the instinct of moral responsibility: the fact that the Christian revelation is one of comprehensive and practical morals, and that the Christian ministry possesses no mystic power apart from its special capacity to bring the Christian system of morals to bear on the minds of men, secures an institution whose express function is, with all therein implied of intellectual and

23*

moral influence, the ethical and spiritual instruction of mankind.   The priesthoods of Greece and Rome were the per-
formers of a certain set of external rites and ceremonies.
They superintended sacrifices; they read auguries; they
swept temples; they dusted images; they laid out banquets;
they arrayed processions.   In the mysteries, they might impart one or two moral truths to an initiated few; but it has
never been proved that the teaching of the mysteries was
pure, and it reached only to the select coterie.   To the people, the priests gave no good instructions, no salutary counsels.   The alteration effected by Christianity was decisive
and all-important.   The perfect type of a Christian ministry has not, indeed, been preserved in its purity in all ages
and Churches.   The reverse has more corresponded with
fact.   Yet it is not easy to present fully to our minds the
difference between even a Mediæval priesthood, with what
of Christianity they taught, and any priesthood of antiquity.   Even a degraded Christian clergy, like that of the
Middle Ages, could not but keep before the public mind
certain of those grand truths and ideas, by which, so to
speak, the moral position of mankind is defined,— the unity
of the Godhead, the immortality of the soul, the essential sin
of selfishness, the infinite evil and danger of wickedness, the
essential joy and eternal bliss of holiness.   When our Lord
commanded his disciples to "Go and *teach* all nations," He
spoke words fitted to change the moral aspect of the world.

I have been compelled to take merely a single glance,
comprehensive as might be, at the new moral principles and
influences introduced by Christianity.   I must hasten on.
But let it be distinctly and forcibly conceived that the religion of Jesus substituted the triune God of the New Testament for the pantheon of mythology; that it gave assurance
to nations, not merely to coteries, of the existence and im-

mortality of the soul and of eternal rewards and punishments; that it re-adjusted the whole ethical system, by making humility, and not pride, its central point; that it annihilated Manicheism by showing the arm of the Almighty severing the light from the darkness, exalting the one to Heaven, and thrusting the other down to hell; and that it substituted, for the priesthood of Paganism, the morally and intellectually educational institution of the Christian ministry.

In even the most cursory glance, however, at the new moral influences introduced into the world by Christianity, it cannot be permitted us to pass by what must be defined as the distinctive fact of the Christian revelation,— that which embraces in itself all its peculiarities, and belongs to it alone ; the fact, namely, that it brought within the sphere of general human vision the Christ of history, the Jesus of the gospels. I would desire you at present to regard this as a simply historical fact, omitting its theological aspects. Consider the Saviour merely as the Christian type of human perfection; as the ideal of virtue and excellence; as the exemplar to whom Christians were to look, in every striving after the better, the higher, the holier. Think how Jesus is portrayed in the gospel narratives. There is, in the drawing of the likeness, a certain rustic simplicity, a certain homeliness as of those peasants who drew it, a sterling heartiness reaching the broadest and deepest human sympathy, of which, perhaps, no better idea could be formed than by comparing it with the style of Bunyan's Pilgrim's Progress, which so closely copied it: yet the lines are of immortal light, imperishable as the light of God's Throne; and as we gaze and gaze upon them, we see that they image forth infinite and unchangeable perfection. So unanimous has been the voice of mankind in setting Jesus at the head of all impersonations of human excellence, that a different view does really not deserve notice. A very able Socinian writer of the present day, while refusing to recognize Jesus as divine, is yet constrained to acknowledge Him an exception to humanity. "He stands," says that writer, "so high, that the purest and noblest elements of our humanity must experience an immense development, and all its coarser adhesions be well purged out, before it can enter generally into any vital communion with Him." Consider then, the fact that this ideal man, with whom, considered merely as a type of human virtue, we are after eighteen hundred years still unable to commune, was first given to the world as an historical fact, first set before the eyes of men, by Christianity; consider that, however men might wander from Him, or, turning to his mother or his brother, put Him from them, His divine endurance, His infinite self-sacrifice, His faithfulness unto death, the unsullied whiteness of that fame on which pharisaic hate and priestly craft could leave not one stain, would always beam out again and again upon the world; consider that He was ever there, drawing men with that eye, in which celestial holiness shone through human tears, drawing them, in the long lapse of ages, nearer and nearer Him, never able altogether to lose sight of Him; consider that, wherever there appeared a new energy to pierce to truth, a new nobleness to aspire after holiness, a new love to consecrate itself for God and man, there was in Jesus an encouragement, an example, a hope to cheer, a guidance to direct: consider, I say, all this and then you may faintly realize, what words are utterly powerless to express, the transforming and irresistible change in the moral position of man, brought about by the mere fact that Jesus lived and died.

The new moral elements introduced by Christianity con-

stitute one great class. Another great class I shall define
as that of the *social* elements introduced by the same
means. And in the term "social," I must comprehend all
that relates, not merely to the domestic, but to the political,
commercial, literary, and artistic provinces of life. The
modifying and quickening elements introduced into all the
social relations and activities, I shall attempt to embrace
in one succinct view like the preceding.

Perhaps the most correct method to be pursued here is
to name one principle, which concentrated in itself an unbounded energy of social change, and whose various applications effected revolution in special departments. This
principle I find in the twofold idea of the unity of the race,
implying essential equality in capability, in merit, in immortality, and the essential nobleness of all natural and
honest work.

The majesty of man, not as the king, not as the warrior,
not as the scholar, not as the millionaire, but simply as the
man, was first explicitly declared by Christianity: and the
essential equality in honor and dignity, of all endeavor, so
it is natural in itself, and pursued with no selfish aim, was
also first proclaimed to the mass of mankind in the Gospel.
The essential unity of the race was exhibited in that the
Saviour took the common nature upon Himself; and in the
express intimation, that all nations of the earth are of one
blood. The essential nobleness of labor was announced,
in the command to do with might whatsoever the hand find-
eth to do; and in the declaration that Christianity makes
not a few things, not a select number of the human faculties, but *all* things new. A few words will suffice to exhibit
the pervasive and inevitable energy of this two-fold social
truth; a truth unknown to heathenism.

It is of the highest importance, it is indispensable, I be-

lieve, to a right appreciation of what Christianity has done
for the world, and an intelligence, in any measure correct,
of the great divisions of human history, that we fairly conceive and master the great fact, which has been so powerfully exposed and illustrated by Neander, and which is one
of those great leading ideas that give character to his invaluable work on Church History, of what he styles the
aristocratism of ancient civilization. This aristocratism
has already met us in the strictly sectional teaching, both
of ancient philosophy and of the ancient mysteries. That
was its moral aspect. But its social aspect was equally remarkable. The civilization of antiquity was the civilization
of a few freemen and a multitude of slaves. Freedom was
synonymous with the privilege of a caste. It was not conceived as a common right which all held directly from God;
in theory it was, perhaps, not defined at all; it was merely
a peculiar possession, which a certain number of men carved
out with their own swords, and thenceforward defended.
This one undeniable fact sets ancient freedom and modern
in antithetic opposition to each other. The one was essentially selfish: the other is not selfish. Freedom, as well as
immortality, was brought to light, when the majesty of man
was vindicated in the person of the man Christ Jesus.

But, again, this inability to conceive equality of social
rights was aggravated in its evil effects by what was its
own inevitable consequence — the proscription, more or less
complete, of various modes in which human faculty is exerted. This brings us face to face with one of the deepest
characteristics of ancient civilization. It was essentially
martial; and it was, in a sense, essentially idle. The warrior was its hero. "The Roman state," says Schlegel,
from its origin, and according to its first constitution, was
nothing else than a well-organized school of war, a perma-

nent establishment for conquest." The Greeks were not so exclusively warlike, but with them too the separation of society into working and unworking castes was distinct. There was associated with idleness in itself a certain idea of nobleness, at least as contrasted with any kind of work of a physical nature. The gentleman was he who had no express occupation, who might fight, or hunt, or legislate, or discuss philosophic subtleties, or admire works of art; but who superintended no manufacture and engaged in no trade. Commerce, it is well known, was in the principal civilized nations of antiquity in the hands of slaves. The freeman, even though a plebeian, would not work. The circumstance was enough to vitiate the whole system of ancient civilization. It bore its most pernicious fruits in that of Rome. The free rabble of Rome, the pauper conquerors of the world, who scorned the slavish arts of trade and handicraft, and had two wants, bread and gladiatorial shows, presented one of the most pitiable spectacles the world has yet seen. Certain modern authors of great name have found the cause of Roman decay in the removal of the old agricultural population of Italy, and have adduced, from the appearance presented by the urban rabble of Rome, an argument applicable to all states of civilization, as to the essentially inferior and unwarlike character of a town population. But these writers seem to me to omit the all-important consideration, that the freemen of Rome were idlers, while the populations of our cities are workers. The invigorating, ennobling influence of labor is present in the one case, and was absent in the other. Mr. McCulloch, and I doubt not many others, have shown that the modern mechanic is as intelligent, as brave, and it may even be, physically as strong, as the agricultural laborer. It is a scientific blunder, as well as a piece of insulting injustice, to

compare the workmen of such cities as Manchester, Liverpool, and Glasgow, with the imperial paupers, who were
fed from the harvests of Egypt, and shouted over the
writhings of gladiators. But labor never became dignified
until it was touched by the golden sceptre of Christianity.

Time forbids me to follow the action of this great two-
fold principle into all the departments of social and national
existence; but it is not difficult to trace its general influence. How would it act in politics? There can be no
question whatever. However gradually it might proceed,
however wisely it might modify by circumstances its complete manifestation, the end at which it would aim cannot be
mistaken. Christianity could not call forth, as if from the
cave in which for centuries they had lain dead, the energies
and activities of the soul of man, and yet leave his political activity, his power of recognizing himself as the member of a national body, and acting freely in that capacity,
still to slumber. Self-government is, beyond question, competent to man; and I know not how any Christian can
either relieve himself from the duty of conscientiously seeking for it, or unconditionally deny it to his fellow-men.
What would be its effect in relation to the physical world?
It would send men to the field, to the mine, to the workshop, with an energy and a sense of dignity never experienced before; it would develop the physical resources of
the planet to their last jot and tittle; it would make fire
bear man's burdens, and the lightning speak his words; it
would lend grandeur to the smoke of the engine and music to the roar of machinery; it would link nation to nation
in commercial brotherhood. One glance along the history
of the three last centuries answers the question, whether it
has done these things. What would be its effect in Literature, in Science, in Art? In every case, it would unfold

the whole nature, exercise the whole capacities, of man; it would ennoble human life and hallow the household affections; it would broaden, deepen, humanize.

It was implied in the change in all man's social ideas which we have been contemplating, but it deserves separate notice, that a different place in the social scale than that she occupied under paganism, should be assigned to woman. In Athens, the focus of ancient civilization, women were little better than slaves. In Rome, they obtained rather more consideration, but they were still, in many respects, deprived of their natural station. Christianity brought emancipation to woman, and with it an inexhaustible store of elevating and softening influences to civilization. It is true, that the change which has in this respect taken place in modern Europe was not exclusively, or at once, owing to Christianity. The barbarians who overthrew the Roman empire, however inferior they might be in other respects, were more perfect gentlemen than their southern antagonists in the important regard of respect and estimation for women. It may be true, also, that the form in which the homage of chivalry to the gentler sex finally passed into manifestation was through the worship of Mary. And it may be true, as represented by Mr. Hallam, that the domestic arrangements of the feudal system favored the development of respect and affection towards the wife and the mother. But all this might have failed of its result if Christianity had not previously prepared the soil. And at all events, the fact remains unassailable, that Christianity does proclaim the equal dignity of woman; and that richer, purer, gentler elements have thus entered into Christian civilization than ever entered into any other. Woman was the Creator's crown-

ing gift to Adam; and Christianity restored the godlike
boon to the world.

I have now endeavored to sketch, in hasty outline, the
principles introduced into civilization by Christianity. It
remains to trace their manifestations in the periods of modern civilization. But it must carefully be noted that our
summary has been gathered mainly from a consideration
of Christianity as revealed in Scripture, aided by hints
from the history of modern times, and that it might be impossible to exhibit all the influences we have discovered,
in distinct manifestation, at any one period. The mode in
which this manifestation took place and may be exhibited
affords, indeed, an emphatic testimony to the celestial origin and perfect excellence of Christianity. Taking any
one age in modern history, it might prove a vain attempt
to show that the essentially Christian principles which we
have seen were dominant in it. But look to the New Testament, and you have these principles *there:* contemplate
the modern epochs at which the nations of Europe have
most certainly made an advance, and you find them, with
new power and breadth, asserting themselves *then.* Their
development was the advancement of the race; and every
onward movement of the race brought out more clearly
their original essence. The lights of history and of revelation thus meet. The divine origin of Christianity is vindicated by the fact that the human race can add nothing to
it, and only in the lapse of long ages can learn to drink of
its living water. When, also, the argument is thus contemplated, the essential nature of Christian civilization is
satisfactorily established; the character of its various periods is rightly ascertained; and the true point of view is
reached from which to discover whether, at any given time,
Christian civilization is more or less fully developed, and

what are the circumstances and influences which imperil its character or hinder its extension.

The history of Europe since the commencement of the Christian era has been variously divided by various historians. It might be exceedingly profitable to consider certain of those modes of division, did our space permit. To do so is impossible. I shall, however, quote the division of Church history, strictly so called, proposed by Philip Schaff, in the general introduction to his great work. It is true that the scope of his division is somewhat too contracted for our entire purpose. But the Christian Church is the central subject of our observations, and therefore it is well to have a distinct view of the various stages of its history.

Schaff, then, divides the history of the Christian Church into three ages, each age containing three periods.

"First Age.

The ancient, or the Græco-Latin (Eastern and Western) Universal Church, from its foundation on the day of Pentecost to Gregory the Great (A. D. 30–590); thus embracing the first six centuries.

First Period.—The *Apostolic* Church, from the first Christian Pentecost to the death of the Apostles (A. D. 30–100).

Second Period.—The *Persecuted* Church (ecclesia pressa), to the reign of Constantine (311).

Third Period.—The *established* Church of the *Græco-Roman empire*, and amidst the barbarian storms, to Gregory the Great (590).

Second Age.

The Mediæval Church, or the Romano-Germanic Catholicism, from Gregory the Great to the Reformation (A. D. 590–1517).

Fourth Period.—The *commencement* of the Middle Ages, the planting of the Church among the Germanic nations, to the time of Hildebrand (590–1049).

Fifth Period.—The *flourishing period* of the Middle Ages, the summit of the Papacy, monachism, scholastic and mystic theology, to Boniface VIII. (1049–1303).

Sixth Period.—The *dissolution* of the Middle Ages, and *preparation for the Reformation* (1303–1517).

THIRD AGE.

The Modern, or Evangelical Protestant Church, in conflict with the *Roman Catholic* Church, from the Reformation to the present time.

Seventh Period.—The *Reformation,* or *productive* Protestantism and re-acting Romanism (sixteenth century).

Eighth Period.—*Orthodox-confessional* and *scholastic* Protestantism, in conflict with ultramontane Jesuitism, and this again with semi-protestant Jansenism (seventeenth century and first part of the eighteenth).

Ninth Period.—*Subjective* and *Negative* Protestantism (Rationalism and Sectarianism), and positive preparation for a new age in both Churches (from the middle of the eighteenth century to the present time)."

This division is comprehensive and useful. Perhaps the way in which the ninth and last period is regarded, is the most open to objection. However the phenomenon of rationalism may be estimated in itself, to give it the name of Protestantism, whether qualified by the adjective "subjective," amounting here simply to individual or personal, or no, is, as I shall afterwards have further occasion to observe, to do profound injustice to the Reformers, and to mistake the true character of the Reformation. The great protest of the sixteenth century was against the *corruption* of a *religion ;* it was the cry of nations to have original Christianity purified from human adhesions: but no process of purification can go the length of purifying away the essence and substance of what is purged; and religion itself is washed away, Christianity itself is annihilated, when reason is exalted above faith. No amount of liberalism, therefore, ought to induce us to consider rationalism a development of Protestantism; and the only true way of regarding it is as a foreign influence, subordinate, possibly, to the further elimination of religious truth, but occupying an essentially different position from that of a religion.

With this qualification — and let me say that it is one which the general tenor of Schaff's work leads me to think he would himself substantially admit — we shall accept his general division, and direct our attention, during the remaining portion of our time, to the leading characteristics of those three ages which he defines. I may remark that, however these ages may be divided into minor portions, there can be no doubt whatever as to themselves. Early Christianity, Latin Christianity, and Modern Christianity, or that since the Reformation, are so evidently the grand natural divisions of the Christian era, that mistake or difference of opinion cannot exist.

In the first age, that of early struggling Christianity, the new principles in the Gospel did not fail to exhibit their power and benignity. I think it admits of satisfactory proof, that the scheme of Christian doctrine in its whole theologic breadth, in its connection with all the provinces of human knowledge and philosophy, was not so fully conceived by the primitive Christians as it has since been. The intellectual worth and meaning of Christianity was not systematically unfolded before the Reformation. But in pure spirituality of devotion, in fervency of personal

piety, the early age stands alone. The light was dewy and
beautiful in that new dawn of humanity. Those were the
days when Christians walked so closely with God, that light
from Heaven beamed visibly around them. Those were
the days when men said of Christians, "See how they love
one another!" Those were the days when, Gibbon himself being witness, the form of Christian morality rose amid
heathen grossness, so pure, so saintly, that the Pagans themselves were astonished and abashed, driven into fiendish
hatred, or won to penitence and adoration. The voice
of Christianity was heard against the licentiousness that
reigned in the temples of Venus; and its eye fell in heavenly pity on the agony of the gladiator. A softer gentleness threw its smile over the faces of men; and, strange as
it might seem, yet in beautiful natural consistency, a new
manliness, a robust valor, recalling better times, also appeared. "In an age of enervated refinement," says Neander, "and of servile cowardice, the Christians manifested
an enthusiasm which gave fresh energy to life, and an heroic faith which despised tortures and death rather than do
what was contrary to conscience. This heroism of the
Christians did indeed strike many as a phenomenon foreign
to the age; they made it a matter of reproach to them that
they possessed a character well enough befitting the ruder
days of antiquity, but little suited to their own refined and
gentle times." It was then that the hardihood of the
Christian faith was proved by its ability to root itself in
blood. The sword which had smitten all the nations into
submission to Rome was unsheathed against the Galileans,
and unsheathed in vain. So intensely and perpetually did
those early Christians realize the belief that the seen and
temporal is but a wavering film over the unseen and eternal, that they hastened even too willingly and joyously to

martyrdom. The mysterious spectacle was presented of a humility and self-negation unexampled in the world, and a fortitude which, from female eyes, could smile calm defiance into the face of death.

That power of Christianity to vindicate the essential majesty of man, to give the same celestial gifts to the babe as to the philosopher, which we found characteristic of Christian principle in the abstract, was now exhibited in practice. "Men," says Neander again, "in the lowest class of society, who had hitherto known nothing of religion but its ceremonies and its fables, attained to clear and firm religious convictions. . . . "Every Christian mechanic," says Tertullian, "has found God, and shows him to you; and can teach you all in fact that you require to know of God; even though Plato (in the Timæus) says that it is hard to find out the Creator of the universe, and impossible, after one has found Him, to make Him known to all."

It is remarkable and undeniable that, from the time of the introduction of Christianity into the world, it was the one principle of vitality and growth amid decay. We have seen how it renewed the character, amid the effeminacy of a decaying civilization. Philosophy and literature speedily acknowledged its power. The philosophic thought of the first centuries was all modified by it. Philosophy attempted to make good its position against it: but that was a vain attempt. Then it assayed to unite with Christianity, but in that, too, it failed. Christianity, it can never be too strongly enforced, is incapable of ever becoming strictly a philosophy. The essential characteristic of philosophy, I shall agree with Mr. Ferrier, though totally disagreeing with him on every other point, is that its method is reasoning. Until the conditions of humanity are changed, this confines it to a class. But religion comes to the mass of men; Christianity speaks to nations; and its method is, therefore, faith. Gnosticism and Neo-Platonism were radically, as the great thinker to whom I have already so often referred suggests, attempts of the ancient spirit of aristocratism in knowledge to introduce itself into Christianity. The endeavor was unsuccessful: but successful or no, the truth remains, that the active philosophic thinking of the time derived its vitality from the position in which it stood with regard to Christianity. Add to this that in Patristic literature, whatever may be its excellences or defects, Christianity produced a series of works of a very remarkable order, of which it may at least be confidently affirmed, that they rose as far above any mythological literature of antiquity, as, in philosophic accuracy and theological breadth, they may have been, in modern times, surpassed.

This hasty glance at the first age of Christian civilization must suffice. That age extended, as we saw, to the end of the sixth century, at which period the victory over Paganism was complete, and the preparation made for Latin or Mediæval Christianity.

In proceeding to consider, in the same brief manner, the civilization of the Middle Ages, it must be distinctly specified that a decline had taken place from the purity of Apostolic times. A vail had gradually been woven, becoming more dense from year to year, over those pure and perfect principles which were embodied in the New Testament. Mankind was not able to look upon the pure radiance of the Gospel; men desired to have that radiance softened and dimmed for their feeble vision; and as of old, the sinful feebleness was permitted to work its own will. A vail passed over the face of Christ as over the face of Moses. Or, to take another illustration from the ancient dispensation, men were not content with the invisible reign of the

Saviour: they desired a king, a Saul; and they had their wish.

Not to tire you with authorities, and to compress the matter into a narrow compass, the principal respects in which the Church at the commencement of the seventh century had departed from the purity of earlier times, may be briefly summed as follows:—1st, In the obscuration of the strictly spiritual nature of Christianity, by a greater or less addition of elements Pagan in their character, specially by a multiplication of forms and ceremonies: 2d, In the circumstance, essentially unchristian in its tendency, of the formation of a sacerdotal caste, in opposition to the idea of a Christian priesthood: 3d, In an abrogation of the original brotherhood and equality of the Christian Church, and a strongly developed tendency to render it, in its constitution, less and less popular, and more and more aristocratic and monarchical.

It is very difficult to present anything approaching to a correct view of such a subject as mediæval civilization, in such space as is now at our command. A thousand years will not compress into a few minutes. But happily we are not without highly competent assistants in making this attempt. Milman, Neander, Schaff, Guizot, and others afford us generalized views of the period which testify their correctness by their radical agreement. The characteristic of the Church Christianity was a vast uniformity: the characteristic of general civilization was an explicit submission to this uniformity. Milman says of Latin Christianity that it was "the Roman empire again extended over Europe by an universal code and a provincial government; by an hierarchy of religious prætors or pro-consuls, and a host of inferior officers, each in strict subordination to those immediately above them, and gradually descending to the very lowest ranks of society: the whole with a certain freedom of action, but a constrained and limited freedom, and with an appeal to the spiritual Cæsar in the last resort." "This," says Schaff, "may be termed the age of *Christian legalism*, of *Church authority*. Personal freedom is here, to a great extent, lost in slavish subjection to fixed, traditional rules and forms. The individual subject is of account, only as the organ and medium of the general spirit of the Church. All secular powers, the state, science, art, are under the guardianship of the hierarchy, and must everywhere serve its ends. This is emphatically the era of grand universal enterprises, of colossal works, whose completion required the co-operation of nations and centuries; the age of the supreme outward sovereignty of the visible Church." M. Guizot confirms this view by his comments on the theological impress which the Church in the Middle Ages imparted to all intellectual exertion.

It is of great importance to understand the meaning of this great characteristic of uniformity, attaching to Mediæval Christianity.

Through all the provinces of nature there can be discerned a great two-fold fact or law; the fact or law of unity in variety. Unity in diversity is the law which in all cases distinguishes creation from chaos. And it is an unchanging principle that the wider the diversity, so it be ruled by one central law, the higher is the achievement of nature, the greater the perfection attained. Now Christianity contains in itself, potentially, not yet, it may be, worked out, the highest possible manifestation of this sublime law. Its unity is in Christ; "one Lord, one faith, one baptism;" its unifying law is love. Therefore, in whatever position a Christian is placed, with reference to the world or to Christians who dissent from certain of his views, he must never, at the risk of abandoning essential Christianity, relinquish the hope of ultimate unity, or deny the obligation of striving to bring all Christians into one great temple, wide as the sky. But Christianity, along with its potential unity, brings also to humanity an expansion, a development, a variety unprecedented and illimitable. It opens, as we formerly saw, all the fountains of the human spirit. It can no more seal up these, in consistency with its true nature, than it can abjure the unity of its great charter of love. Now the Christianity of the Middle Ages was a great attempt — and so far it deserves admiration — to manifest fully the great Christian law of unity: but it omitted the kindred necessity which alone prevents living unity from becoming dead uniformity, the law of variety, the development of the individual life, the sacredness of those countless faculties and peculiarities of man, whose variegated glory and beauty surpass the fields of the earth and the plains of the sky, and will yet render a Christian humanity the richest and most beautiful of all the gardens of God.

While, however, this is true, it were not well to forget that mediæval uniformity by no means suppressed all manifestation of intellectual vitality, petrified strong emotion, or prevented the gradual infiltration, into the mind of Europe, of deeper spiritualities than had dwelt in the systems of heathenism. Everything, indeed, wore a theological aspect; but if the walls of a vast temple shut out the free air of nature, and cast over all a dim religious light, there were, within that temple, many and great activities at work. The faith of the Middle Ages, be it what it might, searched infinitely deeper and rose infinitely higher, than any faith of Paganism. The hymns of the Church, the scholastic reasonings, the devout simplicity and earnest purity of med-

iæval painting, bear witness to the intensity of moral and
intellectual life in those times. All the architectural relics
of antiquity settle into dumb stolidity, or sink into elegant
insignificance, beside the cathedral of the Middle Ages.
All ancient poetry, even including that of Æschylus, is, so
far as I am qualified to judge, a playful dallying with human emotion, compared with the "mystic, unfathomable
song," reaching to the lowest deeps of man's spirit, of
Dante. The Middle Ages present a vast uniformity, but no
blank.

Mediæval civilization has three principal stages corresponding, closely enough, to those three into which we found
Schaff dividing the Church history of that age, but which
it may be well to contemplate somewhat differently. The
first, we shall call the period before the Crusades; the second, that of the Crusades; the third, that of mediæval Catholicism in decay, and the gradual accumulation of materials for the Reformation epoch. I can say but a word of
each of these.

In the first, the period before the Crusades, there is discernible, under countless individual phenomena, the going
out of one great process,—that of gradually working out
from the mind of Europe all remains, not only of the old
Paganism, but of the superstitions of those strong northern tribes which overthrew the Roman empire. The conversion of those tribes was, at first, a very general, whole-
sale sort of operation. But although the Christianity with
which they were indoctrinated was now far from pure, they
were, in the centuries preceding the Crusades, gradually
brought thoroughly to embrace it, and to conceive for it a
deep enthusiasm. It may be affirmed, too, that in relation
to the customs of the barbarians, the influence of the Church
was generally salutary. It specially tended to improve

civil and criminal legislation. M. Guizot tells us that it is
impossible to contrast the codes of the Church with those
of the barbarians, without being struck with the superiority of the former. The Church exercised, also, a human-
izing influence of a more general nature over the barbaric
tribes, softening their rugged manners, and opposing particular customs of a gross or savage nature. It was, besides,
for centuries, the most popular institution in existence; it
afforded the most accessible, perhaps I might say the only,
channel through which talent could find vent; not even as
it sunk deeper and deeper into corruption, could the Church
founded by the Galilean fishermen altogether abnegate its
character as the Church of the people.

The eleventh and twelfth centuries are the era of the Crusades. In the thirteenth the enthusiasm died out. The
Crusades constitute one of the most remarkable and imposing phenomena of history, and exercised, beyond question,
a great influence on subsequent times. The heart of Europe thrilled for the first time to a common impulse. The
consciousness of nations awoke. Christianity advanced to
the East with — ominous token — a sword in its hand. It
had not *come* from the East with a sword in its hand, otherwise it might have been as little successful in its contest
with the West, as it proved in its contest with the East.
But this is by the way. The Crusades were, in the circumstances of the case, thoroughly justifiable on political
grounds; and, since the spiritual essence of Christianity was
now deeply shrouded, there could not, humanly speaking,
have been found any common excitement for the European
nations, uniting so many lofty and noble elements, as that
which sent them to rescue the Holy City from the hands
of the infidel. Historians have enlarged upon the effects
of the Crusades, tracing them in various directions. But

their greatest result, doubtless, was this, — to shake Europe from that comparative lethargy in which it had lain, to exercise the minds of men on certain broad, expanding conceptions, to strike the first spark of life into individual character.

In the centuries immediately preceding the Reformation, the vail which obscured the great principles of Christianity had become very dense. Christendom itself had an uneasy consciousness that all was not well; and I am not aware that, any one has since, been found altogether to defend the time. The various attempts made by councils to effect a reformation of manners indicated, if I may so speak, the sense of shame in the heart of the Christian peoples. Such efforts bore no important fruit, and the darkness grew thicker and thicker over Europe. In various places, indeed, the vail seemed for a moment to be rent asunder, and a ray of the old glory streamed through. Such a ray lingered long among the snows and precipices of the Alps, where the hymns of the Waldenses broke the eternal silence. Such a ray cheered the eye and heart of Wickliffe, and animated him to the denunciation of Roman corruption. Such a ray fell upon the face of Huss, lighting it with the old martyr smile, as he died at the stake. But still the vail was there.

The commencement of the sixteenth century is one of the most singular and critical conjunctures in the history of Europe and the world. An immense addition of intellectual material had been just made to the stores of the West. The revival of letters, in the middle of the fifteenth century, had brought back all the culture of antiquity into the general school-room of Europe. Printing, with all it even then implied, had lately been invented. America and the East Indies had been opened up. The immediate result was a vastly increased intellectual and artistic activity. But the direction taken by modern history could have been predicted from none of these things, and remains to all time one of those sublime Providential lessons, which have been so often given by God, and which man will not learn.

There is no fact in history more certain, than that the revival of letters had no tendency whatever to renovate the Papacy, to re-awaken moral life in Rome and in Europe. The learned refinement of the Popes brought with it the moral apathy of that Pagan lore on which it fed. "Debauchees," "poisoners," "atheists," are the words used by a writer of so temperate Protestantism as Mr. Macaulay, to describe the Popes who wore the tiara immediately before the Reformation. In a most true and literal sense, even the Papacy was saved by Protestantism. It was actually falling back into Paganism: it was rotting away: and that at the very time when the treasures of knowledge, which so many, more or less explicitly, believe and avow to be the one means of moral life for nations, were poured, with unprecedented exuberance, into the lap of Christendom.

In the beginning of the sixteenth century, two spectacles were presented on the stage of Europe. The proud Church of St. Peter's, at Rome, was slowly rising, in pillared magnificence, towards Heaven, as if making *its* appeal for divine countenance: and an unknown Augustine monk, in the convent of Erfurth, his face pallid through fasting and watching, was on his knees, sending *his* earnest prayer to God for light. The fame of St. Peter's went over Christendom. Tetzel came selling indulgences to raise money for its completion. Yes; the somewhat puzzling progress of humanity had brought it to this: Christianity, in the first century, had been preached by Paul; Christianity in the sixteenth was preached by Tetzel! The supreme enlightenment of the Revival of Letters had produced this last remarkable version of the Gospel, proclaimed with the warrant of the Father of Christendom, that if you paid so much money, your sins were forgiven you! But, as I said, Luther was on his knees. Over all the grandeur of St. Peter's, through all the noise which the furtherance of that grandeur made over Europe, above all the false enlightenment of resuscitated Paganism, that still small voice went up — even to the throne of God. And from *it* came the shaping of modern civilization! The Revival of Letters had not got near the heart of nations: on the 31st of October, 1517, Luther posted his theses on the Church door at Wittenberg; and in six weeks, Europe was awake. The philosophy, the arts, the poetry of antiquity had once more risen before the eyes of Europe: and once more God brought life to the world out of a despised Galilee, out of the Convent of Erfurth, and the New Testament of Martin Luther. That enlightenment, which had been mere dead fuel, choking the life out of Christendom, now, kindled by faith, burst forth into a true and dazzling illumination : that Reformation epoch commenced, which, dating from 1517 to 1688, is, I think, take it all in all, the *greatest* in the history of the human race. From this one fact might, I think, be deduced all the canons of history, and a whole philosophy of the human race.

The vail woven by human hands across the brightness of Christianity was now rent asunder from the top to the bottom. Those mighty principles which were, from the first, present in Christianity, came forth from the slumber of centuries. Never before had they obtained so wide a national extension. The Bible, in the vernacular tongues, was, for the first time, put into the hands of the people. Conceive the effect of that one change. " To give the history of the Bible as a *book*," says Coleridge, "would be little less than to relate the origin or first excitement of all the literature and science that we now possess." The idea of a priesthood specially privileged to confer salvation was again struck down, and man once more confronted his God. A Protestant ministry arose; and I think that, if the history of the Protestant nations since the Reformation is considered, it will be found that, however many its short comings, there has never yet acted on the human mind a moral agency, on the whole so powerful and so benign as that of the Protestant ministry. But perhaps the most instructive of all the circumstances connected with the Reformation is the *completeness* with which it vindicated truth. We saw that Christianity introduced into civilization mighty principles, not only of moral but of social truth; that it raised man to his full stature, not only in relation to his God, not only as an individual, but in relation to his fellows. And the Reformation, in again unvailing the glories of Christianity, again addressed the whole nature of man. Moral truth sprung to life, and awoke its slumbering sister, social truth. Christianity led freedom by the hand to bless the nations. Great Britain and North America, the centres of civil liberty for the world, are also, and have been, the great centres of Protestantism.

If we contemplate the epoch of the Reformation, strictly so called, that which commenced with the posting of Luther's theses, and terminated with the close of the Puritan era in Great Britain; and if we embrace, as we ought, all the forms of intellectual activity exhibited by Protestant nations in that period; we shall find reason, I think, for the opinion I have expressed, that it was the greatest time — most abounding in great works and great men — that humanity has yet seen. Luther, Calvin, Bacon, Newton,

25*

Shakspeare, Milton; — these stand in the very foremost file of humanity. The Institutes of the Christian religion of Calvin, published at twenty-seven, the Novum Organon of Bacon, the Principia of Newton, the Dramas of Shakspeare, the Paradise Lost of Milton,— these rank with the solitary achievements of the race, the heirlooms of nations, the palladia of civilizations. And beyond question, the spirit of the Reformation ruled and impelled this magnificent display of power. From the study of Newton to the camp of Gustavus Adolphus, from the slopes of Naseby, where Puritanism rolled resistless down hill after its Cromwell, to the midnight chamber, where all the earnestness of Puritanism was being gathered into one strain of immortal music by Milton, there worked the same mighty impulse, of re-invigorated faith and awakened intellect. Nor least, but perhaps greatest, of the manifestations of the Reformation spirit, was the departure from Delft Haven, in Holland, of that little ship Mayflower, which bore its desolate company of exiles to the deserts of North America, there to found that great Commonwealth, beside which all the glories of Spain's Popish kingdoms of the South were to grow faint and pale, and which, be its faults what they may, was to exhibit the greatest number of self-governing men that the world ever saw.

The history of Europe since the Reformation has, as I said, been shaped out by that event. Yet a doubt will urge its way into my mind, whether we can really view ourselves as heirs of the men of the Reformation, whether we still really breathe their atmosphere and inherit their spirit. We must not be too sure that advance of time has been advance in all respects. That progress of the species is truly a perplexing matter. Tetzel had certainly not progressed beyond Chrysostom or Ignatius. Modern Protestant statesmen seem really tò have made no remarkable advance upon Cromwell. Christian poetry has not been carried far beyond Milton's Hymn of the Nativity. Perhaps we may even yet have something to learn from the times of the Reformation: *possibly*, the wave of Christian Civilization has receded, and is only now gathering for another surge. Let us glance along the intervening space.

Popery, startled by the shock of the Reformation, roused itself in the sixteenth century to a new activity. It shook off the Paganism of the Leos and Bembos. Protestantism thus, as I suppose even Roman Catholics would in a sense admit, was the means of saving Romanism from sheer putrescence and destruction. But the history of the Papacy since the Reformation has proved that the resuscitation of its life was no sound and complete resuscitation, but rather a specious, an outwardly imposing, but an indubitable, lapse into a deeper disease. By associating itself with Jesuitism, it brought the abomination of desolation into the temple of God; and by allying itself universally, even in these days, with European despotism, it has denied the unity of truth, and visibly abdicated its right to lead the human intellect.

Turning to Protestantism, the view is partly cheering, and partly it is not. That intensity of faith, which marked the period of the Reformation, and which has manifested itself at all the great epochs of Christianity, can hardly, even by the most ardent admirer of the present time, be said to be now equally general. And if faith has failed, the shortcoming is important; for it is in faith that all the mighty deeds of nations are performed. But within the last fifty years, there has been a general and unmistakable improvement in this respect.

There is another defect in modern Protestantism, which is to me very evident, and which is of a serious, nay, if suffered to prevail, of a fatal kind. Protestantism has shown a strong tendency to recede from the completeness of what I may call the Reformation idea of truth; to break up that association of political and social with religious truth, which, with the Reformers, was indissoluble. The men who were in the van of Protestantism in the seventeenth century were the men to whom, under God, the world owes Anglo-Saxon freedom. The full development of the idea of intellectual freedom, of toleration, came somewhat later. But there has recently been displayed a tendency to lose more or less partially, more or less perfectly, both the one and the other. This has been occasioned by certain remarkable circumstances, in the general history of the last hundred years. Error and falsehood have, during that time, in two conspicuous cases, assumed the name of excellence and truth: and well-intentioned men have been startled from the real good by alarm at the counterfeit. Milton tells us that Satan, desirous to deceive Uriel the regent of the sun, assumed the shape of a stripling cherub, an angel of light. No doubt the subtle fiend would have adopted the semblance of one of Uriel's well-known and trusted friends. Now, supposing this whole transaction real, one is tempted to ask whether, after having been once deceived, Uriel, ever after, on the appearance of the angel whose shape Satan had assumed, fell into a nervous shudder, and looked with a suspicious, half-averted glance upon his friend. If so, his case corresponded precisely with that of certain modern Protestants. Freedom of judgment, searching of spirits, full and untrammelled use of reason can be separated neither from true Protestantism nor from true Christianity. But rationalism arose and assumed the name both of Christianity and of Protestantism. The assumption of the name of Protestantism was essentially false. The Reformation was, as I said, a return to primitive Christianity: at all events, it was a religion. But the essential idea of religion is bound up with faith, and it at once loses name and nature if it *rests* on reason. Rationalism, whether in its childhood in Britain, its licentious youth in France, its aspiring manhood in Germany, or what is, I think, in certain respects, its *second* childhood among us at this moment, has been and must always be, in virtue of its central principle of deducing everything from reason, not a religion but a philosophy. As a philosophy, it may be good: when it offers itself as a religion, it is infidelity. It has called itself, however, Protestantism, and maintained that it is only a development of the Protestant principle of freedom of judgment. Hereupon start up many good men and hint an impeachment of freedom of judgment itself. Schlegel rushes into the iron embrace of infallibility and Rome. Other German divines, I understand, of perhaps stronger nature than Schlegel, also cower closer and closer under authority and prescription. Among ourselves, there could be pointed out indications of the same spirit. There is great talk of caution, of coming prepared, of refusing to hear what has not been fairly approved and stamped by orthodoxy. Now the very firmness of my opposition to rationalism would set me against the use of such methods to combat it. The adoption of such methods is surely nothing else than a confession that rationalism is powerful. It is surely, also, in this country as weak a policy as it is an unprotestant and unchristian proceeding. The young men of Great Britain, I imagine, will be more apt to obey the apostolic precept of holding fast what is good, by being exhorted boldly to put in force the other apostolic counsel, of proving all things. Cowardice and unfairness will never guard the portals of the Protestant Churches from error;

but there must be an insidious moral poison insinuating itself into the mind of him who would set them there. I do
not say that an open and fair encounter of all forms of
infidelity will in no case lead to submission to it. But on
the other hand, who that knows the truth but will avow
that there lies in it a might, on a fair field, to vanquish error? And whether or not, evil must not be done that good
may come; Satan must not receive the right hand of fellow-
ship though he present himself among the sons of God.

But not only has intellectual freedom been looked at
somewhat askance. Civil freedom, the full, symmetrical
development of all those activities which God has implanted
in man as a social being, was felt by the Reformers, specially by the Puritans of England and Scotland, to be naturally associated with an advance to a higher moral and religious truth. In this they merely brought out, in their
own completeness, the principles which, as we saw in the
outset, Christianity introduced into civilization. But in the
last century the name of freedom was defamed by being
applied to Jacobinism, to wild anarchic Communism, and
principles destructive of civilization. The result has been,
not indeed to put in jeopardy that Anglo-Saxon freedom
which was bequeathed to us from the epoch of the Reformation, but to introduce, into many Protestant minds, a
certain jealousy and apprehension of all political aspiration,
a certain leaning towards political repression, on the one
hand, and apathy, on the other; a favor for galvanized order and ignoble security; a vagueness in the conception of
political duty. The Protestantism of such minds must be
sickly and one-sided, not strongly sinewed, open-faced, and
full-grown, as that which, at the Reformation, wedded civil
to religious liberty. It is altogether too high an honor conferred upon falsehood, to permit it to make us dread truth!

I am profoundly impressed with the idea that the comparatively shrunken and sectional look, which attaches to our modern Protestantism, is traceable, in great measure, to the causes I have now endeavored to penetrate. Protestantism is no longer in possession of the broad fields of political life, and much of the intellectual activity of the age, much of the dominant literature of Protestant nations, has cast off its pervading influence. Once more Protestantism must assay the great Christian duty of making *all* things new.

But there are aspects of modern Christian civilization which are of a highly encouraging character. In the first place, as in Germany the rationalistic infidelity was carried to its highest development, so in Germany it has been met by a counter-revolution, which has long been in process, and of which the perfect triumph is becoming day by day more certain. The modern evangelical school of German theology is one of the most cheering and glorious spectacles presented in the whole course of Church history. Infidelity has been made, in the wisdom of Providence, to serve what seems its natural end, to lead to a more accurate study of Scripture, than was ever before engaged in; and to broaden and deepen the foundations of all the defences of the faith. Had there been no Lessing, Paulus, or Baur, there might have been no Neander, no Tholuck, no Hengstenberg, no Schaff, no Stier. And, let me ask, if these men had simply stopped their ears, and denounced without answering rationalism, would the result have been so consistent with the honor of man, or the glory, or the law, of God? The *use* of reason turned to shame the *worship* of reason.

But next, Christianity has in these last times once more vindicated its true essence by embodying itself in philanthropy, by again breathing in a soft south wind of love over the face of civilization. Among the fathers of the early Church, the saints and martyrs of the olden time, might have walked the holy Howard. His influence is still amidst us, working in each of those countless schemes of beneficence by which our social evils are one by one attacked, which have always been blessed in their promoters, and which will, I believe, be more and more blessed in their objects. With the name of Howard, among the fathers of Christian philanthropy, may be associated that of Wilberforce. The same spirit which put an end to the agonizing atrocities of our prison system put an end to slavery in the possessions of Great Britain. Appropriate work! The Christianity that brought life to the gladiator in those first centuries brought liberty to the slave in these last. And whether the deed was fully and consistently carried out or no by Great Britain, it cannot, I think, be doubted that, in the emancipation of Britain's slaves, the death-blow was given to the universal system.

Last of all, among those cheering and vital symptoms of modern Christianity to which I can refer, our attention is claimed for the modern missionary movement. What Christian heart does not beat high, at the thought of that mild but piercing radiance of divine light, now glimmering visibly along all the borders of heathenism? The thick clouds are edged with white, and seem, after the long night, to be stirring on the mountain-side, as if to collect themselves for finally rolling up, and opening the valleys to the day. It has been said that "beside every group of wild men in the ethnological department of the Crystal Palace, the Missionary could place a contrasting group of their Christianized countrymen." Again, "The Old Book, the Book of our Redeemer's gift and our fathers' faith . . . . has been gradually ascending; taking to itself new tongues, spreading open its page in every land, printed in Chinese camps, pondered in the Red man's wigwam, sought after in Benares, a school-book in Feejee, eagerly bought in Constantinople, loved in the kloofs of Kafirland; while the voices of the dead from Assyria to Egypt have been lifted up to bear it witness." Among the millions of India, there is a listening and a surmise; amid the strange fascinating roar of civilization, advancing from the West, is heard the deep, still music of the Gospel; a quivering here and there, a faint ruddy flush as of life, seems to announce that the swoon of superstition, unbroken for a thousand years, may ere long pass away. The all-important preliminary victory that had to be won over anti-Christian prejudice on the part of the new lords of India is no longer doubtful. The change which has taken place in the way in which Indian statesmen regard, on the one side, the Christian Missionary, and, on the other, the old superstitions, cannot be better indicated than by citing the words in which it has been expressed by one who is in every way qualified to speak, being himself a great Indian stateman :— I mean Mr. Macaulay. In his speech upon the Gates of Somnauth, Mr. Macaulay spoke as follows :— " Some Englishmen, who have held high office in India, seem to have thought that the only religion which was not entitled to toleration and respect was Christianity. They regarded every Christian Missionary with extreme jealousy and disdain; and they suffered the most atrocious crimes, if enjoined by the Hindoo superstition, to be perpetrated in open day. It is lamentable to think how long after our power was firmly established in Bengal, we, grossly neglecting the first and plainest duties of the civil magistrate, suffered the practices of infanticide and suttee to continue unchecked. We decorated the temples of the false gods. We provided the dancing girls. We gilded and painted the images to which our ignorant subjects bowed down. We repaired and embellished the car under the wheels of which crazy devotees flung themselves at every festival to be crushed to death. We sent guards of honor to escort pilgrims to the places of worship. We actually made oblations at the shrines of idols. All this was considered, and is still considered by some prejudiced Anglo-Indians of the old school as profound policy. I believe that there never was so shallow, so senseless a policy. We gained nothing by it. We lowered ourselves in the eyes of those whom we meant to flatter. We led them to believe that we attached no importance to the difference between Christianity and heathenism. Yet how vast that difference is! I altogether abstain from alluding to topics which belong to divines. I speak merely as a politican anxious for the morality and for the temporal well-being of society. And, so speaking, I say that to countenance the Brahminical idolatry, and to discountenance that religion which has done so much to promote justice, and mercy, and freedom, and arts, and sciences, and good government, and domestic happiness; which has struck off the chains of the slave, which has mitigated the horrors of war, which has raised women from servants and playthings into companions and friends; is to commit high treason against humanity and civilization." Still farther east than India, China has heard tidings of a true celestial empire, from the lips of apostolic men, who have cast behind them all the refinement and social pleasure of Europe, as Paul cast behind him the philosophy of Greece and the lordliness of Rome. Beautiful is this return of the Christian morning from the West to the East. Christianity does not now go forth against heathenism, as in the old crusading days, clad in visible armor and bearing an earthly sword. It steps gently like the dawn, its only weapons the shafts of light, wearing the breast-plate of faith and love, and for a helmet the hope of salvation. Clothed thus in the armor of God, if faith does not waver and love continues to burn, it *will* conquer.

IX.

THE MODERN UNIVERSITY;

O R,

EDUCATION IN THE NINETEENTH CENTURY.

SINCE Charlemagne, with the instinct of a true prince, set himself to re-illume the torch of knowledge in the West, then faint and flickering as if about to expire, while it still cast a fair radiance in the East, in the golden prime of good Haroun Alraschid; since sallow monks, in dim cloisters, chid the lagging hours in strains of ancient eloquence and song; even since Pope Nicholas, in the centre of literature and art at Bologna, signed the charter of the University of remote Glasgow;—what a change has passed over the face of this western world! So complete, so profound, so pervasive has it been, that our very words have changed their meaning, and bear the same relation to their former selves, that the crest of the latest cotton lord bears to the banner of the old crusader. Might we not, for instance, puzzle ourselves not a little, in the attempt to reconcile the significance belonging to the term University, in modern times, with that it once bore? The meaning of the word was, at its origin, simple and definite. There had been schools in various parts of Europe. Padua, Naples, Salamanca, Lyons, to mention no more, could each boast a seminary. But the range of subjects over which their instructions extended was limited. In the thirteenth century the school of Paris embraced, for the first time, within its curriculum, the whole circle of the sciences; and, appealing to its *studium universale*, challenged for itself the name of University. The sphere of its influence without was universal, no less than the range of its subjects within. Its decrees affected the deliberations of monarchs. The awe of it lay upon peoples, for it was one of the guardian powers of the faith, and its breath lit the flames of persecution. It was the centre of attraction for all who, not desirous of immuring themselves in monasteries, yet felt the fascination of intellectual light. It alone afforded access to books: and in this lay, perhaps, its greatest power, its noblest distinction. The character of universality and soleness thus eminently belonged to the great school of Paris, and it was well named a University. But can any modern University, expressly so called, vindicate to itself a similar character? Can any Sorbonne now consign its victims to the flames? Can any four walls now inscribe upon their portal that within them alone burns the lamp of knowledge? Did not the University change altogether the relation in which it stood to civilization, when it lost that august and all-important monopoly, the monopoly of books?

It may look pedantic, but yet derive countenance from the aspect of things, to say that the modern University, if we will insist upon confining the word to a significance akin to that it once possessed, has now extended itself over the whole world of civilization. The old walls, beaten down by daring men, conspicuous among them John Faust and Martin Luther, have permitted the light they contained to stream out over the world, kindling illlumination in a thousand places. The old University is still here, but it

26*

does no more than somewhat concentrate the rays it formerly monopolized. It is a class-room, not a University. Knowledge is dispensed in all quarters, with little or no reference to it. If the University must retain the character of universality,— if the University is the sole seat of knowledge,— where can we draw the furrow to mark its present boundary?

All this, it may be exclaimed, is commonplace, and the iteration of a truism might be somewhat more concise. But it will not be amiss to remember, that truism is just the raw material from which truth — practically available in clearing the ideas and dissipating error — is obtained. Truism in itself is useless enough: you do not consider ingenuous youth profoundly instructed when they are familiar with the axioms of mathematics; but when Newton, skilfully availing himself of geometrical truisms, proclaims a truth, at which the Universe opens to the mind's eye in endless perspective, as if again the word had been spoken, and mental had succeeded to physical light, do you not acknowledge a certain virtue in those same original truisms? Is it impossible, to illustrate a small thing by a very great, that we, setting ourselves on some coigne of vantage, and taking in our hand, by way of spyglass, this truism about the unprecedented universality of the modern University, may have some glimpses, both into the nature of education in our day, and into the particular functions of what still calls itself, distinctively, a University?

The class-rooms of our modern University, of which, as we said, the express seat of learning is one, are very numerous. In every reading room, we see such a class-room. Every public library is another. Every Mechanics' Institute is a third. The British Museum must be reckoned among our class-rooms. The exhibition of 1851 was for a season a well-frequented lecture room. The American Congress and the British Parliament are each departments of this extensive Institution.

Who are our professors? They are very numerous. Their uniforms,· their emoluments, their subjects, their modes of tuition, are marked by the boundless diversity of nature. One great class of professors have been styled " able editors" — perhaps with a' touch of irony. Standing in a relation to these, in some respects, it may be, analogous to that in which the tutors in the old University stood to the occupants of chairs, are certain functionaries called reporters. These are seen to advantage in a gallery, scrimp enough of room, overlooking the benches of the British House of Commons. They have in general large heads, and the look of not being apt to be carried off their legs by surges of parliamentary eloquence. Both the editorial professors and their assistants have a number of students so prodigiously great, that it would be absurd to think of collecting them under one roof. So the instruction is conveyed by means of a singular and highly ingenious mechanism, invented by the John Faust previously mentioned. With the aid of this mechanism, vulgarly called a printing-press, the teachings of these learned professors and their tutors are brought within the reach óf millions, and every household becomes a class-room. They compel into their service the intellect, theoretical and practical, of whole Parliaments and Cabinets. The speeches in which honorable members condense the study and reflection devoted by each to his chosen and particular subject, it is theirs to bring into direct communication with the national mind. The practical education, which may consist in observing and considering the relations of the kingdoms of the world, as discussed in Parliament and

Cabinet,— the mental influence which may reside in the mere contemplation, with a comprehensiveness and accuracy not to have been dreamed of in former ages of contemporary world-history,— they are the men who dispense. Did they confine their discussions to the relations that subsisted between Rome and Carthage, between Athens and Sparta, they would run no risk of lacking recognition as engaged in University instruction. But as it is only the commonplace present, of which they take the lineaments,— commonplace as the soil of this present Europe, bearing in it the dust of all former generations, the promise of all future harvests,— they are apt to be thought not at all on a level with gowned professors. Yet what were all the might and power of the Sorbonne, to the influence they now wield over the destinies of men?

But ought we not to assign a separate place to those modern dispensers of knowledge, who are technically called publishers? These have vastly increased the number of pupils, and daringly extended the range of subjects, in our modern University. They also use the mechanism previously alluded to. From all corners of the earth, they bring together stores of knowledge, and pour them out before their students. By a flight equally wide and silent, they pass along the course of time, snatch from every century the treasure it broods over in the gathering twilight of antiquity, and expose the precious horde to view in all thoroughfares. No man can resist their summons, if they only command him to teach. The Humboldts, the Leibnitzes, the Laplaces, the Newtons, the Galens, the Strabos, of science; the Macaulays, the Gibbons, the Humes, the Carlyles, the Hallams, the Xenophons, the Thucydideses, of history; the Wordsworths, the Miltons, the Shakspeares, the Homers, of poetry; in a word, the great speakers, writers, singers of all ages, travel, under their patronage, over all shires, penetrate into all dwellings, and deliver, night and day, their courses of professional instruction. Through the exertions of such men as, say, Henry G. Bohn, every one who can, by any effort of parsimony, muster a shilling a week, nay, a shilling a month, to be employed for literary purposes, who has the necessary intellect, and a certain measure of what also is requisite, leisure, may form for himself, a very accurate notion as to what the past actually was, and how far what learned men have been telling him, of the great authors and actors of antiquity, may be depended upon. There is a certain intimacy with an author, which only a knowledge of the language in which he writes can impart. The mode of expression and the mode of thought are so closely allied, and the former is so graphically indicative of the character of an epoch, that whosoever would dramatically present to his imagination any period of the world's history, will do well resolutely to urge his way to an acquaintance with its language. Who can imagine that all the authors whom Gibbon marshals on his page, stepped along with exactly the same superb strut as the historian of the Decline and Fall? As translated by him, they all do so. But this by no means invalidates the assertion, that the contribution of abstract thought or concrete beauty, which any ancient philosopher or poet made to the stores of the race, can be estimated, with substantial correctness, through translation. On this point, one fact is conclusive. The faith of Christendom rests on translation. Nor has it ever been denied that, whatever their individual defects, the vernacular Bibles convey, on the whole, a correct idea of the meaning and intent of the original writers. Though ignorant of Greek or Latin, the poor man of the present day may hear very distinctly the great voices of Greece and

Rome. He may judge for himself of the nature and range of ancient knowledge, as exhibited,—so the learned inform him,—in its final consummation and perfect form by Aristotle. He may follow Plato in his loftiest flights, and learn what was the highest pitch of spiritualism and purity attained by ancient philosophy. He may form for himself a conception of those wild and gloomy terrors, which he has so often heard connected with the name of Æschylus. He may admire the chaste fervor of Sophocles. He may enjoy the light gracefulness and ease of Livy. He may catch a glimpse of Cicero's grave pomposity, as he elaborates, point by point, his stately argument. He may even, although this is more doubtful, have some idea of the exhaustless vivacity, the hearty, irrepressible, garrulousness, the pre-Raphaelite minuteness and dashing vigor, the fiery vividness and intensity, of old Homer.

We suspect there were no functionaries connected with the ancient University, exactly correspondent to those lecturers, more or less professional, who now, numbered by the thousand, perambulate at least Great Britain and America. These are the irregulars of the army of knowledge, the Cossacks, the Bashi-Bazouks, the guerilla fighters. The most striking characteristic of their efforts is, probably, their variety, including a degree of excellence as well as range of subject. There is, perhaps, no stage of stupidity definable, short of express idiocy, at which it becomes impossible to compose a lecture, to which an audience may be got to listen for an hour. On the other hand, Carlyle, Ruskin, Thackeray, have taken rank among our public lecturers, and, while doing so, have made most important and valuable additions to our literature. Perhaps those old knights of erudition, who used, like admirable Crichtoun, to traverse Europe in the Middle Ages, challenging the learned, at each

University town, to dispute with them, made the nearest approach to our modern lecturers.

This general glance at the world-wide modern University reveals a prospect, which seems to us, on the whole, cheering. Viewed in one very important light, educational systems, and even political constitutions, have it for their object to put tools into the hand that can use them, to enable those specially gifted to speak or to do, to obtain an audience or a field. This object is now, in great measure, achieved. The poorest child is taught to read; and once genius is in these days taught to read, what is it which it may not know? We have heard, it may be, just long enough, of mute, inglorious Miltons. In no age of the world, can such have been very rife. Will and power generally find or make a way for themselves; it is an integral part of their nature to do so. Is it not said that the feeble mushroom will force its way to the light, upheaving stone pavement? Do we not see, every spring, the frail blade piercing the rude earth? Nature, rigidly economical in all her ways, does not lightly throw from her the inscrutable gift of genius. There never yet fell the smallest grain of wheat from the great granary of nature; far less can she afford to lose a Milton, or strike any like him mute. If faculty has not been originally given, no education will supply it. If genius exists, an awakening voice is all that is required. Who is so degraded that he cannot now hear such a voice? If, by some magical exercise of vision, one could perceive, beneath the tattered uniform of a little crossing-sweeper, the faculties of a Bacon, a Newton, a Watt, he might confidently predict that that crossing-sweeper would one day stand before kings.

But supposing there were among our working classes, a few, or not a few, mute Miltons, are we, therefore, to con-

sider them inglorious, are we to pronounce them unre-
warded? Though it is one grand result of the general diffusion of knowledge, that it secures to society talents which
would otherwise have been lost, are we to consider distinction
or wealth the highest reward for which working men ought
to look in pursuing knowledge? The reverse is emphatically the truth. No man has risen to a conception of the
peculiar dignity belonging to him as the possessor of mind,
no man has breathed the atmosphere of the poet, the philosopher, the scholar, who cannot find, in the invigoration
and expansion of his own faculties, and the contemplation
of truth and beauty in themselves, the loftiest inducements
and rewards of study. The ambition to improve one's position in the world is honorable and salutary; it may happen, too, that a mechanical profession has been originally
wrong chosen, and that an ascent to competence or opu-
lence is possible only through its abandonment and an entrance upon literary pursuits. But as a rule, it may be laid
down, that self-culture ought to be dissociated from the
idea of material advancement, and not contemplated as a
means of success. We are deeply convinced that the
aspirations after knowledge which pervade our working
classes are largely vitiated by this taint of selfishness, by
low material ambition, whether directed chiefly to notoriety or to pecuniary profit. To be is in all senses better than
to seem; better, also, than to have. To a true man, fame
is valuable precisely in so far as he can solemnly append
to it his own signature. Biassed as we are apt to be, in
forming a judgment of ourselves, difficult as it is to survey
ourselves and our lives in their bare, objective reality, the
approbation of his fellows will always be an assistance to
a man who can turn it to account. Although every one
ought to retain a right of appeal against the public opinion,

and though that opinion is, perhaps, never quite correct as
to any man, it invariably contains or indicates some important truth, and errs totally in no case. Renown may thus
add substantially to a man's happiness, by affirming and es-
tablishing his self-respect. But the mere exaltations upon
other men's shoulders, the mere being stared at by foolish
thousands,— this, no man of any strength of character will
care for, this only the vain, the prurient, the feeble man will
regard. Nor is the attainment of a high position in respect
of worldly possessions necessary to happiness. One rank in
life may be, in some respects, better adapted to yield enjoyment than another; but it will be found that severely impartial nature works such strange enchantment, by her unnoticed ministers, custom and habit, that there is more of
resemblance between all ranks than of difference between
any. Is it in cruelty or in kindness, that the laborer is just
as warm under his fustian jacket, as the duke under his er-
mine; that the carriage, in which the millionaire lolls to-day,
is not in the least softer or more pleasant to his limbs, than
the cab in which, venturing on a bold stroke for once, he
went with his young wife on a holiday excursion twenty
years ago; that the dinner eaten in the shade of the hedge
in the interval of labor, is no whit less savory or satisfying,
than the turtle and champagne, consumed beneath the blaze
of lamps and to the sound of music? Doubtless it is in
kindness, and none the less so that just enough of beneficent delusion is permitted to secure the upward ambition,
the striving attitude, of all ranks. The toiler will always
think of the padded coach as supporting such aching bones
as those to which he feels it would be such luxury; the
hungry peasant will always think of rich dainties, as enjoyed with that keen appetite which makes his own crust as
sweet, if he knew it, as the rich man's delicacies. But at

all events, we may on the whole, pronounce, that what is
generally understood as success is in no degree essential to
happiness; that, while real wants are supplied, and acquired wants are few, a man is reasonably sure of attaining
the common level of human enjoyment.   What, then, are
those other rewards, beyond fame and fortune, which attend noble self-culture?   They are ill to define; they are
of those things not, seemingly, intended for minute definition: but it is not well with him who can form no idea of
them.   So far, indeed, it is easy to see.   The natural activity of every faculty is productive of pleasure.   The habit,
therefore, of exercising the reason in thought, the imagination in conception, the æsthetic sensibility in the perception
of beauty, the memory, even, in storing up facts, will afford
a most delicate and intense pleasure.   By means of books,
a man makes himself at home in all times and all countries.
Whatever there is in him of curiosity, of sensibility, may
be gratified.   Aided by imagination and sympathy, he may
go round the world in his arm-chair.   But beyond all this,
which belongs to the region of simple psychological fact,
there is a loftier reward attending the highest self-culture,
not by any means definable.   Does not an inextinguishable
instinct tell a man, that by becoming more powerful in intellect, more true in feeling, more wide in knowledge, he
gains a step in the order of being, to which all the distinction of earthly nobilities is but dust and tinsel?   Is there
not an instinct, imperishable as our immortality, assuring
us that there will one day be a grand equalization, re-ad-
justment rather, of ranks, in accordance with the patents
of nobility from Almighty God, possessed by each?   Yes,
in the bare fact that I become a greater and better man,
larger in faculty and knowledge, more fitted to comprehend

this universe and glorify my God, lies the noblest incite-
ment and the proudest reward of study.

It is truly a stirring thought, that the man who bends to
his work in the shop or the furrow can now catch sight, as
if beckoning him to join them, of the great of all time;
that the modern University stands open and cannot again
be closed. It cannot be reasonably doubted that the general standard of intelligence among the broader orders is
higher in these ages than it ever was before. The home of
the modern workman, with its newspaper and its shelf of
books, is a very different place from the serf's hut of the
olden time. Not the shallowest, depend upon it, of our
itinerant lecturers, but casts abroad seeds of thought that
here and there take root. The instances of self-culture,
successful in the most obvious sense, furnished by recent
history, would fill a library.

But we must not allow ourselves to fall into the error of
supposing that we have yet stated the whole truth, or at least
that there is no qualification, of an important kind, to be
made. The modern University is extensive as we have
seen, and stands with its gates wide open. But does capacity to enter correspond to the comprehensiveness of the
invitation given? If the healing waters of knowledge are
abundant, can all men drink of them? To listen to platform oratory, one would be inclined to say that the question is to be met by an unqualified affirmative. But a more
careful consideration reveals the fact that, however the modern University may stand, in regard to the number of its
professors and students, it can bear no comparison with the
old, in reference to the degree of scholarship to which it
can bring its children. We perfect our sciences, of astron-
omy, of history, of politics, filling library after library; we
gather together the flowerage of poetry from the Vedas of

the Ganges to the Sagas of Norway; we heap up, tier after tier, the philosophical systems in which men have attempted to think out the secret of the world : and having made this great treasure-house accessible to all, we are ready to exclaim that the world at length is taught, that ignorance can exist no longer. More, we feel, we cannot do; and it is almost cruel to tell us that our effort is to a great extent in vain. Yet the stern fact is even so.

The physical expansion of modern times — the extension of man's dominion over nature, in all its powers and in all its regions, which has marked the recent period, — has, while adding to the material resources of the race, contributed also, in the strictest sense, to its intellectual advancement. Every practical art has a scientific, a theoretic side. Navigation improves geography; commerce promotes natural history; mining and railway cutting advance geology. But inasmuch as man is capable of only so much work at a time, and the labor of the hand tends to render impossible the proportionate labor of the brain, there can be no doubt whatever that the enormous physical energy of the present time acts as a counteractive to the development of pure intellectual energy among the working classes. Looking broadly, indeed, at the facts of the case, it is safe to make at once the generalization, that a high state of intellectual culture, on the part of the broadest class in any community, is, and must continue, an imagination. The mechanic, the miner, the ploughman, who has to lay down daily his strength and his time as the price of his daily bread, can never become intellectually so cultivated as his brethren of the more leisurely classes. We do not go into any invectives against the mammonism of the times. We are not of opinion that the working classes have less time and strength left for intellectual exertion in the present day, than they had at former periods. On the contrary, it seems to us they never had so much as now. But there are conditions attached to the very existence of human society, under the present dispensation, which confine high mental culture within certain limits. It is easy to draw fanciful pictures, showing well on platforms, and so life-like that even a Lord Stanley deceives by them first himself and then his audience, in which the workman is exhibited, after his ten hours' labor, devoting his hour or couple of hours in the evening, to the pursuit of some science, to be gradually and comfortably mastered. But the workman himself will assure you of the simple fact, of which physiological considerations might have previously convinced you, that his mind, after ten hours' labor, unless of no ordinary calibre, finds science insufferably dull, and if fit for any exertion at all, falls back on novel-reading. The truth is, the highly cultivated have always been, and will always remain, a class. In our days, the class has widened, and it may widen still more: but a class it remains and must remain. There are, first, the professionally learned, those set apart by the community and paid to instruct it, the occupants of professorial chairs and the like. Next, there is the large class of leisure, of necessity belonging to so highly developed a state of civilization as that of Great Britain and America; the nobility of wealth and title, and the whole body of large annuitants. Of this class, the better portion will always signalize themselves by a love of letters. The learned professions make a class by themselves, directly representing a large amount of intellectual culture. We are inclined to think that, among those actively engaged in mercantile pursuits, the opportunities of mental cultivation are not, on the whole, much above those belonging to what is strictly called the working class. The merchant of Man-

27*

chester or New York is, after a hard day's work, almost or altogether as unfit for fresh intellectual exertion as the blacksmith or carpenter. He is also, perhaps, still more apt to lose his leisure hours in ostentatious, joyless, frivolous festivity. His information is apt to be bounded by his daily newspaper. The rule begins to apply to his case, which extends over the whole working class, that the man who is by nature uncommonly endowed, whose mental organization is of extraordinary robustness, will overcome physical exhaustion, improve the fleeting hour, enter for himself the great modern University, and attain a high standard of mental culture; while his brethren in general are capable of but slight mental toil, and will enjoy but little mental pleasure. The Hugh Miller, his hands bleeding, his bones aching, with putting stone over stone in the wet drain, will find relaxation, comfort, and the means of advancement, in the scientific or philosophical treatise; the masons who toiled by his side during the day will drowse and nod by his side, over the evening fire.

A consideration of those conditions of physical labor, by which the workman is prevented from availing himself of the stores of knowledge now at his command, is fitted to incite us to lend all aid and encouragement, so far as is consistent with the requirements, scientifically classified and understood, of the social system, to the efforts made to put a larger amount of time at his disposal. Of all the arguments to be urged in support of their objects, by those associations which set themselves to secure a weekly half-holiday, a diminution of the daily hours of labor, a release of children under a certain age from all physical toil, and so on, the most powerful is that which bears reference to the abundance of materials for self-culture provided for the working man, but which he, shut in by the iron fences of toil, cannot, in any proportionate measure, enjoy. The work of the world must be done. It will not be done without the horny hand and the sweating brow. But it is one of the grandest aims of civilization, so far to relax the intensity of physical labor, that mental labor, with its attendant mental joys, will become more and more possible. It is a poor and pusillanimous political economy, which will altogether sacrifice the mental interests of the community to the physical; which will shrink from continuing the child at school until a foundation for self-culture is thoroughly laid, or which will fear to insist that it remains, during life, at least possible, that a superstructure be raised.

And now, before finally quitting our coigne of vantage, let us have a single look at the old University. Though now but a class-room, it has by no means ceased to have important functions. In the olden time, it was its part to nurse the future. But for its fostering care, infant knowledge might have pined and died. But the babe waxed in strength, and went abroad, proud in acquirement, boundless in ambition, in need of no further nursing, the full-grown, brawny Present. The University, which had been his cradle, could no longer be his dwelling. But the Past, an old decrepit crone, but of great wisdom, and which the world ought not readily to let die, turned into the vacant halls. The University became the protector and preserver of the Past, and the dispenser of its old-world sapience. The Universities in these days guard the books of the sybil; they guarantee to the public that the treasures of antiquity are safe; and they give certification of reasonable correctness in that translation, through which alone men in general will possess themselves of the thought of former times.

But this is not their sole use. They are, so to speak, a standing indication of what education, in the highest sense, must always be. The sermon in their old stones is this, that a certain separation from the stream of general activity, a certain calm and concentration, a certain deliberation and method, are necessary to intellectual culture. "The grand school-master," says Carlyle, "is practice;" and if, in using the word education, we had no special reference to thought as distinguished from action, we should not hesitate to affirm his remark. But by the general consent of mankind, the word is, on the whole, appropriated to that training which results specially in the *knowledge* of old truth, or the discovery of new, which fits out the scholar and thinker, as distinguished from the warrior, the merchant, the politician. And in order to be educated in this sense, in order to attain the power of viewing effects in their causes, of embracing multitudinous facts in broad generalized views, of realizing past times and men in clear imaginative distinctness, of reaching the unchanging, in truth and beauty, beneath that garb which has varied in every age, the calm represented by University life is indispensable. Of course, the mightiest men will prove their sovereignty by triumphing over all rules. A Shakspeare shows you the present, laughing, fighting, dancing, working, weeping, with life in every line of the countenance; yet the wealth of the whole past, the perennial truth and beauty of all time, are in his picture. And he drew that picture for the Globe Theatre, perhaps in brief moments snatched from merriment and the Mermaid Tavern. But the general fact is sure; and the stately old University must ever remain to us, to proclaim that the atmosphere of study is an atmosphere of silence. It is an emblem of the stillness of thought, amid the tumult and haste of action.

For all that is said, on platforms and elsewhere, in these times, on the subject of self-culture, the matter is, by no

means, easy of discussion. The present is a time of boundless possibility, but the perils and temptations to which the
students are exposed may also be said to be boundless. If
there never was a time — and surely there never was —
.when a powerful intellect, carefully, assiduously, deter-
minedly applied, could do more, there never, also, was a
time, when severe toil was more necessary, or when arrangement, selection, sagacity, were less to be dispensed with.
Most earnestly would one say to him who, in the nineteenth
century, desires to educate himself, Beware of seeking for
entertainment, and insisting on the conjunction of amuse-
ment with instruction. The goddess of wisdom, old Pal-
las Athene, was a stern and martial goddess; she wore not
the light scarf of the Naiad, nor courted the graces of the
Paphian Queen; on her head was a helmet, on her brow
the austerity of truth. She required a pure and total al-
leigance, and wisdom and knowledge are apt always to
do so. There are some laws which do not vary; and the
tough sinews of the Norwegian pine will knit themselves
together on the plains of Hindostan, before strength of
character and depth of knowledge are attained without
severe exertion. "Difficulty," said Burke, "is a severe instructor, set over us by the supreme ordinance of a parental
guardian and legislator, who knows us better than we know
ourselves, as he loves us better too. *Pater ipse colendi haud
facilem esse viam voluit.*"

X.

THE PULPIT AND THE PRESS.

In no age of the world were startling novelties transmuted into commonplaces, and paradoxes changed into truisms, so speedily as that in which we live. This remark is
itself a truism, and requires, therefore, no proof or illustration. But it may not be altogether so trite to observe, that
if these novelties acquire a speedy currency, they are apt,
from the very fact, to retain their precise original form, with
the exact measure of truth, half-truth, or mere plausibility,
they at first embodied. An age of travelling is an age of
a thousand acquaintanceships and few friendships. You
see a face, you enter into chat, you become in a few hours
familiar with accent and expression, but next day your
companion takes a different route, and you part for ever.
The intimate and sympathizing knowledge, the gradually-
woven and well-tested bonds of feeling and association, the
habitual regard mellowing more and more into affection,
which are the characteristics of friendship, cannot so origi-
nate. We imagine that our railway-train acquaintanceships have their parallel in our intellectual world : the faces
of truths are seen, but their hearts remain hidden; they
glance past us, leaving, it may be, the recollection of their
outward form, but seldom embraced with thorough and

earnest comprehension. As in the other case, too, there is
an extreme and perilous likelihood that the homely or the
profound thought attract no attention, while the gilded
counterfeit, all smiles and plausibility, be at once and cordially accepted.

It is a remark common among commonplace, that the
newspaper has altogether, or to a large extent, superseded
the pulpit. It was Mr. Carlyle, we think, in 'Sartor Resar-
tus,' who first broadly asserted the fact. 'A Preaching
Friar,' these are his words, 'settles himself in every village,
and builds a pulpit which he calls a newspaper. There-
from he preaches what most momentous doctrine is in him
for man's salvation ; and dost not thou listen and observe ?'
This is but the key-note of a strain which has since been
played with a thousand variations, but without essential alteration of a single note; not a fresh gleam of light has, to
our knowledge, been shed upon the subject; the original
assertion has neither been questioned in itself nor pressed
to its consequences; and in the meantime, in all heads and
over all columns, there float hazy notions of the transfer-
ence of priestly functions from the pulpit to the press,
of the prophetic mission of the journalist, of the destiny of
the broad-sheet to regenerate the world, and so on.

We venture the assertion, that in all this there is a great
amount of superficiality and mistake; that the generalization by which pulpit and press are confounded is false. If
so, the matter may be serious. True generalization is the
ultimate fruit of philosophy; false generalization is error
armed with the sword of logic. True generalization is the
result of accurate induction; the synthesis growing gradually out of the analysis: and on the accuracy of the previous analysis will depend the accuracy of those particular assertions which synthesis empowers. A false generali-

zation covers innumerable particular errors, and prevents, in each case, the truth from being known. In the case before us, for instance, if preacher and journalist are convertible terms, we cease to inquire whether their spheres of operation, their mode of mental action, the nature of their influence, and the tests by which they are to be tried, are really the same or different. By classing them under one appellation, we may be misinterpreting certain of the most important phenomena of our time; we may be introducing confusion into our entire theory of the modern social development. We think it will be found not devoid of interest, and may prove rich in suggestion, to investigate deliberately the whole matter, and endeavor to read off a few of the facts and lessons in world-history, offered by the present aspect of preaching and journalism.

A first glance at the subject reveals almost all that has hitherto been perceived. The influence of the pulpit does not bulk so largely in the public eye as it did in former ages. Not to mention the time when the monastery was the retreat of learning and the source of knowledge, how different was the state of matters when Knox thundered against Queen Mary from the pulpit of St. Giles's, or when the divines met at Westminster! In the whole age of the Reformation, the pulpit was, more or less expressly, a political institution. The preacher was a politician. His words, delivered to his congregation, determined royal marriages, thinned or crowded the ranks of political parties, directed the movements of armies. Whatever may now be discussed in the leading article of a modern newspaper, was then more or less directly treated of in the pulpit. Knox, it has been said, was a kind of king in Scotland; Henderson was one of the leading statesmen of his day. The blind veneration for the clergy which had marked the ages of

Popery, was succeeded by a more reasonable deference, that seemed as secure. Endowed no longer in the popular esteem with religious infallibility, the ministers could not alienate that power which was the necessary result of their intellectual superiority — their breadth of view and extent of culture. They were the guides of public opinion. They had the ear of the community. The necessary result was, that they wielded indirectly a vast civil power; that the attempt to put down Knox would have been resented as we should now resent an interference with the freedom of the press, and that the prerogative of Charles was less powerful than the popularity of Roundhead preachers. The altered state of things is obvious. The Church has receded from direct political influence, and the press has advanced in towering prominence. Queen Elizabeth tuned her pulpits; a politician of the Long Parliament hearkened diligently for the public voice as expressed by the clergy; a modern politician trims his papers, or rather finds that it is no longer possible to trim them, and takes to trimming his own sails instead. It never occurs to him to ask what is the burden of the discourses of Henry Melvill or Mr. Binney; but he quietly endorses the mandate of The Times. The Covenanting ministers have been much blamed for their doings in Leslie's camp on Doon Hill before the battle of Dunbar; it is upon 'our own correspondents' that the wrath of all who dare to be angry on the subject is poured, when they look towards the Allied Camp of Sebastopol. The united and resolute demand· of the London press, on certain subjects, no ministry can defy; we are not sure that any ministry could long defy, on an important question of general policy, the full power of The Times. The Good Regent leaned on Knox; Sir Robert Peel formally thanked Capt. Sterling for his leading articles. To one who reads

The Times carefully during the sitting of Parliament, it becomes almost startling to observe how parliamentary measures are suggested, decreed, or whiffed aside, by that remarkable power. It is one of our distinct political agencies, an unforseen growth among British institutions, and very singularly supplementing our constitution. Nature and fact always outrun theory; a Times newspaper is too much for an Abbe Sièyes. And not only by direct political discussion do our newspapers and magazines govern us: they affect our whole mode of thought. Gradually springing out of our system of social life, they now overshadow it; and it would not, perhaps, be carrying the analogy too far to say, that in that gourd-shadow only stunted herbs and sickly flowers will grow. But we need not extend these remarks. The tendency in the public mind is not to underrate but to exaggerate the power of the press, and as all the information necessary to our discussion is patent to every reader, we are safe in assuming it in his possession as we proceed.

The broad view we have taken indicates that first impression, beyond which, we have said, there has yet been no progress. In general, the impression is, beyond question, correct. But does it exhaust the subject? The influence of the pulpit has receded from observation: has it ceased to act? There are certain facts which may lead us to hesitate before returning an answer in the affirmative. It is clear, to begin with, that the press has the lion's share of declaration and of declamation on the subject. It is heard perpetually; it alone speaks directly on political questions; and its tendency is decided to sneer at and underrate the intelligence and influence of the clergy. On questions of foreign policy, too, where Englishmen in general are peculiarly ignorant, and in all economic discussions, the influence of

the press is paramount. But a keen observer may have
perceived, that there is a class of questions in connection
with which that influence, as exerted on Parliament, very
remarkably fails. These are questions which have more or
less a religious character. We shall instance one or two,
irresistibly suggestive of some other influence to counteract
that of journalism.

The voice of the ruling portion of the London press is
unanimous on the subject of the admission of the Jews to
Parliament. The whole of that intellectual world specially
represented by the press approves the measure. Yet it has
been lost in the Houses, and will probably continue to be
lost. Again, the ruling press of London demands, with im-
portunate unanimity, that the British Museum and the picture galleries be thrown open to the public on Sundays.
We do not think there is any probability that Parliament
will accede to the demand. The opening of the Crystal
Palace may be regarded as a separate question, and here,
too, there is the like unanimity on the part of the press,
with the like refusal on the part of Parliament. On the
subject of education, the dominant London press may be
said to have but one opinion. The theological distinctions
which encumber the question are declared unworthy of discussion. They are made the subject of fierce and uncompromising derision. A system of national education is im-
portunately demanded. When you enter Parliament, the
scene is completely changed. The network, which before
seemed of dew and cobwebs, to be brushed aside with careless facility, is converted into a fence of iron. Scheme after scheme is proposed; scheme after scheme is discussed;
speeches are spoken by the stricken hour, day after day,
week, perhaps, after week; honorable members draw upon
their vital energies to the shortening of their invaluable

lives; page after page is printed on broadsheet and in blue-book; and the conclusion is—nothing! Theological questions determine the issue. You are in a different atmosphere from that of the press.

What is the cause of all this? We believe it is, that the indirect influence of the clergy is far more powerful than is believed. It pervades the vast middle class. It tells in elections. Not concerning itself with subjects of general politics or social economy, not consciously intermeddling, save in a very small and silent way, in any department of politics, it exercises a mighty and penetrating influence in what is perhaps the most natural, appropriate, and healthful manner. The great fact is unquestionable, that in the whole range of questions connected, directly or indirectly, with religion, the press speaks on one side, and Parliament votes on another. The fact must be accounted for; and we are inclined to believe that the Radical journalist was, to a certain considerable extent, in the right as to fact, though in the spirit of his remark we do not in the least agree, when he declared, in reference to political action, that 'the white chokers are choking us all.' Of the relative influence of the pulpit on our general modes of thought, we do not yet speak.

We have found that the exclusive political influence which we are at times apt to attribute to the press, is by no means in its possession. In cases in which the influence of the Church admits of being exhibited—and we might have cited questions more distinctively ecclesiastical, in which ecclesiastical influence is still more direct—that influence is easily traceable. But may this not lead us further to a distinct limning out of the several spheres of the modern pulpit and the modern press? May we not have discovered a key, not only to the peculiarities of their respective political in-

fluence, but to their action upon our whole social life? Let
it be remarked, that we institute a historical, not a philosophical inquiry. We do not ask, what are the legitimate
provinces of religion and literature, of press and pulpit, as
they might be fixed by theory, but what are the provinces
which the course of events—the application of new mechanical agencies, and the unconstrained progress of the
human mind — have assigned them?

As Christianity embodied in itself principles which searched
more deeply into human nature than any system which
ever acted upon the human mind, as it touched deeper affin-
ities, and awoke more comprehensive elements of joint and
several action, than had previously entered into civilization,
so the Reformation brought these into more perfect development and wider action than had been witnessed in any
previous century of the Christian era. It awoke to new
energy forces which had been but partially engaged in working out the Reformation itself. As a rule which may be
pronounced universal, revolutions were in former ages effected by conscious, intelligent, reasoning units, and by unconscious, unreasoning, merely consenting masses. It looks
different in Greece and Rome, but was not in reality so:
the freemen themselves were in those kingdoms a class. In
certain countries, at the era of the Reformation, the people
were enlightened and convinced by a gradual and sponta-
neous progress; but even in such instances the heads of the
movement were the powers that be; and in countries which
will occur to all, the Reformation was almost entirely a political revolution. But it was, humanly speaking, the last
great intellectual revolution which can be so characterized.
When it was completed three great fetters were for ever
struck from the limbs of those nations which accepted it as
the latest development of civilization. Slavery had been

28*

previously destroyed in Europe; ecclesiastical infallibility was now discarded; and the monopoly of knowledge was doomed by the discovery of the printing-press. Modern history is the mad gambolling, or the free and graceful movement, of the nations from whose limbs these fetters fell away. Proclaiming loudly the doctrine of private judgment, the political theologians and theological politicians of the Reformation allied themselves with another power, whose epoch was inaugurated by the printing-press — the power of education. Education and the printing-press opened new fields of information and speculation to multitudes, who had never dreamed either of extensive information or original speculation. New departments of intellectual exertion required new intellectual laborers. May it not be, then, that it is not so much the contraction of the sphere of religious and clerical influence which marks the modern age, as the expansion of the whole province over which intellectual influence is exercised? May not all, or almost all, that is done by the newspaper, the magazine, and the volume, be *supplementary* to what was done of old time by the pulpit? May not the press and the pulpit be the types and representatives of perhaps the most grand and important of all the developments of the great modern principle of *division of labor?* May they not symbolize a separation between the distinctively moral and the distinctively intellectual provinces, paralled in no previous age, but necessary to the consummation of human culture? To ask the question, is to receive its affirmative answer. It becomes perfectly evident to one who glances along the period of our modern development, that there has grown up a demand for knowledge which the pulpit cannot supply, and which, it does not seem unreasonable to say, it ought not to supply. A vast and powerful profession has arisen to meet the new demand.

It is in the natural course of events that press and pulpit have been severed, and, if we look fairly into the phenomenon, we may find that it is by no means a cause of lamentation.

They are nowise the deepest influences of which we are the most conscious. Unconscious influences, which emerge into consciousness only in the pain or dreariness of their discontinuance, are the most powerful. A child is not conscious of its mother's love. It is around him like mild sunshine pervading the atmosphere, coloring all things, but itself unseen. It smiles upon him in his sleep. It makes a little place of rest around him, in which every wind is tuned to melody. It is when it ceases that it is known. It is when the mother's smile of universal indulgence, of unconstrained, uncalled-for care, is taken from the face of the world, and stern, exacting, merciless demand is written in its every iron line, that the want is felt. The most powerful influences of nature are all of an unobserved, steady, gentle nature, realized most acutely in their cessation. So it is with light. So it is with dew. So it is with the gentle rain that droppeth from heaven. The healthful operations of nature are never spasmodic; a fact, by the way, which we commend to Professor Aytoun, as the strongest and most strictly scientific proof producible that the spasmodic school in poetry is a mistake. We imagine that the influence of religion, and, we scruple not to say, of the clergy, in our modern system of life, is somewhat of this sort. Sitting monotonously in your pew from Sunday to Sunday, hearing the same psalms or hymns sung, listening to sermons which have at least that characteristic of art, that they can be contemplated as wholes as soon as the exordium and first head are despatched, and having texts repeated in your ear with which you are not only perfectly familiar, but which

constantly recur from Sabbath to Sabbath, you are apt to
conclude that your mind is altogether unaffected, and that
a total cessation of attendance would occasion no change
whatever in your prevailing moods and opinions. But experience of a foreign land, where there was no weekly worship, might work a change in your impressions. The Sabbath bell has a sacredness and a charm when heard across
the sea. You might perceive a something stealing over the
mind difficult to define, but marking a real and by no means
auspicious change; a certain spiritual dryness; a comparative
absence of reverence and child-like looking of the soul
towards Heaven; an infrequency of scriptural associations and
imagery; a discontinuance of that mental condition which
belongs to the state in which life is a prayer and work indeed
worship. We do not here speak at hap-hazard; we believe
that we mention a fact. And we cannot doubt that an influence of the nature we have indicated, very largely pervades British society. Nay, we are inclined to think that,
however unseen, this influence does more really to mould
the national character, and has a more powerful hold upon
the public mind, than that of the press. The modern church
may be different from the old cathedral. The solemnity of
Gothic pillars and dim-lit lofty isles may be wanting But
merely to look upon the faces of a congregation met on that
business so inseparably associated with man in all ages — to
worship God — merely to do homage weekly to the Most
High—this must send earnest influences into the recesses of
the soul.

May it not have been in the essence of Protestantism thus
to separate, and we may hope, spiritualize, the clerical influence? The religion which Paul preached was to change
institutions from within. It freed the slave, yet it left on
him his bodily fetters. It encouraged no rebellion to the

ruling powers, but it breathed a spirit into civilization which was to cause it to arise on new pinions, leaving its old form to moulder in the dust. We think this consideration sufficient to impose at least a caution upon those who rashly exclaim that the clergy ought to strive to regain an influence, which it is by no means proved they have lost, by preaching upon the characteristics of the age, having recourse to fresh stores of scientific imagery, and so on. Such general declarations we always hold conclusive evidence that the speaker has regarded the subject only in that broad, unreflecting way so characteristic of a journalistic age. It is of course the duty of the Christian clergy to apply Christianity to every new want and development of the age; to show how the imperishable spirit can enter into all forms, and animate all agencies. It is its duty, too, as it is that of every body of men, to watch with reverence and joy the unveiling of the august brow of Nature by the hand of science, and to be ready to call mankind to a worship ever new. But the day which witnesses the conversion of our ministers into political or philosophical speculators, or scientific lecturers, will witness the final decay of clerical weight and influence. The developing powers of civilization have relieved the clergy of certain functions, put these into different hands, and remitted them to purely pastoral work; are we to make these circumstances positive arguments why they should merge the specialties of their office in a score of vapid, indefinite, and, perhaps, ephemeral novelties?

It may be worth while to look this great result of Protestantism fairly in the face. It brings us, if we mistake not, into the neighborhood of truths of the very highest importance, available for the destruction of errors which exercise a subtle and pernicious influence on our national life. Is there not a rightness, a propriety, a consistence at once

with nature and Christianity, in encircling the clerical profession with an exclusive spirituality, in defining its functions
as more strictly pertaining to the Sabbath, and, while nar-
rowing the sphere of formal worship, in extending the sphere
of a worship as truly real and Christian as formal worship,
over that whole field of life which the New Testament seems
to point to its embracing?   "The hour cometh," said our
Saviour to the woman of Samaria, "and now is, when ye
shall neither in this mountain, nor yet at Jerusalem, worship
the Father."   "Whether therefore ye eat," says the apostle
Paul, "or drink, or whatsoever ye do, do all to the glory
of God."   And again, "Whatsoever ye do in word or deed,
do all in the name of the Lord Jesus, giving thanks to God
and the Father by Him."   Has the Christian world yet
really possessed itself of the significance of such words as
these ?   Has it fully appreciated the fact that Christianity
is a consecration *of* life, not of times, seasons, and places,
in life ?   Has it fully apprehended the scope and effect of
that transmutation, by which, when steeped in the light of
Christian devotion, all the natural operations of the human
brain and hand cease to be common and unclean ?   To go
to church every day, there to offer up prayers to a God more
propitious than elsewhere, to have places of worship always
standing open, that the passer by may turn aside to worship,
to have days of religious holiday scattered over the year,
— all this has a look of sanctity and religion, which prevails
greatly with excitable young persons, with Puseyite weak-
lings, and the like.   But the spirit of true Christianity, of
true and robust Protestantism, is the breath of a stronger
life than this.   It does not call the mechanic to the church:
but it makes the workshop a temple.   It hallows the duties
of the six days, and makes all true work worship.   Over
the husbandman in the field, over the miner in the pit, over

the sailor on the ocean, it spreads the canopy of one wide
temple-roof. The week-day psalm is the immeasurable hum
of labor, the ringing of a thousand hammers, the roar of a
thousand engines. The week-day prayer is the earnestness
with which a man bends to his work, feeling himself God's
workman, and looking up for his blessing. And the grand
division of labor which we have discovered has marked off
a clergy for the week-day. The literary class is the priesthood of the laboring days. It is their function to aid, so far
as is necessary by speech, the general work. It is their
function further, to bring out in full and vigorous action all
those powers of intellect, imagination, sensibility, which
expatiate in the fields of science, philosophy, and poetry,
whose direct operation is distinct both from conscience
and the devotional faculty, but which are of God's appointment, and in their natural development as beautiful and
sinless as the trees of the forest and the lilies of the field.
To minister to these powers truly and well, to be led aside
by no sinful and debasing selfishness, to write and speak as
God's servants, are the duties of the week-day clergy. The
duties of the Sabbath clergy are as well-defined as theirs,
in correspondence with the general distinction between the
week-day duties and the Sabbath duties. In the one case,
there is the worship of labor; in the other case, the worship
of rest. We cannot here enter upon any proof or discussion with regard to the duty of Sabbath-keeping. We must
suppose readers to agree with what is our profound conviction, that, were the Bible not once consulted on the subject,
the natural and unbiassed heart and conscience, collaterally
assisted by the physical and mental powers, would urge upon
man one day in the seven of worshipping rest. The man
or nation has fallen from a normal and a felicitous condition,
which does not weekly lay down the instruments of physi-

cal and intellectual toil, and permit the purely devotional part of human nature to arise towards God. To aid men in this worship of rest is the business of the clergy, distinctively so called. They guide in the worship of rest, in that Sabbath worship, strictly a type of the celestial, in which labor is suspended. To confound the functions of the two orders of clergy is an important error. The sermon must not be a leading article, or lecture: the leading article or treatise must not be a sermon. The sermon is adapted to that state of mind in which worship is the work: the leading article to that state of mind in which work is worship. Whatever is bad in its kind is unchristian: nothing that is good in its kind, and remains in its place, is profane. The distinction between profane and religious literature is false and pernicious. No moral tagged on to the end or inscribed on every page will make a slovenly treatment of a scientific or historical subject Christian : no absence of direct reference to religion can make a thorough treatment of natural truth profane.

It cannot be too often repeated that there is, in the actual world, no such thing as a mathematical line. We do not pretend to lay down with geometrical exactness the line between the clerical and literary classes, between the duties and functions of the Sabbath and those of the week-day. But we are convinced that the principle we have indicated, that of the comparative severance between spiritual and intellectual truth, is one of vital importance to an intelligence of the modern epoch. And it would be to the advantage both of the press and the pulpit that there was a better understanding as to their respective spheres and functions. Meanwhile we turn again to the ecclesiastical clergy.

It is not demanding too much in favor of the body of these men to say, that, apart from their strictly professional

labors, they exercise, from their position, a moral influence
upon the community of a nature on the whole benign.   It
is difficult, in this relation, to speak of the Churches of
Scotland and of England indiscriminately.   We do not by
any means assail even the relative morality and godliness
of the English clergy.   But, excluding the Dissenters, there
are circumstances which render it difficult, from the com-
plication of questions entering into the consideration, to
form a judgment beforehand of the probable standard of
morality among the English clergy.   On the one hand, there
are higher prizes in the English Church than are held out
by any ecclesiastical body in Scotland; on the other, there
is a possibility, if not a probability, of drudgery and poverty, and there are circumstances of favoritism, to be contemplated by one entering the English Establishment, which
do not present themselves to the aspirant to the ministry in
any Scottish denomination.   Striking the average over the
island, we think it must be conceded that, in the vast majority of cases, the incitements of ambition, and the desire of
wealth, would urge young men to look towards some other
profession rather than the Church.   It is a supposition, not
only warranted by all human charity, but urged upon us by
the facts of the case, that the large majority of young men
entering the ministry are drawn towards it by noble and
lofty motives — by a certain revolt of the celestial principle within from the materialism and mammonism of our
age — by a felt affinity with works of benignity and advancement — by an experienced power to find a life-occupa-
tion and a life-enjoyment apart from the common aims and
vulgar ambitions of the world.   This *a priori* consideration
is strengthened by regarding the average character of our
clergy.   With the most perfect deliberation we express the
conviction, that the Christian ministry of the British Isles

is at present, on the whole, a glory and a blessing to the land. They have their shortcomings, and there are exceptions; but there is enough left to justify our assertion. Somewhat to our surprise, we have lit upon a most gratifying confirmation of our words in one of the books of Mr. Thackeray, a man who is fearless not only in attacking the bad, but also, what is now, perhaps, still more difficult and dangerous, in acknowledging the good. Mr. Thackeray writes as follows: — "And I know this, that if there are some clerics who do wrong, there are straightway a thousand newspapers to haul up those unfortunates, and cry, Fie upon them, fie upon them! while, though the press is always ready to yell and bellow excommunication against these stray delinquent parsons, it somehow takes very little count of the good ones — of the tens of thousands of honest men who lead Christian lives, who give to the poor generously, who deny themselves rigidly, and live and die in their duty, without ever a newspaper paragraph in their favor. My beloved friend and reader, I wish you and I could do the same; and let me whisper my belief, *entre nous*, that, of those eminent philosophers who cry out against parsons the loudest, there are not many who have got their knowledge of the church by going thither often. But you who have ever listened to village bells, or have walked to church as children on sunny Sabbath mornings; you who have ever seen the parson's wife tending the sick man's bedside, or the town clergyman threading the dirty stairs of noxious alleys upon his sacred business, do not raise a shout when one of these falls away, or yell with the mob that howls after him."

This is as appropriate and consistent with fact as it is generous. The yell of triumph emitted by the London press when anything seems to cast discredit on the clergy — as on the late occasion of Archdeacon Sinclair's charge — is peculiarly offensive, and not less peculiarly absurd. If the clergy are affected with a most objectionable theological nervousness, and do at times, in their public appearances, justify the charge of wordiness, we should think no journalist in the kingdom, with a spark of common honesty in his composition, would stand to a denial that the morality of the press is incomparably inferior to that of the pulpit. The subject is one on which we could expatiate indefinitely. but it is quite unnecessary. It is matter of common notoriety that journalism has become almost universally a trade, and that the most earnest, perhaps the only hopeful, exhortation one would address to journalists, is, that they should conduct their trade on the safest *commercial* principle, and stick to honesty as the best *policy*. The dishonest recklessness occasionally exhibited in the London press gives rise to really startling reflections.

Since we have partially contrasted the professions of which we treat, in a moral point of view, we may contrast them briefly as spheres of talent. We find the expression of a very general idea on this subject in the last number of the " Westminster Review; " — " Given a man with moderate intellect, a moral standard not higher than the average, some rhetorical affluence and great glibness of speech, what is the career in which, without the aid of birth or money, he may most easily attain power and reputation in English society? Where is that Goshen of mediocrity in which a smattering of science and learning will pass for profound instruction, where platitudes will be accepted as wisdom, bigoted narrowness as holy zeal, unctuous egotism as God-given piety? Let such a man become an evangelical preacher, he will then find it possible to reconcile small ability with great ambition, superficial knowledge with the

prestige of erudition, a middling *morale* with a high reputation for sanctity. Let him shun practical extremes, and
be ultra only in what is purely theoretic; let him be strin-
gent on predestination, but latitudinarian on fasting; unflinching in insisting on the eternity of punishment, but dif-
fident of curtailing the substantial comforts of time; ardent
and imaginative on the pre-millennial advent of Christ,
but cold and cautious towards every other infringement of
the *status quo*. Let him fish for souls, not with the bait of
inconvenient singularity, but with the drag-net of comfortable conformity. Let him be hard and literal in his interpretation only when he wants to hurl texts at the heads of
unbelievers and adversaries, but when the letter of the
Scriptures presses too closely on the genteel Christianity of
the nineteenth century, let him use his spiritualizing alem-
bic, and disperse it into thin ether. Let him preach less of
Christ than of Anti-christ; let him be less definite in showing what sin is, than in showing who is the man of sin; less
expansive on the blessedness of faith, than on the accursed-
ness of infidelity. Above all, let him set up as an interpreter of prophecy, and rival ' Moore's Almanack ' in the pre-
diction of political events, tickling the interest of hearers
who are but moderately spiritual, by showing how the
Holy Spirit has dictated problems and charades for their
benefit, and how, if they are ingenious enough to solve
these, they may have their Christian graces nourished by
learning precisely to whom they may point as the "horn
that had eyes," "the lying prophet," and the "unclean spirits." In this way he will draw men to him by the strong
cords of their passions, made reason-proof by being bap-
tized with the name of piety. In this way he may gain a
metropolitan pulpit; the avenues to his church will be as
crowded as the passages to the opera; he has but to print

his prophetic sermons, and bind them in lilac and gold, and they will adorn the drawing-room table of all evangelical ladies, who will regard as a sort of pious "light reading" the demonstration that the prophecy of the locusts, whose sting is in their tail, is fulfilled in the fact of the Turkish commander having taken a horse's tail for his standard, and that the French are the very frogs predicted in the Revelations.

'Pleasant, to the clerical flesh, under such circumstances, is the arrival of Sunday! Somewhat at a disadvantage during the week, in the presence of working-day interests and lay splendors, on Sunday the preacher becomes the cynosure of a thousand eyes, and predominates at once over the amphitryon with whom he dines, and the most captious member of his church or vestry. He has an immense advantage over all other public speakers. The platform orator is subject to the criticism of hisses and groans. Counsel for the plaintiff expects the retort of counsel for the defendant. The honorable gentleman on one side of the House is liable to have his facts and figures shown up by his honorable friend on the opposite side. Even the scientific or literary lecturer, if he is dull or incompetent, may see the best part of his audience slip out one by one. But the preacher is completely master of the situation — no one may hiss, no one may depart. Like the writer of imaginary conversations, he may put what imbecilities he pleases into the mouths of his antagonists, and swell with triumph when he has refuted them. He may riot in gratuitous assertions, confident that no man will contradict him; he may exercise perfect free will in logic, and invent illustrative experience; he may give an evangelical edition of history, with the inconvenient facts omitted. All this he may do with impunity, certain that those of his hearers who are not sympathizing

are not listening.   For the press has no band of critics who
go the round of the churches and chapels, and are on the
watch for a slip or defect in the preacher, to make a "feature" in their article.   The clergy are, practically, the most
irresponsible of all talkers.   For this reason, at least, it is
well that they do not always allow their discourses to be
merely figurative, but are often induced to fix them in that
black and white, in which they are open to the criticism of
any man who has the courage and patience to treat them
with thorough freedom of speech and pen.'

We do not deny that there are touches of truth here; perhaps, as the daguerreotype of the particular minister whom
the writer had in view, the description has certain points of
accuracy and suggestion.   But, as a fair representation of
the talents, requirements, and difficulties of the popular
preacher, it is grossly and palpably at fault.   Pass from the
particular to the general, and it is at once seen to fail.   The
methods by which the depicted personage is so easily to secure popularity, are not an altogether unfair representation
of Dr. Cumming's general manner; but it is Dr. Cumming's
manner alone; we cannot recall a single instance of similar
methods having been similarly successful.   The other two
points, besides dealing in prophetic lore, which can be partic-
ularized in this description of the popular preacher, are the
general assumption of glib mediocrity, and the assertion of
public irresponsibility.   We can adduce a fact or two which
cut the theory, in both respects, across, as with a scythe.
First of all, it is a fact for which we can vouch our own experience, and for which we appeal fearlessly to those who
are acquainted with the state of, at least, our Scottish Universities, that a very large proportion of the highest talent
in the college class passes into the Church.   We do not refer to the mere plodders, to the slow, sure. unimpassioned

followers of the steps of their fathers, who are removed equally from blunder and brilliancy, but to the really superior fellows, those who are beyond question the most substantially and symmetrically gifted, who display a fine, glad recipiency for every kind of culture, and are devoid neither of character nor of originality. Of these we assert that a very large proportion out of all our college classes enter the ministry. Whatever, therefore, may be the effect of the clerical profession on ability, it cannot be asserted that it does not set out with its full share of the youthful talent of the country. We shall grant that, in this respect, there may be a decided difference between England and Scotland. That fatal influence, which, wherever it comes, eats out excellence like a canker; that pernicious principle, which is a practical infraction of God's laws, to the extent of impiety and blasphemy; that formula, by which there is a local habitation, a name, and a certain consecration given to what nature, in her effort towards perfection, sets herself, specially and universally, to combat; that legalized injustice to the individual and the nation, by which the one is crushed below the level to which inborn and most sacred impulses compel him to aspire, and the other deprived of that inheritance of talent which God alone can give, and which is the most princely of his earthly gifts, — favoritism, casts its shadow over the English Church. But it cannot be doubted that even this evil, precious as the talent is which it must turn aside from the Church, does not altogether avert ability. Let any one, who imagines that it does, read the life of Arnold, and consider who were his class-fellows at Corpus. But, next, let us see how the reviewer's pleasant little theory will consist with the success in general attained in the clerical profession. If so shabby an outfit of ability is needful as that of which he favors us with a catalogue, it is abundantly clear that pop-

ular preachers must be plentiful.   Taking one thing with
another, no test of the talent required in any profession is
more reliable than the relative number of those who win its
prizes; and, in the same general view, no test of real talent
is superior to that of legitimate and noble success in life.   It
is superior even to the competition in an University class.
Every psychologist knows that, however true to their peculiar standard, and however valuable in practice, all the
schemes by which the human mind is mapped into express
faculties and emotions, are incomplete, and may be fallacious.
In accordance with such schemes, every system of academic
education must be framed.   The consequence is that, though
on the whole accurate in fixing the relative talent of those
whose intellectual culture they subserve, they cannot be
deemed infallible.   In the individual case, there may be a
balance of faculties too subtle for any analysis generally applicable.   There may be some lurking capacity or aptitude
which has been brought into no psychological category.
There may be some new and delicate mental coloring which
meets all attempts at classification with the defiance of genius.   But nature is true to herself; she will recognize her
own most cunning workmanship; and therefore it is, that
in the general commerce of life, in the struggles for professional preferment, in the natural outgoing of feeling and faculty in congenial action, there may be displayed or developed capacity to convince or sympathy to draw, whose existence had been indicated by no previous test.   Now, whatever may be the cause, success in preaching, as tested by
popularity, is at least as rare as success in any of the learned
professions.   There are, in round numbers, twenty thousand
preachers in this island.   Of these it may, on the whole, be said
that they desire popularity; not by any means for its own
sake, or known by that name, but as a necessary form of evi-

dence that their ministrations are impressive. In Scotland, as every one is aware, there is abroad among the clergy an earnest spirit of emulation and noble ambition; they strive with all their energy to excel; and among the junior clergy of England, the same fact must, despite all hindrances, hold good. Yet, how many of our clergy attain even a local celebrity? How many of them attain a national reputation? To the first question, we shall answer, Not so much as ten per cent.; to the second, Not so much as five. We found that the clerical body secured to the full its share of the nation's talent. We now find that, when this talent is applied to its peculiar work, applied with determined energy and desire to succeed, it is only, at the utmost, in five cases out of a hundred that success is attained. How is this? It can be accounted for only by supposing that pulpit popularity is not so easy to secure as our reviewer imagines. Call it what you like — tact, fancy, feeling, fluency — the popular preacher must possess some quality which is uncommon. Men of acknowledged talent have egregiously failed as preachers. Foster desired earnestly to succeed, strove resolutely, and emptied his chapels thoroughly. Arnold would have valued pulpit acceptability very much, but he never, to any extent worth remark, obtained it. We could point to men in our own day of powerful logical faculty, of vast knowledge, of unquestioned piety, who have never, though they would conscientiously have prized it, reached popularity. We would advise the reviewer to make the experiment on his own behalf. Let him try to become a popular preacher. He may find it not so easy to make the egg stand on end.

Our own impression is, that a universal mediocrity of character is precisely what never succeeds in the pulpit. Dull uniformity, however proper and orthodox, has not a

chance. It is rather some conspicuous quality in which
a particular man is different from all others, that attracts
attention; and even this must be of a peculiar nature. The
result of mature consideration has with us been, that we
can neither explain the phenomenon of popularity, nor lay
down rules for its attainment. The preacher, too, is born.
Like the poet, he may have a feeble logical faculty; like the
poet, he may abhor the investigation of evidence, the
details of fact, the study of statistics; but, like the poet, he
must possess some indefinable gift, by virtue of which men
flock round him and love to listen.

A valuable light is cast upon this subject, as we pass on
to consider that other assertion of the Westminster critic
as to the irresponsibility of the pulpit orator. Counsel re-
plies to counsel, honorable gentlemen upset the arguments
of honorable gentlemen, but there is no voice or answer as
the honey-dew of pulpit oratory falls upon the congregation.
The preacher, is, therefore, shall we conclude, irresponsible?
Of course. Precisely as the newspaper editor is irresponsible, who pens his articles without even the criticism of list-
less eyes and nodding heads. Precisely as the Westminster writer is irresponsible, when he sends his manuscript by
post to his literary liege lord or corrects the proof when it
is to come before the public eye. Strange to relate, the irresponsible editor writes as if a responsibility lay upon him;
he fancies he beholds the eye of the indulgent reader — the
most merciless of human existences — following his pen.
Singular to consider, the Westminster author writes in the
lively consciousness of the fact, that if the public dislike his
lucubrations, his wary superior will indicate, in terms of op-
pressive compliment, that the article, or articles, must be
discontinued. Might not one who enlightens the world on
so large a scale as our clever friend, have hit upon the pro-

found observation that, in order to be popular, a man must be liked? Byron thought that Roberts must have known from the sale of his review that there could be no very extensive selling without buying. The Westminster writer would have puzzled him with his popularity without preference. As a rule, men prefer dozing on the sofa to dozing in church; where there is much sleeping, there will soon be vacant pews. The fact of the matter is obvious, and to overlook it is to practise a singular *legerdemain* upon one's self. The hiss is unnecessary in the church; audible criticism is quite superfluous; a respondent might often be a valuable assistant in keeping up interest. The cessation of the steady, clear, piercing, united gleam of a thousand eyes is sufficient; the restlessness and indifference of the congregation announce the departure of popularity as certainly as the most fierce outcry of a public assembly. And has the reviewer fairly considered all that the popular preacher has to do, all with which he has to contend? The advocate, the honorable gentleman, and the speaker on a public platform — particular difficulties as unquestionably lie in their several ways — have all one great advantage. Their subject is new, its interest is fresh. But the preacher discourses on themes with which his audience have been familiar from infancy. Whatever expectation hangs upon his words has peculiar reference to himself; a new truth is not looked for, but he is expected to set some old truth in a new light; he has to create an interest, and sustain it from week to week, though his doctrinal beliefs are marked by no novelty, and the sources of almost all his imagery have been drawn upon a thousand times. If he becomes monotonous, if he fails in animation, if he is too shallow or too profound, too exclusively commonplace or too erudite, too barely logical or too loosely rhetorical, his popularity is sure to decay. Dr.

Cumming is, we have said, an individual and peculiar instance; his style of preaching is his own; it is a style which hardly exists in Scotland, the land of preaching, and which certainly leads to no popularity in North Britain. To preaching in general all we have said applies.

Our observations have unconsciously assumed an apologetic tone. We have had to clear away a certain amount of rubbish before proceeding on our way. We must now somewhat alter the tenor of our remarks. It cannot, we think, be denied that there are grounds for the prevailing idea, that the clerical intellect lacks the clearness and logical power pertaining to the advocate or journalist. Be he what he may in his own sphere, a minister makes a bad platform speaker and a bad book-writer. A reporter will tell you that clerical speeches admit of remarkable condensation, and if the books produced by acceptable preachers within the last thirty years were collected, they would form a pile of confusion, commonplace, and verbosity worthy to enthrone a modern goddess of dulness. In the case even of preachers of commanding genius, the general literary inability remains. Dr. Chalmers was a man of such genius. His original endowment was, we are assured, one of the noblest to be met with in these latter ages. In the pulpit he was irresistible. He gave an impulse to the moral and intellectual life of Scotland. His books are valuable, and may live long. They are great masses of truth and fervor. But, as we peruse them, the feeling that their author was a preacher at all times, and a preacher only, is perpetually present; we long for the calm tracking of ideas which we expect in a book; we want the deliberate meeting of objections, the accurate observance of plan, the gradual evolution of the argumentative chain, which ought to characterize a production intended for a world-wide audience and a lasting

fame. Butler could not preach like Chalmers, but what a
different author is Chalmers from Butler! The Scottish
preacher could never divest himself of the consciousness of
his congregation, and books which are magnificently-ex-
panded sermons must be denied the approval of art.

We cannot ignore the phenomenon we have been considering. In business-like dealing with facts, in logical acute-
ness, the clerical body seems beyond question deficient.
The reason is easily perceived, and nowise compels a conclusion generally unfavorable to the intellectual capacities of
the clergy. It may be, that the clerical profession furnishes a more *complete* practical culture for the mind, while
law and journalism foster *particular* faculties. Two young
men of equal capacity part company after quitting college,
the one becoming an advocate, the other a clergyman. For
ten years they follow their professions. The lawyer has
acquired the eye of a lynx; he can untie the most intricate
knots; he can think out a whole train of argument from
the trace of a foot on the sand. But his soul is clear, cold,
passionless; it cuts like a razor, but suggests that the final
end of the human mind is to have a razor's edge. The
clergyman has fallen far behind his classfellow in argumentative skill. His mind has been engaged in spreading, di-
lating, representing, attiring ideas, not in grappling with
new facts, and searching, with swift urgency, for the links
of that harness by which they can be yoked to a conclusion.
He has been in the habit of addressing himself to the emotions as well as the pure intellect. He has made it his
business to bring to act upon men those subtle but potent
influences, which it is useless, if not impossible, to attempt
to reduce under logical formula; influences of reverence,
of admiration, of love, of the contemplation of moral excellence; and familiarity with such influences, both as

preacher and pastor, is to him that culture which perpetual consideration of facts in their logical relations is to the lawyer. The journalist occupies a middle position between advocate and preacher. He dare not be so diffuse as the pulpit orator; he must not be so barely argumentative as the special pleader. His mind is furnished with a perpetual gymnastic in discussing the endless succession of new events. He must generalize with speed, he must arrange with clearness, he must accustom his memory to carry facts. His teaching function is now extremely limited; Mr. Cobden used to think it ought to be dispensed with altogether. In a platform speech, in a discussion relative to business matters, he will be more curt, clear, and pointed, than the clergyman. But we may well doubt whether his profession is so noble a culture as that of the latter. It is remarkable, by the way, that men who have failed signally as preachers have notoriously succeeded as journalists, while we are not aware of the case having been reversed.

In one respect, however, the circumstances of the journalist are more favorable to mental health than those which encircle the clergyman. The preacher may be keenly alive to all that is necessary to maintain him in his popularity; but he is under great temptations to mistake the meaning and limits of that popularity. In no position in the world is there so great an aptness to confound the voice of a few with the judgment of mankind, the partial applause of a generation with the admiration of posterity. We are so much the creatures of influence, consciously or unconsciously, that there is no man who values intellectual health, and does not care for sugar in the mouth, but will desire to work in secret, and to know as little as may be of his celebrity. Mankind, besides, is, on the whole, savagely exacting; there can be no doubt of it: and as it is well always to know under what adamantine conditions we work, it is perilous to have the world's criticism tempered by the indulgence of a congregation. The popular minister is surrounded by an atmosphere artificially heated; his cheek is apt to flush unhealthily, his joints to relax. And on the instant when he steps into the arena of literature, the authoritative tone of his office, which has become habitual in his canonicals, is an argument against him. One would think it possible, however, at least partially, to counteract those influences. A minister who has formed a complete idea of the action of his functions on his mind, and who knows accurately his position in relation to his fellow-men, may attain a very noble character. The legal mind is clear as crystal or as ice; it thinks and writes in uncial characters. The journalist is sharp, but may be hard, and has no time for reflection. In the clerical character there may be both stem and foliage.

We are accustomed to hear nothing but laudation of the influence of the press on the public mind. Yet it is only in its exterior and obvious action that it has yet been considered. We are well assured that careful reflection will reveal to every thinking man certain perilous circumstances which attend it. Let not the foolish mistake be made, of supposing that we in any sense or measure assail the press. Such a procedure is out of the question. But by looking into it, by knowing it well in its advantages and dangers, we best learn to appreciate and use it. Might not a somewhat cynical admirer of the good old times inquire, whether, in order to the efficient transaction of the world's business, it is after all necessary that every person know what every other person is about? In former days, action proceeded quietly; every day's events now produce an immeasurable hubbub of talk. To compare great things with small, the drowsy roll of the old stage-coach is exchanged for the roar

of the railway train. The maxim about minding one's own
business is obsolete. A man is now behind his age if he
does not mind the business of the King of Siam. Looked
at in a planetary point of view, the earth has become something of a chatterbox in her old age; she is no longer content with her daily achievement of work; the universal
press may be considered the tongue with which she proclaims
it through the solar system. It is more than questionable
whether the vast multiplicity of the matters brought by the
press before the mind does not distract as well as teach. It
can hardly be considered questionable at all, that it tends
to destroy reflection. One sometimes fears that men at
present forget the end of knowledge in its quantity, and do
not think of its quality at all. In a remarkably interesting
and suggestive German book, by L. Bucher, published in
Berlin in 1855, we have met with one or two ideas on this
subject as true as they are trenchant. The author considers
the daily press of England fitted to blunt the memory and
deaden thought. "The custom," he says, "of enjoying
each days's spiritual nourishment on a dish of the same size,
and, if possible, in the same quantity, renders the memory
waste and the judgment dull." With a keen eye, he detects
evidence of this in the fact that our journals now experience
extreme difficulty in devising methods to impress the 'weight-
ier matters on the attention of their readers. All resource
in diction and style has failed to fix the eye as it glances
over the wavering sea of words: and italics, large letters,
and lines far apart, express the difficulty. The truth of this
we must acknowledge. By gazing perpetually upon the
pageantry of the world-drama, our eyes become insensible
to its splendors. We resemble men who work in a yard
where iron vessels are built; the perpetual hammering causes
deafness to the ordinary tones of the human voice. And,

what is singular enough, our standard specific at present for the cure of this deafness is the introduction of new hammerers! Go over the whole range of the human faculties, and you will find that the haste, multitude, and tumult of interests which occupy the modern mind, are perilous to their most lofty and noble action. The oak may buffet with an occasional tempest, and strike its roots the deeper, but it grows in calm.

We found the Reformation to have heralded the great modern division of labor between press and pulpit. In all directions, this principle of division is now carried out. The result has been an unprecedented advance by the species. But Sir William Hamilton has reminded us that "the cultivation of the individual is not to be rashly confounded with the progress of the species." Tennyson long since pointed to the advancement of the world and the withering of the individual; and other high thinkers have of late discerned a danger to completeness, symmetry, and freedom of character, from the extreme division of labor. Now, perhaps, more than ever, the wise man would choose the part of Pythagoras at Samos, would pass from the crowd, and develop his mind symmetrically by making a synthesis of knowledge. At all events, it must become certain to every reflecting mind, that, for a healthful development of the whole character, there is required some calming influence to overarch, like a sky, the din of this ceaseless journalistic commotion. The rest of religion is more than ever precious and necessary. If the Church stepped boldly forward, casting aside even apparent nervousness at the facts of science, and endeavoring to improve in many respects the culture of her candidates for the office of the ministry, her mission might be illustrated instead of obscured by her separation from the press.

Of all the symptoms which might be collected of a distempered restlessness, a febrile, joyless excitement, as characterizing large classes of London society in the present day, none could be more expressive or more mournful, than the way in which the great body of the newspapers uniformly refer to public worship. The one broad, bold, undisguised idea entertained and expressed of it by them is, that it is a thing of dreariness and gloom. Truly, from whatever cause, the Sabbath has become a weariness to all that is represented by the leading journals of London. The feeling takes various forms of manifestation. Now it is that of contemptuous assertion of the dulness, the ignorance, the inefficiency, of the clergy. Now it is that of indignant appeal against the refusal of the British nation, as represented in Parliament, to sanction a Parisian Sabbath, and provide, on that day, public amusements for the populace; who, it is piteously reiterated, must be driven to the gin-palace, since the dingy and wearisome church can present no attractions. Often it is that of entreaty to the clergymen to be more scientific, or philosophic, or literary, in one word, and, in whatsoever way, interesting. Now we leave totally out of sight the question of the abilities, earnestness, or piety, of the metropolitan clergy. But is it not melancholy, is it not ghastly and appalling, that it could be in the *power* of men to blind altogether the eyes of their fellows to the blessedness of merely worshipping God? Might not one weep to think that, among multitudes of men in this century, — men of genius, of culture, the rulers of the age — there cannot arise the very idea of a portion of the human life, in which selfish entertainment is not at all contemplated, in which the question is not of being interested or uninter_ ested, but in which man stands amidst his fellows, and uncovers his head before his God? Surely if in former times

men sought, from week to week, the hallowing influences
of worship, never were they so required as now. When
one listens to the central roar of London; when one paces
our hurrying quays; when one enters an Exchange in any
of our great cities; when one watches by night the tongues
of flame licking upwards through the darkness, the clouds,
for leagues on leagues, touched with a sombre but sublime
illumination, in our manufacturing districts; when, in any
way, one catches, so to speak, the bloodshot eye, or feels
the fevered pulse, of the nineteenth century; can he resist
the feeling that now, of all ages, there is most need of intervals of silence and repose, of seasons of reflection and
worship, of times when the mind is laid open to the influences of divine contemplation, and the earth is forgotten
and the soul seeks to envelop itself in the calmness of heaven?
The sky must be clear of clouds, before the stars can be
seen or the dews can fall. The ambitions and interests of
earth must be swept from the mind, before the heavenly
influences can descend to reinvigorate or refresh. What
man can say that his Sabbath practice approaches the ideal
of a Christian Sabbath; but surely the *rationale* of the
Sabbath and of worship is not difficult to find.

XI.

THE TESTIMONY OF THE ROCKS:

A DEFENCE.*

THOSE of our readers who have made themselves acquainted with an article entitled "Genesis and Science," which appeared in the fifty-fourth number of the *North British Review*, will perceive without surprise that we have deemed it our duty to make that article the subject of particular comment.

* This article was written and published in successive numbers of the *Edinburgh Witness* after the present volume was mostly in type. It did not therefore originally enter into the plan of the work, and it may strike the reader as not being entirely in harmony with the other contents. But the marked ability displayed in the discussion, and the great interest which the subject is now exciting in this country, together with the author's sanction, have induced the publishers to give the essay a place in this volume   In its original form it excited so much attention in Scotland that a pamphlet edition was called for, and in a prefatory note to that edition Mr. Bayne proceeds to remark as follows :

"The author does not profess to be a geologist in any sense implying that he has made Geology his exclusive or his principal study. He has devoted to it a considerable measure of attention, and believes that he has made himself master of its main lines of argument and of its general scheme. But he claims only to represent that large class of men, of University education, who, feeling themselves personally concerned with those questions at issue between geologists and theologians, have made it a duty to acquire sufficient geological knowledge to enable them to follow and appreciate argument on the subject. Science must abdicate all claim to an influence at once general and rational, if none but professional men of science can deal with its logic.

If there is anything strictly new in the following pages, it is the definite statement of the *method* attributed, in the Age theory of reconciliation between Scripture and Geology to the Mosaic record. Although this has been implied in many works, the writer has not seen it expressly stated.

He is particularly anxious to have it understood that, however dangerous he may consider the tendencies and effects of a certain system of Mosaic Geology, he reflects upon the sincerity, the Christianity, or the liberality of no man and no Church in still maintaining it. His own sincerity must excuse any emphasis which he may use in warning against perils which he cannot help perceiving."

We are anxious to make it clear at the outset for what reasons and with what aims we address ourselves to this subject. Neither with the *North British Review* nor with the writer of this article have we, on account of the way in which Mr. Hugh Miller is alluded to by the latter, strictly speaking, any ground of quarrel. What exception we take is to the opinions expressed, and has no reference to the mode of expressing them. The reviewer pays a becoming tribute to the genius and worth of Mr. Miller; and the *Witness* would poorly represent the principles of feeling and action bequeathed to it, by its great founder, if it discovered in manly, plain-spoken, argumentative opposition, anything fitted to compromise dispositions of friendliness. In perfect consistence, however, with friendliness of disposition towards Mr. Miller, it was possible for the writer of the article before us to do him abstract injustice, and, while so doing, to deal unintentional blows at truth itself. And this, in our view, represents the actual state of the case.

Injustice is here done, first, to Mr. Miller. It was the highest ambition of his life to serve his God and his country, and the principal way in which he hoped to do so was by applying his geological knowledge to the defence of holy Scripture against infidel assaults masked by science. It was not as a geologist, it was not as a logician, it was not as a literary composer, that Hugh Miller aimed principally at distinction. The deepest vein in his nature was his Christianity; and it was as a Christian that his loftiest aspiration displayed itself. To have told Hugh Miller that he had yielded a hair's breadth of the defences of Bible Christianity, would have been to have told him that he had shed extinguishing drops on the altar-fire which warmed and lit the inmost shrine of his own existence. " It is done," he said, referring to *The Testimony of the Rocks*, on the last day of his life, just before the nervous organization finally rebelled against that tyrant soul which had made it serve too well, — "It is done." He spoke the words, not in vain exultation, but with the serene and noble satisfaction of one whose work was finished, and who in that already saw a reward greater than any which man could bestow upon him. And what was the work which he believed he had completed? He believed that he had taken the torch of science out of the hand of the infidel, and set it to burn in the temple of the Lord; he believed that he had exhibited, more plainly than had previously been done, the harmony and accordance between the word and the works of God; he believed that he had pushed that great enterprise which had been begun by Chalmers, whom of all men he most gratefully named his father on earth, further towards its goal: he believed that he had done the Christian Church a service. In the article in the *North British* entitled "Genesis and Science," it is distinctly represented that Mr. Miller, in his last work, instead of carrying forward the standards of Christianity, carried them back, — that, as a Christian apologist, he did not therein advance, but recede. So far as this reviewer and the *North British Review* speak for any Church, that Church is put in the position towards Mr. Miller, not of one thanking and honoring for service, but of one expostulating against undue concession, or repelling actual assault. We believe that this is not just to Mr. Miller, and, so believing, feel that it is appropriate in us to attempt to restore him to the place among the faithful defenders of Christianity which is his due.

But the injustice done to Mr. Miller is comparatively of slight importance as a reason for replying to this article, if, as we maintain, in the next place, it inflicts injury on the cause of truth. The name of Hugh Miller might well be left to guard his reputation. But we believe that the interests of truth are here imperilled, and that in a very critical manner. Let

it be understood that we do not consider the questions which
have been raised in connection with the first chapter of Genesis as at an end. We do not commit ourselves irrevocably to
any dogma in the case. But so far we can go with unwavering confidence. The *path* indicated in *The Testimony of the
Rocks* is that in which advance towards clearer light is possible; the *key* to the sublime problem has there been given;
while the theory preferred in the article under notice, — the
theory best known as that of Dr. Chalmers, — cannot lead to
truth or reconciliation, but must imperil the one, and render the
other impossible. It is well here to speak with emphasis, because it is of an important part of .the defences of Christianity
that we speak. It is our solemn conviction that, excluding the
express historical evidence of New Testament facts, no argument for the divinity and inspiration of Scripture in the whole
range of apologetics is more express, distinct, irresistible, than
that to which *The Testimony of the Rocks*, to say the very
least, points the way. It is an argument which might be said,
with hardly any figure, to convert faith into sight. Already it
appears to us sufficient to convince any reasonable man, we
say not of the being of God, or of the general truth of Christianity, but of the positive, supernatural inspiration of Scripture; and were it once perfectly elaborated, as perhaps ten or
twenty years may see it elaborated, it might, we maintain, be
fairly pleaded as literally and demonstrably equal in strength
to the rising of one from the dead. In one word, the Christian apologist is already able, by Mr. Miller's theory, and will
become more and more conspicuously able, to propose to the
infidel this dilemma: Either a wandering tribe of the Arabian
Desert was acquainted, three thousand years ago, with the
most recent revelations of science, or the first chapter of Genesis was written by the inspiration of the Almighty. Our readers will agree with us, that *if* such a weapon has been brought

to the Christian armory, it would be unwise in the Church to cast it aside.

In the further discussion of this subject we shall first briefly point out wherein the writer in the *North British Review* misconceives, and consequently misrepresents, Mr. Miller's course of argument in *The Testimony of The Rocks*. We shall then endeavor to show how much more sound, definite, and satisfactory, considered as a defence of the inspiration of the Mosaic records against the assaults of skeptical geologists, is the theory supported by Mr. Miller than that maintained by this reviewer.

SCOPE OF "THE TESTIMONY OF THE ROCKS."

The writer in the *North British Review* has fallen into complete and fatal error in his conception of the general argument in *The Testimony of the Rocks*. "In the chapter on the Palæontological History of Plants," says the reviewer, referring to Mr. Miller's scheme of harmony between Genesis and Geology, "a corroboration of the theory is sought in the alleged 'resemblance, almost amounting to identity,' between the classification of modern botanists and that discovered in the various fossiliferous strata." The writer then proceeds to show that this corroboration is not made out. To all that he says, however, there is a simple answer to be given. The whole allegation of Mr. Miller's having sought such corroboration is a delusion. We are here stating not an argument, but a fact. We point to an entire misapprehension of what Mr. Miller did or intended to do; and the bearing of our allegation on the succeeding argument consists merely in its pointing out how imperfectly the reviewer understood the book he reviewed. Considered in connection with the science of Christian apologetics, *The Testimony of the Rocks* consists mainly, though not, indeed, entirely, of two parts; first, a contribution to the argument from design in support of the doctrine of the being and unity of God; second, a contribution to the argument by which the works of God are brought to bear testimony in favor of his inspired word. The reviewer confounds the two. They do not, however, even stand and fall together; they are absolutely distinct. Sweep away Mr. Miller's whole theory of the reconciliation between Geology and Genesis, and his argument for the being and unity of God, founded on modern systems of botanical and zoological classification, might remain as clearly recognized a contribution to natural theology as any chapter in Paley: deny all validity to his reasonings in the domain of natural theology, and you must still try on its own merits his theory of Mosaic Geology. The mistake fallen into by the reviewer is a remarkable, and not a very excusable mistake. We can hardly believe him to be fully aware of what his words imply when he disparages Mr. Miller's argument in support of the being and unity of God derived from the palæontological history of plants and animals. He may reject the theory of *The Testimony of the Rocks* on the first chapter of Genesis, but we venture to say that he cannot reject the preceding argument. Modern botanists and modern zoologists, — thus argues Mr. Miller, — acting in complete independence of Geology, have, by natural reason, matured a certain classification of plants and animals. This classification is an example of the working of human intellect. In the records of a bygone creation, proceeds Mr. Miller, it is found that a classification which may be pronounced all but identical with this was historically developed. Hence an argument for the being and unity of God. The problem of natural theology is to ascend from the human mind and the visible creation to the Divine mind and the unseen Creator. By a process of observing, comparing, reasoning, the human brain works out,

from the extant creation, one classification: in the lapse of bygone ages, a similar classification was evolved. Is it possible,
on a comparison of the two, not to perceive that a mind of
which the human is an image, — a mind that can compare and
design, — a mind that is one, — had part in the bygone creation? It may be, that the state of science does not yet admit
of the detailed elaboration of Mr. Miller's argument; but to
deny that it *does* admit of elaboration, would be very like sapping the whole edifice of natural theology. To our own minds
that argument is one of the grandest contributions, if not the
very grandest, ever made to natural theology. A watch, said
Paley, reveals design; therefore a watch can be constructed
only by mind. A flower, he added, reveals design; therefore
a flower must have been created by mind. But for Paley's
watch Mr. Miller substitutes the superb machine of modern
classification, put together, in its thousand complications, by
the human mind. *That*, he says, is, sure enough, the result of
design, the work of mind. Here then, — and he turns on the
skeptic, — is the precise counterpart of the magnificent watch,
found in the silent desert of bygone ages, — its wheels, its
springs, its hands, the same; will you deny that mind was at
the designing of it, — that a reasoning soul like that taken
upon him by Jesus Christ inserted *its* wheels and chains?

Mr. Miller walked about Zion, and went around, marking
well her bulwarks, and telling the towers thereof; with the eye
of a skilful general, he embraced in one view the various
points of defence; and, in *The Testimony of the Rocks*, before
proceeding to prove the integrity of the Mosaic record, he
deemed it fitting to silence certain of those batteries of Hume
and the materialists, which are still from time to time sullenly
firing. And this is the true account of that argument from
Palæontology which his reviewer so strangely misconceived.

But, next, it is a mistake to represent, as this writer does,

that Mr. Miller in the Age theory, puts the third day of creation for the fourth. From the circumstance that Mr. Miller,
on a particular occasion, and to a popular audience, restricted
himself to three of the creative days, and from not observing
which days these were, the reviewer concludes them to be the
fourth, fifth, and sixth, instead of, as they are, the third, fifth,
and sixth. In his popular lecture, Mr. Miller said, that in the
geological record he could expect to find reference to but those
three days on which creation of organic existences took place.
He omitted, therefore, the first two days and the fourth day.
But, even in that lecture, he does not say that he makes the
day of plants fall on the fourth, instead of the third; and in his
other lectures he so explicitly assigns to each day its own work,
that the reviewer is left with but slight excuse. In both cases
the third day is that in which flourished the forests of the Carboniferous epoch. In the lecture implicitly, and in other parts
of Mr. Miller's work explicitly, the period assigned to the
appearance of the sun and moon is that succeeding the Carboniferous epoch, namely, the Permian and Triassic. It is a valid
objection to the literary arrangement of *The Testimony of the
Rocks*, that it discusses the question of the Mosaic and Scientific Geologies in two different places, and in ways which it may
require a moment's reflection to reconcile; but more than a
moment's reflection is not necessary, and this it was the reviewer's duty to have devoted to their comparison.

We shall quote here a passage from *The Testimony of the
Rocks*, which will at once show how Mr. Miller distinguished
three of the creative days, as preëminently geological, from
the others, and exhibit the essential features of his theory of
reconciliation between Genesis and Science. " What may be
termed the three *geologic* days,—the third, fifth, and sixth,—
may be held to have extended over those Carboniferous periods
during which the great plants were created,—over those Oölitic

and Cretaceous periods during which the great sea-monsters
and birds were created,—and over those Tertiary periods during which the great terrestrial mammals were created. For
the intervening or fourth day we have that wide space represented by the Permian and Triassic periods, which, less conspicuous in their floras than the period that went immediately
before, and less conspicuous in their faunas than the periods
that came immediately after, were marked by the decline, and
ultimate extinction, of the Palæozoic forms, and the first partially developed beginnings of the secondary ones. And for
the first and second days there remain the great Azoic period,
during which the immensely developed gneisses, mica schists,
and primary clay-slates, were deposited, and the two extended
periods represented by the Silurian and Old Red Sandstone
systems. These, taken together, exhaust the geological scale,
and may be named in their order as, — *first*, the Azoic day or
period.; *second*, the Silurian and Old Red Sandstone day or
period; *third*, the Carboniferous day or period; *fourth*, the
Permian or Triassic day or period; *fifth*, the Oölitic and Cretaceous day or period; and *sixth*, the Tertiary day or period."

It is of the highest importance, in considering the claims of
the theory of reconciliation between Genesis and Geology
maintained by Mr. Miller, to discriminate between its essential
characteristics, and what are, more or less, external and adven-
titious. Attracted by its novel and imposing aspect, and dazzled by the splendor of poetry with which Mr. Miller has
invested it, we are apt to conclude that the succession of visions under which, in *The Testimony of the Rocks*, the revelation of the first chapter of Genesis is represented as having
been made to Moses, is inseparable from the general theory.
Such, however, is not the case. Certain facts and sequences
revealed in the rocks have a correspondence with certain facts
and sequences revealed in the first chapter of Genesis, — a cor-

respondence so clear and so precise, that it cannot possibly be accounted for except on the grounds of supernatural revelation to the writer of the books of Moses. This is the proposition on which Mr. Miller's theory radically rests. The *mode* in which the revelation was made is another question : it may have been by a succession of visions, or it may not; the point of importance is, that the correspondence exists. For óur own part, while deeming the hypothesis of a series of visions one of singular aptness and beauty, and while believing that its acceptance can involve no consequence dangerous to the doctrine of inspiration, we do not profess strictly and literally to maintain it. We conceive that it weakens rather than strengthens the theory of the periods of creation, in exposition and support of which it is put forward. Had Moses seen in vision what the geologist can now see by aid of science, it seems hardly possible that he should not himself have possessed, and transmitted to succeeding generations of the Jewish people, a scientific knowledge of the history of creation. But not the slightest indication exists that Moses scientifically understood what he was made the instrument of revealing ; and it is certain that no succeeding generation before the present could scientifically explain his writings. If the vision theory, strictly so called, compromises this fact, the vision theory must be abandoned. The apologetic worth of the argument from the geologic period lies in the circumstance that the first chapter of Genesis is a scientifically exact revelation, but was, in the wisdom of God, uncomprehended for many generations; that it is written in characters of perfect definiteness, but in characters belonging to an unknown tongue ; and that, only when at length the light of science is flashed upon the inscription, — only when the lost language is studied and known, — is its meaning plain and unmistakable. This argument must on no account be put in peril. But not only is the hypothesis of a series of visions

31*

connected in no essential manner with the theory of harmony between Genesis and Geology, as maintained by Mr. Miller; — it is not absolutely necessary, to impart value to the theory in question, that the geologic days, corresponding to the days of Genesis, be ultimately discriminated in Mr. Miller's precise manner.   It is our belief that very few changes will ultimately be found necessary in his scheme of division; but the great point is, that the mind of the Church should be directed to the availability of the Age theory as a scheme of harmony; and the service here done by Mr. Miller is to point out in what general manner Geology in its present advanced state may be brought into accordance with that theory.   He himself distinctly states that our conceptions of the first two days-periods are not yet exact.   If he has not, however, finally and perfectly triumphed, he joined a school which must finally and perfectly triumph; and *The Testimony of the Rocks* is to be regarded as a most important contribution to the literature of that school.   This is sufficient to vindicate for Mr. Miller the claim to an honored place among Christian apologists.

THE OPPOSING SCHEME OF MOSAIC GEOLOGY UNTENABLE.

To avoid technical terms, and to make no demands on scientific information, in a matter which may, we are convinced, be decided on the grounds of common sense, we shall inform our readers in one word wherein the radical difference between the theory of Mr. Miller and that of his reviewer consists. The theory which the reviewer declines to abandon is, that about six thousand years ago the earth was the scene of that chaos described in the first chapter of Genesis in these words, — " And the earth was without form, and void; and darkness was upon the face of the deep."   In this view the entire series of geologic creations is ignored; from "the beginning" to six thousand years ago is one mighty hiatus. According to Mr. Miller's theory, on the other hand, the creative work recorded in Genesis is in correspondence with that revealed in the rocks : the days of Scripture are extended periods of time ; and the chaos which is referred to in Genesis preceded the geologic series, instead of occuring at its close. The essential difference, then, is as to the position of the chaotic period. Those who agree with our reviewer place it immediately before the appearance of man ; those who follow Mr. Miller place it before the commencement of the geologic ages. If science negatives a recent chaos, the theory of the former falls at once to the ground.

Mr. Miller first enunciated his refutation of the theory of a recent chaos to a popular audience, in a popular lecture. The scheme of such a composition did not admit of a detailed or exhaustive exhibition of proof. The lecturer was compelled rather to choose, from a mass of evidence, one or two easily apprehended and pointed proofs, such as could be speedily despatched on a public platform. Two such proofs he selected, — the first drawn from old and new coast lines, — the second drawn from the unbroken succession of animal and vegetable life through the whole vast duration of the Tertiary period. These proofs appear to us in themselves conclusive. The reviewer does not attempt to fix the age of the present coast line at less than 2600 years ; and we presume no geologist would consent to set it under 3000 or 4000. He offers a suggestion or two against the relative age assigned by Mr. Miller to the old coast line ; but to these we cannot attach any force, and are confident that, were the opinion of British geologists universally taken on the subject, an immense majority would declare that Mr. Miller's calculation of the combined ages of the coast lines, — 6500 years, — was far too moderate. The second argument, — that derived from the continuation of types of life, — is still more powerful. It is hardly a correct representation of this argument to state it as based on the fact of types of life having been carried forward "from one epoch to another." The whole question relates to one époch, the Tertiary. If a chaotic period preceded the creation of man, it *must* fall, — this all concede, — at the very end of the Tertiary period. It *must* fall, not only after the original creation of vast numbers of plants and shells now in existence, but after the first creation of the badger, the wild cat, the fox, the red deer, the hare, and other denizens of our woods. The theory of the opponents of Mr. Miller is, that while these were in existence, a chaotic break took place, — they were all exterminated, and then all again created. Do we not almost instinctively recognize in this something unlike the general method of Divine workmanship? The sudden extermination, moreover, must have taken place in a well-peopled world, and the sudden death of its myriads have converted its surface into a vast cemetery. But no tide-mark has been left of this wave of universal death. As the succession of life can be traced for six thousand years, it can be traced during previous periods.

These, exclusive of certain considerations adduced in other parts of the volume, are the arguments brought forward in *The Testimony of the Rocks* against the theory of a recent chaos. But it would be, we repeat, a most inaccurate representation to say that these arguments, or any which the popular form in which *The Testimony of the Rocks* was drawn up enabled Mr. Miller to use, exhaust the proofs to be advanced against that view. Several years ago, Dr. Pye Smith, one of the most sincere and devout of Calvinistic divines, was so completely convinced by a general survey of the evidence which negatives a recent chaos of universal extent, that he proposed his scheme of a chaos merely local, in order to reconcile Geology with Scripture; and, says Mr. Miller, "be it remembered, that between the scheme of lengthened periods, and the scheme of a merely local chaos which existed no one knows how, and of a merely local creation which had its scene no one knows where, geological science leaves us now no choice whatever." The plain fact seems to be, that the very affluence of the proofs at his command prevented Mr. Miller from attempting synoptically to draw them out. It is said that a man who has a strongly marked genius for any one branch of knowledge will not improbably be a bad teacher in that department: he will be apt to outrun his pupils, and fatally to over-rate the facility of his favorite pursuit. In the same way, a reasoner who is, so to speak, superabundantly convinced of the soundness of his theory, may half-unconsciously assume that it is unnecessary to exhibit all its grounds. But if Mr. Miller exhibited no more proof against the proposition of a recent chaos than what at first occurred to him, and was adapted to a popular audience, it is fair, especially when we consider that death has palsied the hand which could have drawn many another shaft from that well-filled quiver, that we should remember the fact, and view the theory in connection with the whole range of the evidence adducible in its support.

It is of course out of the question that we should point out here the whole compass of that evidence. We may refer, however, to one or two important portions of it, not directly cited by Mr. Miller in support of his theory.

Evidence which to us appears of a conclusive character is afforded on the subject by certain American rivers. Between Queenstown Heights and the Falls of Niagara there is a gorge a considerable number of miles in length, which has been hollowed out by the Falls. Sir Charles Lyell pronounced a period of 35,000 years necessary to have completed the work of erosion. If you grant but a half or a fourth part of the

time, you must' allow that the river has been flowing from a
period antecedent by a thousand years to the creation of
Adam.   But America furnishes a series of examples similar
to that of the gorge of Niagara.   We find Mr. M'Ausland, in
his very valuable work on Scripture and Geology, quoting the
following passage from Professor Hitchcock's well-known
work: — "The Niagara gorge is only one among a multitude
of examples which might be quoted, and some of them far
more striking to a geologist.   On Oak Orchard Creek and
the Genesee River, between Rochester and Lake Ontario,
are similar erosions, seven miles long.   On the latter river,
south of Rochester, we find a cut from Mount Morris to Port-
age, sometimes 400 feet deep.   On many of our south-western
rivers we have what are called caverns or gorges, often 250
feet deep, and several miles long.   Near the source of the
Missouri River are what are called the Rocky Mountains,
where there is a gorge six miles long and 1200 feet deep.
Similar cuts occur in the Columbia River, hundreds of feet
deep, through the hard trap rock, for hundreds of miles, between the American Falls and the Dalles.   At St. Anthony's
Falls, in the Mississippi, that river has worn a passage in
limestone seven miles long, which distance the cataract has
receded.   On the Potomac, ten miles west of Washington,
the Great Falls have worn back a passage sixty to sixty-five
feet deep, four miles continuously; — a greater work, considering the nature of the rock, than has been done by the
Niagara."   This list is far from exhausted; but it is already
of sufficient length.   There is probably not one of these
instances in which a geologist would not declare the river
in question to have occupied its bed for more than six thousand years.   It may just be maintained, though hardly, we
should think, by any one making pretensions to geological
knowledge, that a watery chaos may have covered the whole

face of the earth, but that these rivers, though temporarily swallowed up in the universal ocean, may have resumed their courses. We shall not consider this a hypothesis against which it is necessary to argue; but if there is any mind to which it presents itself with force of evidence, we would point to a case in which such an idea cannot be even entertained. In the volcanic districts of Auvergne, in France, instances are presented of an erosion similar to that exhibited in America, gorges being cut for hundreds of feet through the solid granite on which they rest. The precipices cut by the waters stand there in their nakedness, and the point is distinctly discernible where the work of erosion began. The rock through which it has penetrated was thrown out by the neighboring volcanoes. Of this no doubt can possibly he entertained. The rock must have been emitted before the erosion began. But the erosion has been proceeding for periods to which the six thousand years of human chronology are as yesterday. In this case too, then, the rivers enveloped in the surrounding ocean must have been lifted from their beds, to be gently replaced as the six days' work proceeded. But how was it with the neighboring volcanic craters? Were the loose pumice-stones and scoriæ with which they are covered also spared by the dark and boundless tide? In 1831 Graham Island was flung up by volcanic action from the bosom of the sea. It became three miles in circumference, and two hundred feet in height. Then the volcanic action ceased. In three or four months it was swept out of sight by the waves, and existed, says Mr. Miller, "but as a dangerous shoal." If the sea, merely dashing on its borders, had such power over Graham Island, would not the universal ocean have swept flat the sugar-loaf cones of Auvergne? But there they stand, peaked and sharp, covered with lava which was ejected from the volcanic craters. If the geologist can make any one assertion whatever, he can say that no wave ever dashed against their summits.   Need we any further proof against a recent chaos?

OBJECTIONS TO THE AGE THEORY OBVIATED.

The negative evidence in favor of the scheme of geologic periods, — that consisting in an exhibition of the scientific grounds which prove the hypothesis of a recent chaos to be no longer tenable, — having been indicated, it would now be the natural sequence of argument to present, at least in outline, the positive evidence which may be brought forward in support of Mr. Miller's theory.   But we deem it advisable first to turn our attention to the removal of certain objections, which may present themselves to the ordinary student of Scripture, and which may seem to forestall and forbid all scientific argument in the case.

It may be objected, first, that the days of the first chapter of Genesis are obviously natural days, and that violence is done to Scripture by regarding them in any other light.   This objection has great influence, if no great weight, and comes supported by the prejudice of three thousand years.   Yet we are persuaded that, if calmly contemplated, it can, in accordance with the profoundest reverence for God's word, and the deepest principles of reasoning, be conclusively set aside.   In the first place, it is on all hands conceded that the word "day" has been used by all nations to express indefinite periods of time.   In the next place, we learn, from the fourth verse of the second chapter of Genesis, that such a use of the word "day" was not rejected by the authority from which the inspiration of both chapters emanated : "These are the generations of the heavens and of the earth when they were created, in the *day* that the Lord God made the earth and the heavens."   Nor in other parts of Scripture are similar examples wanting.   Mr.

M'Ausland, after referring to several passages of Scripture in support of the theory we now maintain, cites, with great aptness, the passage in the book of Daniel in which the "vision of the morning and evening" is made to embrace a period of "two thousand and three hundred days." Next, it is worthy of being remarked, as is done by the writer whom we have just mentioned, that Josephus and Philo among the ancients, and Whiston, Des Cartes, and De Luc among the moderns, argued—on grounds, of course, entirely independent of science —that the Mosaic days were protracted periods. But lastly, —and this is to us by far the most conclusive argument of all,—it is to be maintained that the subject matter of the revelation made in the first chapter of Genesis is in itself sufficient to render a deviation from the common historical practice in the use of the word "day," probable and natural. Our opponents may argue that the style is simply historical. But on any showing, the first chapter of Genesis is a historical narration of a kind altogether unexampled. It is as completely separated from any human coöperation or action as the purest prophecy. In such a case, there was at least no presumption against the attachment to the word "day," of that meaning which it bears in prophetic passages. And if the works of God, the sole testimony on earth that can plead authority in the interpretation of the word of God, distinctly exhibit that God *did* so use the term, will mere human preconception be permitted to put that testimony to silence? No philological argument will ever prove the first chapter of Genesis to be ordinary history. Its language might take that *form*, because, in the infinite wisdom of God, it was intended that to the human instrument, Moses, used for its transmission, it should appear historical, and should remain sealed in mystery until brought forth in these latter days, to the confusion of the infidel, and the edification of true believers. It was necessary

32

that its language should not externally and at first sight appear prophetic. But the *substance* of the revelation, known to God only, did not, and could not, pertain to the domain of ordinary history; and when the works of God have enabled us to understand the full significance of the revelation, we may surely admit that it was just, wise, and right in the Almighty to use certain terms in its transmission in a sense which in other parts of Scripture is appropriated to prophetic revealings. When Scripture history describes scenes in which man has acted, the language of men in its common acceptation is used; when Scripture reveals what, covered up in the future, is seen by the eye of God only, it adopts a language not in all respects the same as that of every-day life; and when the sacred volume calls from the past the history of that great creative work in which the hand of God alone was engaged, it is fitting that the language which is used should be that adopted in other parts of Scripture, when man stands aside, and God alone acts.

Passing from this objection, it may be right to allude, in one word, to the impression subsisting in certain quarters, that the Age theory puts in peril the reason annexed to the Fourth Commandment. We confess that this objection appears to us devoid of all semblance of force. Nay, it might, we think, be maintained that the Age theory alone exhibits, in all their Scriptural and scientific breadth, the grounds of the Sabbatic rest. The scheme of the geologic periods points to the resting of God as a *fact*. Since the appearance of man in the world, the work of creation has ceased. No species is known to have come into existence since the procession of being was closed by its king. Here, then, is direct confirmation of Scripture. And if the redemption of man is God's Sabbath-day's work, and the reasoning head of this lower creation is permitted, on each recurrent Sabbath in the natural year, to praise and magnify his greatness and mercy in that work, shall we say that the sanctions attached to the Sabbath-day have become, on account of the light cast by science on God's word, less binding or less sacred?

But, once more, it is flatly affirmed, in opposition of the Age theory, that the successions recorded in Genesis and those revealed in the rocks do not correspond. This assertion is made by the reviewer in the *North British*, and it is manifestly that on which he mainly depends. If it can be conclusively defended, although the opposing scheme would not yet be established, the scheme of the periods would certainly require to be abandoned. It is proved, then, that animal life existed on our globe in the geologic periods corresponding to the first, second, third, and fourth Mosaic days, in the account of which days in Genesis there seems, at a first glance, to be no mention of life; while the creation of creeping things, usually allotted to the fifth Mosaic day, occurred at a much lower point in the scale. Such is the argument of our opponents. It is quite impossible for us to state here the acute and admirable reasoning by which Mr. M'Ausland strives, in meeting it, to show, entirely from Scripture, first, that the expression "the Spirit of God moved upon the waters," amounts to a declaration that certain forms of life were generated on the first day by the creative Spirit; and second, that the Hebrew original does not warrant the allotment of creeping things to the creation of the fifth day, but solely that of the creatures which are presented to us by the fifth geologic period. To that reasoning we attach great weight, and commend our readers to make themselves acquainted with it. But we would call their attention at present more particularly to another argument, — one whose force cannot, we think, be denied, and for apprehending and weighing which no scientific knowledge is necessary. It is simply this; that, even if we conceded, as we by no means do, that the theory of the periods anticipates in certain particulars the recorded appearance of animals, it is yet, in this respect, in incomparably closer correspondence with the Mosaic account than the theory to which it is opposed by our reviewer. It is *alleged*, though most strenuously denied, that in one or two points the one theory makes the rocks announce special processes of creation earlier than Moses; but it is *allowed* that the other theory makes the Mosaic narrative not declarative of the time of creation at all; it is *allowed* that by it the creation of vast forests and countless animals took place before the Mosaic record gives any surmise of the appearance of tree, of animal, of light itself. There may be difficulty as yet in fitting, word for word, by the one theory, the writing in the rocks to the writing in the Bible. The commas and dashes may not be finally set. But the other theory sweeps the whole revelation of the rocks aside, and, in so sweeping it, renders the Mosaic revelation not a revelation of *the* creation at all, but only that of a recent, and, in comparison with the others, a momentary creation. The supporter of this theory obliterates by one stroke of his pen every chronological mark given in the Mosaic days. He declares that light was *not* first poured on this world six thousand years ago, but perhaps six millions of years. He declares that plants were *not* first created six thousand years ago, but unnumbered ages before. He declares that creeping thing, fowl, fish, and mammal, were *not* first created six thousand years ago, but at some unknown time in the preceding eternity. It will of course be responded that, according to the theory we assail, no succession is alleged, and that it is only when correspondence is affirmed that chronological sequence can be demanded. We are willing to attach all due weight to this consideration; but let it have no more than is its due. Which theory, then, is nearer to the truth, more evidently on the way to the truth? — that which has still but to remove a difficulty here and there, to fit one or two still dubious correspondences, but which boldly maintains its capability of exhibiting the Mosaic record as a strict account of the evolution of creation on our world since the beginning? or that which to each Mosaic day prefixes a broad and sweeping negative, and declares that each successive operation there recorded did not then first take place, but untold ages before? Is the one theory to be condemned because in one or two cases it does not consider a Mosaic affirmative to have implied a negative; and the other to be preferred, although it embraces, under one unsuggested negative, the whole magnificent procession of creation, from the primeval fire to the end of the Pleistocene epoch? The state of the question is not that of no difficulty on the one side, and all difficulty on the other. By the theory of the reviewer, that account which sets out from "the beginning," and ends with man, passes over without a hint the whole of that work of creation which Geology has revealed. The theory *compels* us to assume an immense gap in a narrative which has the appearance of being connected. This is really an insuperable difficulty. The opposing theory is not yet finally, minutely, and unassailably established; but we deliberately profess, on the strength of it, to find in the first chapter of Genesis a consistent, unbroken narrative; we acknowledge no suppression, but such as the mode and extent of the description rendered absolutely necessary; we begin with it at the beginning, and it leads us to the Sabbath of rest, in which the creative work on our world has ceased.

THE POSITIVE EVIDENCE FOR THE AGE THEORY.

God created man in his own image: we can never too vividly remember the fact, or too deeply ponder its significance. In the noblest working of man's highest powers is to be found the best assistance afforded by the whole domain of

32*

nature towards explaining and illustrating the methods of
Divine operation. The consummate human artist is distinguished from inferior painters by his power of producing a
great effect with slight expenditure of effort or use of material.
His eye pierces at once to what is essential and distinctive,
seizes the whole of that, and leaves the rest alone : his hand
glances for a few moments about the canvas, and the likeness
is unmistakable. A burnt stick is to him more than a complete set of colors to another ; a few lines drawn by him
signify more than the most complex and elaborate light and
shade from an unskilful hand. In this power of narrating
much in little space, modern science has somewhat curiously
furnished a parallel to the achievements of supreme artistic
skill. The telegraph transmits, in a few abrupt and discon-
nected sentences, those particulars which make up the essential history of a protracted period ; and the art — a very
important art — of transmitting telegraphic intelligence,
reaches perfection when every item of real moment is transmitted, and not one unnecessary word enters into the composition of the telegram. The first chapter of Genesis may be
most accurately conceived either as a succession of descriptive
sketches from the hand of an infinitely skilful artist, or as a
sublime telegram, composed with absolute skill, and bringing
us tidings from a dim and remote antiquity. Considered as
pictorial sketches, the records of the successive creations are
of course not exhaustive ; but it may be boldly affirmed, that
in no other instance, whether in the Bible or out of it, has so
much been conveyed in so small space. The resemblance, the
likeness, is unerring. These outlined sketches are as true and
sure *representations* as if they detailed every motion of every
created animal, and showed the light falling over every leaf
and wave : but, being sketches, and sketches produced with
the smallest possible expenditure of means, they contain dis-

tinctive features, and distinctive features alone. Considered, on the other hand, as sentences of a sublime and wonderful telegram, the descriptions in Genesis are not detailed : were they so, all the chronicles of human history would dwindle into smallness compared with the long annals of those ancient centuries. But were they not here before us, conception would fail to realize, faith would be unable to accept as possible, that marvellous selection of particulars by which the essential history of the planet, probably for millions of years, is condensed into one short chapter. And let it be particularly remarked that, whether the theory of the natural days or that of the extended periods is adopted, this character of condensation and selection must be imputed to the Mosaic account of the creation. Both parties find in one chapter an account of the creation of a world and its inhabitants : both must admit that much has been omitted. On neither hypothesis, therefore, can a negative be inferred because a positive is asserted.

We must offer yet another illustration of the method pursued in the Mosaic record of creation. The discovery and definition of that method are the distinctive merits claimed by the advocates of the Age theory. On a clear and definite apprehension of that method depends the ability to understand, to test, to apply, the Age theory. We have given one illustration of the method of the Mosaic account of creation from science, and another from art; we take our third from nature. In a clear day, when you look upon a mountainous horizon in the far distance, you perceive a delicate film of faint blue or pearly gray relieved against the sky. The outline of that film, faint though it be, is, for every kind of mountain-range, definite and unchangeable. The horizon line of the primaries will be serrated, peaked, and jagged. The horizon line of the metamorphic hills will be more undulating and rounded. The

horizon of the tertiaries will be in long sweeps and tenderly
modulated curves.   In each case, the line of the horizon tells
more than can be told in any other conceivable way, of the
character of a whole district of country.   Those minute jags
and points of the primaries are dizzy precipices and towering
peaks.   The glacier is creeping on under that filmy blue ; the
avalanche is thundering in that intense silence.   Rivers that
will channel continents and separate nation from nation are
leaping in foamy cataracts, where you perceive only that the
tender amethyst of the sky has taken a deeper tinge.   That
undulating line of the crystalline hills tells of broad, dreary
moors, of dark, sullen streams, of sparse fields of stunted corn.
That sweeping, melting, waving line of the tertiaries tells of
stately forest and gardened plain, of lordly mansions and
bustling villages.   Now, the Mosaic record of creation gives the
horizon lines of the various geological periods.   Its descriptions are unerringly exact, considered as horizon lines.   It
is impossible to exchange the one for the other.   There is no
confusion between them.   They reveal the very largest possible
amount concerning the several periods in the very smallest
possible space.   When we investigate those periods in detail,
when we enter the valleys folded up under those horizons, we
find that only under such horizons could such valleys have
been ; that those horizons really, had we but known it, revealed
the character of the underlying valleys.   In order to prove
them untrue, we have to show, either that other valleys than
those we have found must have been under such horizons, or
that such horizons are only vaguely and at hap-hazard related
to such valleys.

It is agreed on all hands that the first verse in Genesis, "In
the beginning God created the heavens and the earth," does
not fix the antiquity of the actual matter constituting our globe.
It is, however, natural, nay, imperative, to consider the term

"beginning" to have a special significance for our world. Science has now distinctly and finally declared that what may, for our world, be peculiarly called the beginning, was in fire. The eye of science first rests on the earth as a burning mass, of a temperature whose fierce heat cannot be conceived. However long that fire-period may have lasted, it was strictly the beginning. A description which, after alluding to it, sets out from its termination, omits nothing.

"And the earth was without form, and void; and darkness was upon the face of the deep; and the Spirit of God moved upon the face of the waters." This verse, according to the theory we now oppose, is separated from that immediately preceding by all the geologic ages. Not only from the beginning of things is it divided, but from the special beginning of this world, — from that period of fire when it was unfitted to support animal or vegetable life, when it was draped by no clouds and embraced by no atmosphere; — when it was not an ordered planet, but a raging, flaming chaos. By the theory finally embraced by Mr. Miller, on the other hand, this verse is the natural sequel to that which referred to the beginning of the earth. Formlessness, voidness, and — whenever the fire was sufficiently cooled to admit of the formation of water — a universal, boiling ocean, to whose surface no ray of light could penetrate; — such was the state of the world immediately after the commencing fire-period. In describing it the man of science would in vain seek for more apt or expressive terms than those used in the second verse of Genesis.

"And God said, Let there be light; and there was light." At what precise point in the evolution of the creative plan light penetrated to the surface of our planet, and shed a faint glimmer through the dense vapor which rose from the seething wilderness of waters, science cannot declare. At a certain

point, however, light did so penetrate. On this Geology
speaks plainly. The universal ocean appears to have first
wrapped the world, when the molten granite had, to a certain
extent, cooled. Then commenced the deposition of the
gneisses, the mica-schists, and the clay-slates. These rocks,
particularly those of the two former series, are contorted and
twisted in a manner which completely distinguishes them from
all succeeding rocks. To use the expression applied to them
by Mr. Ruskin, they "tremble through their every fibre, like
the chords of an Æolian harp." They were manifestly formed
in a sea at first surging and tossing on its bed of fire, and
thereafter gradually cooled. This fact explains peculiarities
in their form, which otherwise mock all conjecture. But if
these rocks were deposited in the ocean succeeding the ancient
fire, beneath the vapors of a boiling sea, there can be no
doubt that for a long period they were enveloped in blackest
night, and that at a certain moment this darkness was faintly
penetrated. Genesis informs us that the first day's work was
completed when the diffused radiance first shimmered through
the brooding darkness, and there was on this earth light.
Darkness and light,—these are the two essentially descriptive
words in the Mosaic telegram, embracing the period between
the earth's beginning and the close of the first day. To
assume that this positive account implies the negative declaration that, when the ocean became tepid, and light was groping its way to its surface, no minute creature, no *Oldhamia
antiqua*, no trilobite, moved in its depths, is entirely gratuitous,
and proves that the whole method of the Mosaic narrative has
been misconceived. The important fact is, that science cannot
possibly describe those early ages, except in a manner to agree
with the first verses of Genesis. The inspired word closes
the first great period with the appearance on earth of light,
and the man of science can fix upon no scientifically estab-

lished occurrence of that primeval time so magnificently
decisive, so sublimely closing one era and commencing another,
as even this same penetration of light.

The work allotted in Genesis to the second day is the formation of what, in our translation, is rendered a "firmament,"
but which all now agree in considering rather an expansion or
atmosphere. Mr. Miller regarded the geological interpretation
of the work of this day, which he believed to have fallen on
the ages succeeding those of the metamorphic rocks, as peculiarly difficult. Mr. Ruskin, on the other hand, considers it
exceedingly easy. We are, on the whole, inclined to think that
though much may still be done towards defining the limits of
this day's duration, and towards scientifically working out the
processes by which the mighty operation of dividing the waters
which are under the firmament from the waters which are
above the firmament, was performed, the operation itself can
be already with sufficient clearness apprehended. The distinctive features of the creative work were still those pertaining, not so much to the earth's surface, as to its meteorological
phenomena. The first grand advance had been the pervasion
of the vapors which encompassed the earth by light. But for
a protracted period the faintly-illuminated steam could not be
again condensed, so as to fall in rain. It was only as the earth
cooled, and the temperature of the air fell, that sudden and
local condensation of the vapor could take place. When it
could take place, the second day's work was done. And assuredly this arrangement of the clouds over the face of the sky,
this fitting up of that marvellous apparatus by which unnumbered rivers were to be filled and unnumbered harvests to
ripen, was the chief and distinctive operation of that early
time. To this assertion science cannot but yield assent. It is
a wondrous tale that those few rain-marks on the Old Red
Sandstone tell. The few insignificant plants and living crea-

tures which then also existed were altogether unimportant as characteristic of the period, compared with that great process of separating "the waters which *fall* and *flow*, from those which *rise* and *float*." The *North British* reviewer is here of a different opinion. We cannot agree with him. We concede at once that during the Silurian and Old Red Sandstone periods there existed several species of plants and animals. But to mention these in the record in Genesis would have been a departure from the whole method of that record. Their presence was not distinctive. They passed away after having done little. For us their importance is past. But it has at this day the profoundest and loftiest interest for all men, to know when the Almighty bade the cloud gather up its stores to water the fields we *now* till, — when the vast, vague, colorless mist drew itself up in draperies of gold, and purple, and scarlet, round the chamber of the blue, — when the tempest was first tamed to the steady gale, and the trade-winds were bid to blow, — when that innumerable army of the rain, whose cloudy banners kindle the sky over *our* heads into beauty, was first appointed to its mighty work of furrowing the mountain, and fertilizing the valley, and shaping the face of the earth, æon after æon, as the Creator wills. Be the Bible inspired or no, we shall never recognize any description of the progress in creation during those ages as essentially and scientifically true, which does not, as is done in Genesis, pass over all other things as comparatively unimportant, and throw out into boldest relief the proclamation of this " most magnificent ordinance of the clouds."

On the remaining days we need not linger. The third, — that during which grew the forests of the Carboniferous era, — is described in Genesis as that of herbs and trees, and of the separation of land and water. What were then the distinctive features of the period? Science points them out

as two. Such forests have never clothed the world as those
of the Carboniferous era; and, in order to their growth, it was
absolutely necessary that the extent of land should have been
very great. In other words, the separation of land and sea,
and the growth of a vast flora, distinguished the period; and
when we state the fact, we find ourselves almost necessarily
using the words of Genesis. The fourth day was that on
which the sun first shone out upon the world. Light had been
announced before. The sun now appears. We are compelled
to assume it as declared that the sun was not visible until the
fourth day. And, wonderful to say, science shows this to have
been the case. *The plants of the great Carboniferous epoch
are such as must never have been touched by a sunbeam.* They
are such precisely as would have grown in a humid atmosphere; their wood is not hardened, as that of plants on
which the pure sunlight falls. In the Permian and Triassic
ages, trees of tough fibre, and with season-rings, are found;
and the Permian and Triassic periods coincide with the fourth
day of the Mosaic account. The fifth day was that of mon-
strous creeping things and of birds. Its correspondence with
the Liassic and Oölitic periods is unmistakable. The aerial
phenomena of our world were now no longer the most striking,
novel, or important. The earth was a prepared stage, and the
interest concentrated itself on the living creatures that moved
upon it. The inspired telegram, therefore, speaks of these.
Last of all, at the close of the sixth day, that of the Tertiary
periods, man was created; the final picture has for its centre
a king. The mighty work was finished. The cycle of operations which had begun with the raging flame, and which for
long ages had been carried forward by the wild ministry of
volcano and deluge, was brought to a termination. The Sabbath of creation dawned. Do you doubt of the reality of this
Sabbath? Do you question the reasonableness of its being,

33

as it were, the motive and impulse of the Creator in conferring on man the gentle blessing of Sabbath rest? Then look around, and compare the present scene with those of the bygone days. Think of those periods of fire and flood, of darkness and tempest, of gigantic birds, and dragons at whose huge bones we even yet shudder; and then remember the soft falling of the sunbeam on the flower, the gentle lapse of the streamlet in the glade, the tender warbling amid the golden-green of the spring woods; and be assured that the one discord in the Sabbatic harmony of terrestial nature comes from the human heart; that the sin of man alone blots the Sabbath light resting on the face of the earth; that, compared with the long week-days, the human period is the Sabbath of the world, and that man is the great Sabbath-breaker.

OPPOSING THEORIES OF RECONCILIATION BETWEEN GEOL-
OGY AND REVELATION: THEIR APOLOGETIC VALUE.

Having, we venture to hope, set before our readers with sufficient distinctness the true purport of the theory of recon-ciliation between Genesis and Geology supported in *The Tes-timony of the Rocks*, and having glanced at the leading arguments for and against that theory, we are in a position to return to that most important question to which we referred in the outset, — Whether this theory is a retrogression or an advance in the line of Christian apologetics, — whether the views of Mr. Miller, or those of his reviewer, are of greater avail in defence of the Christian Revelation?

The theory of natural days has somewhat to commend it. It has a clear, compact, what might be called commonplace aspect. At first sight it appears business-like and practical. It comfortably avoids generalization, it requires little illus-tration, and it gets rid of what appears a suspicious sublimity.

It seems difficult to assail, and yet it gives perfect freedom
to speculation.   Drawing a ring-fence round the garden of the
revealed word, it permits as much digging and planting in the
country beyond as the most ardent philosopher could desire.
The rocks are simply put out of account.   The inspired record
is assumed to know nothing concerning them.   The Bible is
declared to be the domain of an implicit, unquestioning faith,
which does not desire to see : over the geologic ages a curious
reason may expatiate at will.   We need not be surprised that
such a theory proves attractive to certain minds.   Combine
true devoutness with sincere love of science, a sense of the
need of perfect freedom in the exercise of reason with earnest
acceptance of the Christian revelation, — let a sharp logical
faculty be united with an undue appreciation of the natural,
healthful, divinely-appointed functions of the speculative and
imaginative powers, — and you have a mind to which this
theory is naturally agreeable.   Many persons also, whose
minds are not of this order, but who have for a long period
regarded the old view as satisfactory, may be expected, though
good geologists otherwise, to attach undue importance to arguments which convinced them in their youth, and unconsciously
to put prejudice for logic.   Having been hitherto at rest, these
persons will too easily mistake change for danger, and think
it safer to remain in their little canoe than to scale the sides of
the larger vessel.   Yet it is difficult to conceive the two theories set fairly in contrast, and the belief still retained that
Mr. Miller's is a less complete defence of the inspired volume
than the reviewer's.   In every point of vital importance the
one triumphantly succeeds, the other signally fails.   Each
apparent advantage pertaining to the theory of natural days
is found on examination to be a counterfeit.   If it seem clear
and compact, it but substitutes the littleness of human conception for the sublimity of the Divine operations.   If those

who rest in it have a feeling of safety, it is but that of the garrison which too timidly shuts itself up in a little fortress, leaving the whole of the open country to the enemy. If it appear to vindicate the honor of God, and to prove the integrity of his revelation, it in reality puts both in peril, by separating between the word and the works of the Almighty. Let us carry out a contrast between the two theories somewhat in detail.

It is undeniable, to begin with, that the theory of natural days breaks the continuity of the Mosaic record, while it is perfectly preserved by that of Mr. Miller. If we can point to a period which was, for this world, literally and scientifically the beginning, and to epoch after epoch succeeding, in which the leading features of the Mosaic and geologic records are unmistakably identical, there is no hiatus in the inspired narrative; the most rigorous philologist may be appealed to for his testimony to its magnificent symmetry and its marvellous condensation. Thus we are enabled to proceed by the theory of Mr. Miller. On the other hypothesis, the small conjunction "and," which so naturally links the first verse in Genesis with the second, forms an objection, in the mouth of the philologist, which may really be pronounced insurmountable. Either this conjunction passes over an immensely extended period of time without hint of its existence, or calls that the beginning which can with no definiteness or accuracy be so defined. The latter is, we believe, the alternative most generally accepted. The "beginning" is declared to have extended to the end of the geologic epochs. But how can it be considered correct to include under the same term a period of flaming ruin, when life was impossible on our planet, before its molten surges had hardened into the adamant that was to bear a world, and periods in which the fire had subsided, — periods when plants grew and creatures lived, — periods when light fell through a

transparent atmosphere, and animals breathed which were to
subsist along with man? Compared with the human period,
the geologic ages are as week-days to a Sabbath; but it is a
positive mistake to describe them as chaotic. They are marked
off from the chaos as clearly as from the time of man. They
belong no more to the "beginning" than to the last creation,
which, according to our opponents, occupied the six natural
days. Philology and Geology equally protest against a use
of the term "beginning," which would extend it beyond the
fire-period. Shall we disregard both sciences, and reject the
continuity, completeness, and harmony of the Millerian theory,
merely that we may confine to spaces of four-and-twenty hours
those days of creation in which that God was at work who has
told us that with Him a day is as a thousand years, and a
thousand years as one day?

In the next place,—and this is a point of fearful importance,
—it must now be distinctly conceded that the theory of natural
days cannot be authoritatively accepted and taught by the
Churches without occasioning a vast amount of unbelief. It
seems to us that if an angel were sent from heaven to proclaim
to theologians the special temptation and peril of the time, he
would declare it to be that of taking up a station apart from
and behind the genuine enlightenment of the century. Man
is the chief instance of God's productive power here below.
His eye is an instrument of infinite delicacy, adapted for beholding the works of God. His hand is endowed with inexpressible cunning, to follow up the discoveries of his eye. His
mind is the most wondrous specimen of Divine workmanship
of all; and to it, aided and guided by Divine Providence, and
acting through the senses, is it appointed to work out man's
task in time, and to rear the great temple of civilization. To
work with hand and brain is a duty proclaimed by man's conscience, and enforced in his Bible. It is no less than irrever-

ence to God to scorn or defame those results of human inquiry in which instincts implanted and capacities conferred by God have proceeded to their natural goal. Now, we are perfectly sure that no Protestant Church would for a moment deliberately contemplate this. But *one* point can no longer be doubted, that, namely, if the theory against which we contend is identified with the Protestant creeds, the conviction *will* sink into the mind of the scientific part of the community that the Churches are behind the age, that they fear the light, that they would put out the eyes of reason. Whatever may be the case in individual instances, or with peculiarly constituted minds, science will no longer believe in a universal chaos covering the face of the earth some six thousand years ago. On this point, the unmistakable, irresistible tendency is to that authoritative unanimity of science with which it is in vain to contend, — that authoritative unanimity whose seal secures belief beyond the walls of the school, which makes us credit the theory of gravitation though unacquainted with the arguments of Newton, and rely on that of the circulation of the blood though we never followed the demonstrations of Harvey. When scientific men are thus unanimous, argument ceases. The Churches might then fondly dream that the danger was past. But the religious and philosophical history of the last hundred years renders it easy to see what the result would be. Science would assume the attitude of Galileo; pitying toleration would supersede both assent and attack; and the highest culture, separating itself from Christianity, would exhibit to us in England and in Scotland what it has already so long exhibited on the Continent, — a refined, a self-satisfied, a most plausible Paganism.

Further, the theory we oppose is *avowedly* unable to contribute anything *positive* to Christian apologetics. Did we even grant all its pretensions, its attitude would be entirely negative.

It aims at no explanation ; it demands and it offers no confirmation of the word from the works of the Creator; it seeks not victory, but only peace; it spreads over the geologic ages a ghastly silence, a Godless desolation, and calls this the tranquillity of triumph. But the theory of Mr. Miller is a new, a positive, a weighty addition to the external evidences of Christianity. The argument it affords is clear and convincing. The Christian apologist, armed with its reasoning, may challenge the skeptic to produce, from all the records of mythology, ancient or modern, northern or oriental, any correspondence between cosmogony and science which will for a moment compare with the correspondence it exhibits between the geologic periods and the Mosaic days. To this challenge the skeptic will in vain attempt to respond. Point after point of marvellous correspondence the Christian apologist can urge on his observation, pressing him, meanwhile, to explain how the Hebrew leader, legislating for an uncultured tribe, became possessed of those unsurmised secrets three thousand years ago. To omit other instances, let one express and striking argument in favor of inspiration afforded by this theory be particularly considered. We cannot be far wrong in stating that, ever since wit and blasphemy cemented an unholy union, the Mosaic declaration of the appearance of light in our world before the sun was visible has been a favorite subject for infidel derision. The opportunity of attack was indeed tempting. Men naturally associate light with the sun and moon, and their separation seems at first sight flat nonsense. For three thousand years the Christian apologist could only say that so it had been· For three thousand years the mysterious oracle was unread. In the nineteenth century, science comes forward distinctly to inform us that, during three sufficiently discriminated periods, there was light on this world, while the sun and moon were invisible. In the fourth period the heavenly luminaries were unveiled. And, lo! this is what is declared in Genesis. How, we ask, did Moses know that fact? How did he know that, first when the impenetrable veil of steam covering the primeval ocean became less dense, light shimmered faintly through? How did he know that no clear sunbeam ever found its way to the Carboniferous forests? Could he discriminate the properties of light, separating those which color and harden from those which only irradiate? The fact comes upon one like a flash of lightning. The book in which, three thousand years ago, the aerial conditions of our planet for uncounted ages before man appeared on the world are unmistakably described, *must* have come from God.

Once more, not only does the reviewer's theory break the continuity of the narrative in Genesis; — it destroys the completeness of the word of God considered as a whole. It confines revelation to a part of the world's history. It removes from its ken protracted periods in which, as the rocks cannot but be regarded as demonstrating, the Almighty was at work with our planet, and race after race of plants and animals were showing forth his glory. Turning to the other theory, we see revelation synchronous with the history of our planet. The word in which the redeeming Christ is revealed becomes precisely commensurate with the time in which the creating Christ has exhibited, on our planet, his creative power. The closing books of the New Testament tell us of a fire which will in the latter time envelope the world. The first book of the Old Testament, read by the light reflected from the works of God, points us to a commencing fire in which the planet, as now constituted, had its beginning. From fire to fire spans the arch of creation; from fire to fire spans the arch of revelation; Christ the alpha and the omega of both.

END OF SECOND SERIES.